PRACTICING THE CITY

# PRACTICING THE CITY

## *Early Modern London on Stage*

*Nina Levine*

Fordham University Press
New York 2016

Fordham University Press also publishes its books in a variety of electronic formats. Some content that appears in print may not be available in electronic books.

Visit us online at www.fordhampress.com.

Library of Congress Cataloging-in-Publication Data

Levine, Nina S., (date)
Practicing the city : early modern London on stage / Nina Levine.—First edition.
pages cm
Includes bibliographical references and index.
ISBN 978-0-8232-6786-6 (cloth : alk. paper)—ISBN 978-0-8232-6787-3 (pbk. : alk. paper)
1. London (England)—In literature. 2. English drama—Early modern and Elizabethan, 1500–1600—History and criticism. 3. English drama—17th century—History and criticism. 4. City and town life in literature. 5. Theater and society—England—London—History. 6. Theater—England—London—History—16th century. 7. Theater—England—London—History—17th century. I. Title.
PR658.L58L48 2016
822'.309358421—dc23
2015009510

Printed in the United States of America

18 17 16 5 4 3 2 1

First edition

# *Contents*

# *Acknowledgments*

Among the pleasures of writing this book have been the many conversations and collaborations that have shaped my thinking along the way, and I have much to acknowledge here. I wish especially to thank Jill Frank, whose generosity of mind and spirit has been sustaining. She's read every chapter, followed every thread, and adduced clarity from complexity while never forgetting to ask about the politics. I'm happily indebted to Greg Forter, who's about as ideal a reader and interlocutor as one could hope for; to Kate Brown, whose capacity for intellectual play pushed me further than I might ever have ventured alone; and to David Lee Miller, whose generosity has made all the difference in the project's final stages.

At the University of South Carolina, I've benefited from a remarkable medieval and Renaissance cohort—Lawrence Rhu, David Lee Miller, Ed Gieskes, Andrew Shifflett, Esther Richey, Holly Crocker, and Scott Gwara. That Harry Berger, Jr. has generously graced us with extended visits over the years has only added to this sense of community, reminding us why what we do matters. Among the many other friends and colleagues who have made the department such a good place to teach and write, I'm especially grateful to Susan Courtney, Rebecca Stern, Cynthia Davis, Amittai Aviram, Meili Steele, Brian Glavey, Debra Rae Cohen, Leon Jackson, John Muckelbauer, David Shields, and Tony Jarrells. I'm grateful as well to department chairs Steven Lynn and Bill Rivers and to Dean Mary Anne Fitzpatrick for her generous support.

Without the Folger Shakespeare Library, this book probably wouldn't have been written, or at least not in the form that it has taken. The starting point for the project was a remarkable Folger Institute seminar on social and cultural history organized by David Harris Sacks, and I'm indebted to David and his all-star panel. Fellow seminarians James Siemon and Lena Cowen Orlin couldn't have been more collegial or welcoming. For me, as for so many others, the Folger Library is a kind of second home, and here I thank Gail Paster, Barbara Mowat, Kathleen Lynch, and Owen Williams, along with a remarkable staff of librarians, for their intellectual support and expertise over many years. I'm grateful as well for a Folger short-term fellowship that allowed me to do crucial research in the project's early stages.

If it's possible to institute collaborative networks from above, the Shakespeare Association of America conference is exemplary. Among the many with whom I've had the pleasure of sharing writing and conversation over the years, special thanks go to Valerie Forman, Mary Bly, Anita Sherman, Mario DiGangi, Mary Ellen Lamb, Natasha Korda, Ted Leinwand, John Archer, William Ingram, William West, Alexandra Halasz, Mary Floyd-Wilson, Dan Vitkus, James Siemon, Adam Zucker, Andras Kisery, Musa Gurnis, Lowell Gallagher, Shankar Raman, Frank Whigham, Susan O'Malley, and Rosemary Kegl. I'm grateful as well for invitations to present my work from Christy Desmet and Frances Teague at the University of Georgia, and from Gary Taylor and Sharon O'Dair of the Hudson Strode Center at the University of Alabama.

At Fordham University Press, I'm indebted to the late Helen Tartar and honored to count myself among the scholars she supported. Tom Lay has been a strong advocate throughout, and I've valued his expert shepherding of this project. I'm also deeply grateful to the readers for the Press whose astute comments and suggestions have, I hope, made this a better book.

The University of South Carolina has been generous in its financial support. A Provost's Arts and Humanities Grant funded research travel and teaching release for a semester, a College of Arts and Sciences Professional Development Award funded summer support, and a Research Professorship in the Department of English allowed me a much needed teaching release for writing and research.

At the center of this book are those with whom I've long practiced the collaborative art of living, and here my love and appreciation go to my family, Emily, Carol, Karen, Emily X, Douglas, and Beverly; and my extended families, Marsha, Lane, Jill, Larry, Alexander, and Abigail. And, most of all, to Arnie, for these many years.

# *Introduction*

## Presupposing the Stage

CORDATUS O, marry, this is one for whose better illustration we must desire you to presuppose the stage the middle aisle in Paul's, and that [*Pointing to the door on which Shift is posting his bills*] the west end of it.
MITIS So, sir. And what follows?
CORDATUS Faith, a whole volume of humour, and worthy the unclasping.

—Ben Jonson, *Every Man Out of His Humor*

By the sixteenth century's end, London had arrived on stage. Not only was the commercial theater now a prominent fixture within the growing metropolis—the city's "ornament," Thomas Heywood would soon proclaim—but the metropolis itself was fast becoming a popular dramatic subject.[1] In *Every Man Out of His Humor*, Jonson prominently marks this convergence of city and stage when Cordatus steps forward at the start of Act 3 to enjoin spectators "to presuppose the stage the middle aisle in Paul's" (3.1.2–3).[2] Performed at the recently opened Globe Theater in late 1599, *Every Man Out* is Jonson's first experiment with a London setting, and the invitation "to presuppose" seems calculated to play up the scene's audacious replication of one of the city's most prominent public locations. Cordatus's invitation indeed commands attention in its seeming boast to reduce the Bankside's newly acclaimed world stage to an explicitly city stage, an urban simulacrum bounded by Paul's Walk and populated not by princes and monarchs but by a parade of city types—knights, courtiers, overdressed gallants, bumbling rustics, doting citizens, threadbare rogues, even a leashed greyhound and a cat in a sack.[3]

But what does it mean to *presuppose* that the stage is the city? *Every Man Out*'s unusually lengthy induction offers one answer with Asper's arch pronouncement that the play is a "mirror" in which the audience "shall see the time's deformity / Anatomized in every nerve and sinew" (Induction, 116, 118–19), and we might read Cordatus's directive as simply updating this classic formulation by holding up the mirror, with surgical precision, to "the middle aisle in Paul's" near to its western door.[4] Yet the request complicates even as it recalls mimetic traditions. Reaching out from the onstage audience to the play's own spectators, Cordatus's invitation does more than just ramp up interest in the scene to follow. It boldly solicits what playgoers already know about the city, presumably from their own experiences of streets, neighborhoods, and the daily concourse of St. Paul's cathedral. It also solicits their preconceptions about dramatic representation. Paradoxically invoking and confounding expectations for a local mimesis, Jonson aligns his urban turn with what promises to be a new mode of theatrical practice.

The features of this new urban poetics turn on the insistent doubling of the city within the space of the theater, a doubling that is at once obvious, in plain sight, as it were, and, at the same time, operating behind the scenes. First among these features are the experimental freedoms that come with city subjects—the "*licentia* or free power" (Ind. 262) of dramatic invention that Cordatus endorses in the play's induction and the Paul's Walk scene then embodies, in its colloquial dialogue, for example, or in the random circulation of characters like Clove and Orange, the two gallants who wander onto the scene supposedly "by chance" (3.1.40), as if they themselves had mistaken the Globe's stage for the vast central aisle of Paul's.[5] Other features turn on the ways in which the stage's redoubling of the city is profoundly bound up with, and complicated by, the everyday experiences and perceptions of the city's population. The effects of this redoubling are often paradoxical, as *Every Man Out*'s intrusive metatheatrics repeatedly demonstrate, dislocating spectators in the very act of locating them within the city and prompting an awareness of distance and difference even in the moment of identification. The stage's urban turn no doubt catered to the increasingly commercial metropolis, trading in a repertoire of local stories that, as is now commonly assumed, had the power to shape or make the city even as they reflected it. But what *Every Man Out* also suggests is that by taking the city as its subject, the stage introduced a new dimension into theatrical experience, opening up a reflexive space between the city and stage in the here-and-now of performance, a space in which, I want to argue, Londoners might begin to "practice" the city. This is a book about the stage's traffic in this practice.

In its broadest terms, *Practicing the City* seeks to explore responses to the unprecedented urbanization of late-sixteenth and early-seventeenth-century London. It considers how local residents conceptualized and experienced an increasingly diverse metropolis and how the local theater worked to mediate this experience. It tracks these responses across five plays, moving from histories to comedies, from *1* and *2 Henry IV* and *Sir Thomas More* to *Englishmen for My Money* and *The Roaring Girl*. What connects these plays, other than their London settings, is their engagement with new forms of urban activity, forms that extend well beyond the getting and spending conventionally associated with city plays. Encompassing a wide range of everyday practices—involving credit and labor relations, foreign language lessons, and the temporal measures of plague time and playgoing—these activities are all linked to, and shaped by, the exigencies of commerce. Yet my interest in these activities lies less with their specific economic uses than with the kinds of cultural work they enable by bringing together the city's diverse population in networks of association and exchange. Although early modern London was crisscrossed by multiple and overlapping networks, not all of them models of urban association (think of the notorious surveillance networks set up by the Crown), the plays I examine in this study explore a subset of local networks that encouraged relations across difference within the city, crossing boundaries of neighborhood and parish, for example, or divisions between citizens and strangers. One of the organizing premises of this book is that these networks—at once mobile and unstable, and thus subject to debate and alteration—allowed the local population to work out new forms of sociability within the unsettled urban milieu.

Central to my argument is the question of the stage's place within this milieu, and following recent work on early modern drama, I assume that in its urban turn, the stage shaped, and even transformed, local responses to the pressures of contemporary city life. At the same time, though, I want to follow Jonson's call "to presuppose" in order to raise, and complicate, questions about theater's role in the constitutive processes of urban commonality. If the early modern London amphitheaters offered a new instrument or technology for "collective thought," as Steven Mullaney has recently argued, and if the plays performed on that instrument were "designed to resonate with an audience newly uncertain of its individual or collective identities," then those plays that took London as their subject must have resonated in ways that were strikingly close to home.[6] As the choric apparatus in *Every Man Out* repeatedly demonstrates, to put the city on stage is to provoke self-awareness and understanding on the part of both playgoers and playwrights, and with it a more engaged and participatory theatrical experience. This is not to suggest that we see city plays as offering an early version of Brechtian dramaturgy, but it is to propose that in its urban turn, the London stage opened up the contemporary scene to multiple and newly divergent levels of meaning and interpretation. In this, I argue, even as the theater modeled networks of association on stage, it was beginning to operate as a local network in its own right, enabling the city's population to experiment in the complex reciprocities of new modes of urban belonging.

## *Presupposing*

Before turning to a more detailed account of these experiential theatrics, and to an overview of the book's individual chapters, I briefly want to look at some of the prevailing suppositions about urban collectivity and the city stage, the critical medium in which my own rehearsal of London plays takes place. For much of the latter half of the twentieth century, studies of early modern London began with statistics, drawing on demographic tables and employment figures to document the city's growth from a walled medieval enclave to a sprawling modern metropolis.[7] What the numbers tell us is that waves of migrants flooded into the city and suburbs, by some estimates upward of 8,000 a year: young men from the provinces hoping to apprentice with one of the great companies; Protestant refugees from France and the Low Countries setting up shop in the liberties; gentlemen pursuing legal careers or those, more frivolous, who simply wanted "to see and shew vanity"; and streams of vagrants and unemployed desperate for work or charity.[8] London was quickly becoming a place in which "strangers are likely to meet," to borrow from Richard Sennett's characterization of later urban settlements.[9] And by 1600, the city ranked among the largest in Europe with a population of 200,000, double what it had been only twenty years before; it would double again by 1650.[10] This factual accounting underlies what has been an abiding question in this urban story: What bound metropolitan London together in the face of this rapid change? Or to put the question differently, how did this unsettled population understand itself within a city in which urbanization was paradoxically "a function not so much of residence as of mobility," as Margaret Pelling reminds us?[11]

The answers vary and are not without debate. In the 1970s and 1980s, historians were divided over the question of the city's stability. Some claimed that economic strains and social polarization, in the 1590s especially, created a state of crisis and disorder. Others argued that the city remained relatively stable and resilient in these years, largely because of its consolidating institutions, a revisionist view advocating not crisis but cooperation and consensus among citizens and city rulers.[12] Within the last two decades, however, social history has shifted away from these broader questions about stability and institutional structure to concentrate instead on the experiences of city residents themselves. In place of grand narratives of social and economic change, historians now offer microhistories of the everyday practices of ordinary Londoners as they worked, shopped, gossiped, suffered disease and hardship, and marked births and deaths. As Julia Merritt characterizes this approach in a recent essay collection, the aim is to look "behind the larger processes of change at work in the early modern capital in order to consider the human, the particular, and the personal."[13] Rather than taking the city's official regulations and idealizing discourses at face value, as a factual record of urban practice and attitudes, historians now consider how the population might have *used* those rules or reinterpreted community ideals in their day-to-day activities. The assumption here is that social relations at the local level are at once complex *and* unstable in the sense that they are always changing in an "ongoing process of rearticulation," as Keith Wrightson puts it.[14] Rather than assuming a model of normalizing consensus and stability, these accounts understand conflict and debate to be part of the processes of urban collectivity, including debate about who belongs to the community.[15]

As this work persuasively documents, local perceptions of metropolitan London were hardly monolithic at the start of the seventeenth century.[16] Moreover, as London became increasingly "pesterd with people," as John Stow memorably put it, urban experience was less and less defined by neighborly relations and the kinds of face-to-face transactions associated with smaller and more homogenous communities.[17] It is true that the livery companies, or trade guilds, continued to regulate lives and livelihoods within London, and in 1600 roughly two-thirds of the city's male population were "free" of a company, and counted as citizens. Yet it is also the case that the percentage of citizens within greater London was declining.[18] As new arrivals poured into the city and suburbs, more and more of the population was officially among the disenfranchised. Women and substantial numbers of subsistence migrants, along with the city's foreign population, all lived outside the assimilating corporate structures.[19] Yet as the ranks of the enfranchised thinned, the role of livery companies within the city was not simply, or immediately, supplanted by new administrative organizations. Local and state governments did begin expanding their reach in this period, instituting mechanisms of poor relief and plague control to manage the burgeoning population.[20] But London was still far from the large-scale governmental systems that would divide and regulate the city according to the scientific and political technologies Michel de Certeau describes in his well-known formulation of the modern "concept city."[21]

Instead, metropolitan life most likely resembled "a complex web of interwoven communities."[22] As Jeremy Boulton's research shows us, even as neighborhoods continued to define daily activity, with many residents spending their lives within the jurisdictions of local parishes, the increasing claims of extra-parish associations, including company membership and new trading networks, exerted outward pressures on parochial insularities, particularly for those with means.[23] The recent outpouring of cultural history on early modern London has done much to document the population's movements within the overlapping networks that increasingly defined urban life—circles of credit, for example, or science and medicine, or the supposedly nefarious associations linking the city's criminal underclass.[24] The livery companies were themselves beginning to look outward from the city's strictly defined borders, extending their reach within a metropolitan community that included the suburbs and liberties as well as the city center.[25] Even London's own history, newly rendered by antiquarians like Stow in annals and surveys, was increasingly understood as part of a complex web of local topography linking the city with the suburbs and the past with the present.[26] As has been much discussed, the effects of these widening networks were far reaching, shaping new formations of state and nation.[27] But the proliferating networks of exchange and communication also reverberated locally, particularly as they served to link residents not only to outlying provinces and foreign markets but to the so-called "strangers" and "foreigners" who resided within their midst.

What emerges from this impressive body of cultural history is a highly complex, multi-layered mapping of urban formation, and a dynamic historiography that productively reinforces the equally complex work of cultural geographers on city space. "No space disappears in the course of growth and development: *the worldwide does not abolish the local*," Henri

Lefebvre observes in his influential work on the production of city space.[28] Instead, urban space comprises a diverse and layered structure "more reminiscent of flaky *mille-feuille* pastry than of the homogeneous and isotropic space of classical (Euclidean/Cartesian) mathematics," he argues, elaborating a figure of "hypercomplexity" that aptly characterizes the interpenetrating networks and pathways of early modern London.[29] Concerned with distance in relation to proximity, and movement in relation to stasis, cultural geographers argue for a dynamic model of spatial practice that, to borrow from John Agnew, understands culture in terms of "a changing matrix of practices and ideas that *actively* mediates" spatial levels and locations.[30] "Rather than a 'metric' space, divided into compact areas," Agnew contends, "place involves a conception of 'topological' space in which diverse scales are brought together through networks of 'internal' and 'external' ties."[31] These models of spatial processes invite us to think about urban experience beyond specific city sites and even beyond familiar spatial configurations, like city and court or city and suburbs, and to focus as well on the layered networks of mobility and exchange that served to connect disparate populations and locales within greater London.

What then is the stage's role in this accounting? If, as most assume, the theater was crucial in shaping urban experience for a diverse population, how exactly did it interpret or give meaning to that experience? Central to these questions has been the broader debate about "the place" of the London stage.[32] For much of the twentieth century, scholarship on city plays emphasized the stage's distance from the city proper, literally marked out by its place in the liberties and suburbs, out of reach of city authorities, but also set apart ideologically by its promotion of moral traditions and values at odds with the city's "capitalist enterprise."[33] Presupposing an opposition between city and stage, this work focused on satiric or so-called city comedies, said to offer a "radical critique of their age."[34] Challenging these assumptions, recent work on London's cultural production has largely understood the theater as aligned and to some extent complicit with the city and its developing structures of market and state formation. Lawrence Manley advances what is perhaps the most fully articulated version of this position. Placing the city at the center of England's transition from feudalism to capitalism, Manley contends that London literatures, including drama, responded to the "profoundly unsettling experience" of urbanization by inculcating "new forms of sedentarism, ways of perceiving the self and society that encouraged settlement and civility, allayed anxieties, and encouraged innovation."[35]

What follows from this conceptual shift is a new model of dramatic production that insists on the stage's centrality to the commercial city, inviting us to see the theater as "a place of business," as Douglas Bruster puts it, and therefore as "part of a complex of centralizing institutions."[36] This model has the advantage of expanding the subgenres of London drama far beyond the confines of satiric comedy, to include a range of plays with city settings. It also opens up new ways of thinking about collective urban experience. If earlier studies saw the stage's cultural work as rejecting commercial urban values in favor of the communal values of the past—appealing to "an older world which was still 'normal,' a world of small communities," as L. C. Knights put it—late twentieth-century historicist and materialist approaches emphasize a collective experience that coalesces the city's diverse population within the here-and-now of urban life.[37] In this view, the stage operates as a kind of urban guidebook, as Jean Howard has argued, modeling new forms of civility and cultural competencies, "rendering the *un*familiar intelligible," and "*creating* rather than simply calling upon an audience's sense of itself as knowing urban dwellers."[38] To the extent that this theater regulated even as it educated local residents, explicitly London plays also suggest a more coercive construction of the urban collective, aligned with what Manley refers to as urbanization's evolving moral technologies, which "organize and discipline populations" within large scale settlements.[39] By rewriting "belonging" within the city's commercial structures, this recent work productively resists those who would simply oppose urban collectivity with an idealized notion of harmonious community. Yet what often disappears within these larger narratives of cultural change is the story of the particular and the personal, and with it the capacity of both playgoers and playwrights to interpret and invent the city in ways not yet fully institutionalized or determined.

My work seeks to explore these possibilities for interpretation and invention among ordinary Londoners. It does this in part by following the example of social and cultural historians who, as Merritt puts it, have begun "to reinstitute citizens as active participants in the changing city—not simply as passive observers of a developing cityscape, but as individuals making creative, pragmatic responses to a changing urban environment."[40] As should be evident throughout this book, my thinking about city plays is indebted to these developments in early modern historiography, and my project aims to explore what this analytical model of urban experience holds for plays that take London as their subject. To this end, my approach shifts attention away from institutional structures and focuses instead on the exchanges and communications connecting disparate populations and locales within greater London. What this permits is a view of a stage linked not only to city government and commerce, and therefore instrumental in inculcating civic sensibilities and values, but also, and crucially, to the everyday activities of the local population. This is not to say that city residents didn't live within a matrix of institutional structures, their actions inscribed within the *habitus* of an increasingly commercial metropolis, but it is to acknowledge the possibility for mobility, change, and disagreement *within* those shaping structures. It is also to open up the question of urban identity and belonging to the multiple ways collectivity was coming to be defined, and practiced, in this dynamic urban environment.[41]

Following the so-called "spatial turn" in early modern studies, recent work on London literatures has begun to turn attention to the multiplicity of urban experience, often in ways that run counter to the familiar oppositions of city and court or city and suburbs that figured so centrally in earlier studies. The portrait of the city emerging from this work is at once theoretically informed and richly archival, documented by a wealth of artifacts and genres, as exemplified by Karen Newman's comparative study of London and Paris, which traces "an ideology of the urban" across a range of cultural texts, from maps, surveys, guidebooks, buildings, and bridges to ballads, poetry, and plays.[42] The spatial turn has also brought more attention to the movements of city residents, as shown in Mary Bly's work on the cultural geography of theatrical production within the city's liberties, or in Adam Zucker's exploration of the "social logic of wit," the geographic fluencies by which fashion-conscious Londoners enhanced their status within the city.[43] With its focus on practices that operate across difference and division within London, my work adds to this increasingly complex portrait of a city mapped by the activities of its residents. But what sets it apart from other recent studies of urban sociability is that it takes the question of plurality as central to what it means to "practice" the city.

Focused on London's changing networks of communication and exchange, *Practicing the City* affirms the complexity of the theater's engagements with urban life. Plays that take the city as their subject no doubt attempted to instruct a diverse population in the social competencies of urban living, including playgoing itself, and thus worked to inculcate shared habits of mind. But by repeating the city on stage, city plays were also doing something else, engaging in a new form of theatrical practice contingent upon the multiple experiences and perceptions of local audiences.

This practice, I argue, enabled local residents to unsettle and reconfigure their place within the expanding metropolis, to become aware of and to experiment with new forms of alliance and association, sometimes collaboratively and sometimes at odds with each other. Focused on the interplay of local experience and theatrical practice, this book seeks, then, to delineate a new mode of theatricality that has the capacity to exceed its own boundaries and intentions. It also seeks to raise questions about the politics of the theater's urban turn. If plurality is "*the* condition" of all political life, as Hannah Arendt contends, then the city plays I explore in this study present an unusually powerful form of politics.[44]

## *Taking Place*

Each of the plays in this study invites local audiences to confront questions of plurality at the heart of the city. Each play explores these questions by staging encounters across social and geographical boundaries, between citizens and strangers or tradesmen and nobles, for example, or between city and court or city and suburbs. Set in the familiar and often intimate spaces of contemporary London, each play mediates these encounters in relation to new modes of urban activity and association. Yet the point of this intense localizing is not just to model solutions to urban problems or to administer correctives. Indeed, if the metatheatrics of city plays are to be credited, it is also to insist that playgoers become aware of, and maybe even struggle with, their own place within the city scene. The stage's urban turn could be said, then, to exemplify theater's longstanding associations with democratic practices, opening up forums for public discussion and rational debate along the lines of those modeled by Cordatus and Mitis in *Every Man Out*, and in the chapters that follow I am interested in how city plays structure these forums. But I am also interested in how these plays encourage playgoers to go beyond the constraints of these structures by granting them the freedom to experiment in new forms of urban association. What this entails is thinking about how the stage's performance of the urban scene operates at a more experiential level, as a medium that dislocates and unsettles audiences even as its dramatic fictions locate and stabilize. For it is in the stage's capacity to operate as a medium as well as a model for the urban experiences of local audiences, I suggest, that London plays begin to complicate the collective activity of theatrical practice itself.

My focus, then, is on city plays that engage the urban experience on multiple and overlapping levels and thereby give us access to these highly complex mediations. The plays' local engagements are most visible at the level of representation, with dramatic narratives that vividly recreate the familiar activities of everyday life, trafficking in the "deeds and language such as men do use," as Jonson puts it in the prologue of *Every Man in His Humor.*[45] Yet one of the difficulties of city plays is that their surfaces seem so transparent and *un*mediated. Recall, for example, T. S. Eliot's often quoted remark that Middleton's comedy is "photographic" and that, in the end, the prolific London playwright "has no message—he is merely a great recorder."[46] Recent work, of course, views city plays not as documentary snapshots but as complex dramatic narratives, yet the question remains about how to understand their mirrored surfaces. My approach considers how these representations might play out within London, accruing meanings and interpretations not always controlled by playwrights and acting companies. *Every Man Out*, for example, for all of its experimental staging, replays what for the times was a fairly conventional critique of Paul's Walk, taking the cathedral's congested nave as a microcosm of the commercial city. Yet to the extent that the scene solicits the audience's suppositions about Paul's, it provokes multiple and potentially divergent views of the familiar location. The cathedral's great concourse served, after all, as the city's informal newsroom, as a clearinghouse for foreign reports and local gossip in close proximity to the city's book trade. Mention of Paul's might thus have prompted some in the Globe's audience to become aware of an incipient competition between Jonson's urban theatrics and the fledgling news trade, a competition elided by the play but no less present to London playgoers. It is partly by way of these complex and sometimes unpredictable engagements with the local scene that city plays themselves begin to generate dense webs of urban experience.

Less visible but no less crucial, the plays also engage the city at a formal level in the sense that urban experience is not simply reflected in their surfaces but, as Manley observes, "inhabits their very forms."[47] Some of the best work on London literature in recent years has traced these formal concerns, exploring the interplay between generic and economic development, for example, or between changing urban genres and broader questions of urbanization and cultural change, as exemplified by Manley's sweeping genealogies of civic description, encomium, epic, pageantry, pamphlets, verse satire, epigram, and stage comedy.[48] The question motivating my own interest in form focuses more specifically on relations between the stage's formal innovations and new modes of urban association. We might glimpse these relations in the generic hybridity of the *Henry IV* plays, materialized by credit networks that anachronistically link fifteenth-century dynastic history to late-sixteenth-century London, or in the dramatic unfolding of a play like *The Roaring Girl*, whose innovative topicality reiterates new forms of temporal experience within the commercial city. Yet, as the plays of this study suggest, the relationship between dramatic form and new forms of exchange and communication is rarely straightforward or precisely homologous. Rather than simply reinforcing the plays' ostensible messages about metropolitan life, these formal experiments tend to deepen and complicate their meanings in ways that also complicate the audience's experience of the city within the space of performance.

There is also a third, and related, level on which these plays engage local networks—that of performance itself. Reinforcing recent work on generic form, performance studies are helpful here in turning attention to the theater's attention to what plays could "do" as well as what they might "mean." As Mary Thomas Crane has shown, in its general, non-theatrical use in the period, "to perform" meant "to carry through to completion; to complete, finish, perfect," a usage that contains the idea of performativity, "in that it involves turning something immaterial (a duty, a promise, a contract, the pattern of a ceremony) into a material thing."[49] As a theatrical term, she writes, performance insists on its status as material practice, or activity, as do other common terms for playing in the period, words like "use," "exercise," and even "practice" itself.[50] The Privy Council's letter of 1598, for example, authorizes the Admiral's and Chamberlain's Men "to use and practise stage playes," on the assumption that the actors will "be the better enabled and prepared" for court performances.[51] Here, to "practise" means to rehearse, in the sense of performing an action repeatedly so as to become more proficient, as one would a skill, and in using this term, the council may also have hoped to legitimate playing by linking it with other arts or professions within the city.[52] But plays that take London as their subject point to yet another variation on the repetitions of theatrical practice and performativity. To perform or "practice" the city, these plays suggest, is to engage in a form of redoubling that in repeating urban activities on stage opens up possibilities for theatrical agency and collective experience that is as fluid and contingent as it is fixed or predetermined.

We tend to assume that the London theater created a common understanding or collective experience predicated on the communal space of the theater itself. The city's purpose-built amphitheaters fostered a "theater of a nation," Alfred Harbage concluded more than a half-century ago, arguing that the public stage brought together a diverse audience to share in the unifying values of a popular tradition.[53] So too, explicitly city plays may be said to promote a "theater of a city," in Howard's more recent formulation, with the commercial theaters making city space "socially legible" to Londoners of all ranks and occupations.[54] The theater's power in these accounts resides in its capacity to assemble a cross-section of the city's demographic, aligning them in an act of common spectatorship, interpellated through the shared values and behaviors enacted before them. And it's this accommodating capacity that Jonson invokes in *Every Man Out* when Cordatus finishes his introductions at the start of Act 3 by promising the audience "a whole volume of humour, and worthy the unclasping" (3.1.6–7). The theater is figured here as a book, a massive folio of encyclopedic knowledge to be revealed for the instruction and edification of the Globe's several thousand spectators. Yet the metaphor sits oddly beside the call to presuppose, issued only a few lines earlier. As if to disavow the possibility of a more participatory and fluid theatrical experience, Cordatus's ceremonial unclasping of the volume seems to revert to the induction's insistence that authority resides in a written text, in a form of poetic truth that would fix collective understandings of the contemporary city along with the passive spectators themselves, subjecting both to the satirist's correction.[55]

But if the call to presuppose is a rhetorical ploy, and a means of reforming rather than validating local experience, it nonetheless marks out the possibilities for alternative, and even competing, ideas of theatrical practice. It suggests that the stage's capacity to operate as a medium involves more than the passive spectatorship of common virtues and values, a view the play itself seems to endorse with its onstage audience of Mitis and Cordatus, who "liberally / Speak [their] opinions upon every scene" (Ind. 153–54). Most crucially, the call to presuppose reminds London audiences that the performance of the city on stage cannot be confined to a book or even to the space of the theater but that it instead takes place within a wider context of local practices and mediated exchanges. Invoking a theater that is at once fixed *and* mobile, localizing *and* dislocating, and that licenses audiences even as it attempts to control them, *Every Man Out*'s mixed messages register a central contradiction of city plays. The call to presuppose may recall the fluid theatrical practices of early Tudor interludes and morality plays—their playing spaces literally taken from the space of the audience, marked out by a cry of "Make room!"—yet Jonson's innovation is to reenact this fluidity *within* the walls of the purpose-built Globe, and within the space of theatricality itself.[56] Set apart from the city, the amphitheater stands at a distance from the events it describes, but not completely, Jonson suggests. As the work of Robert Weimann and William West persuasively shows us, what's crucial about the Elizabethan stage are its bifold capacities—to present and represent, or to localize and dislocate—which in turn promote new understandings of how knowledge is produced and experienced.[57] City plays, I would add, exploit these existing contradictions, for by literalizing the play of location within contemporary settings, they push the theatricality of the Elizabethan stage to its limits.

Of course, as West observes, the notion of a self-divided theater is not limited to the early modern stage but suggests "an incommensurable and irreducible difference" located in theatrical signification itself.[58] It is precisely this question of irreducible difference that Samuel Weber takes up in his recent book *Theatricality as Medium*. Weber explores the stage's mediating capacities in examples that extend from Greek tragedy to *Hamlet* to twentieth-century theater and film, but his astute observations about theater's disruption of proper place seem especially relevant to the constitutive contradictions of early modern plays about London. Weber begins by resisting efforts to limit the notion of medium to a transparent and self-effacing *means* of representation, following Aristotle's remarks in *The Poetics*. Neither transparent or self-effacing, Weber claims, the theatrical medium is instead defined by an in-betweenness that exposes rather than masks the "irreducible difference" within signification. In Weber's formulation, the theatrical medium enables events "to take place" on stage, and yet it paradoxically reveals the "place" these events "take" to be a stage, reminding us that on stage "no action is ever fully self-present."[59] What follows from this, Weber contends, is a recognition that theatrical events "can neither be contained within the place where they unfold nor entirely separated from it."[60] Because they are constituted by difference rather than identity, theatricality's displacements have the effect of making a space for repetition, alteration, and the processes of "reiterative openness."[61] What "'happens' on the stage," Weber writes, "is not the communication of something new, in the sense of content, but the variation of something familiar through its repetition. Repetition thus emerges as a visible, audible, and constitutive element of the theatrical medium."[62]

The plays I explore in this study are all striking examples of theatricality operating as a medium in which the events taking place on stage show themselves to be part of theater's "reiterative openness," part of an ongoing scene that is quite literally repeating across London. In some cases, the repetitions are at once obvious and confusing, as exemplified by the metatheatrical interplay of Jonson's Paul's Walk scene, in which the choric commentary of Cordatus and Mitis is comically echoed by the choreographed spectatorship of characters within the scene and, it would seem, by the Globe's own audience. A complex and seemingly literal redoubling is also on display in the topical mirroring of a play like *The Roaring Girl*, which playfully confronts audiences with a recognizable London personage in the form of Mary Frith. But one of the premises of this book is that a similarly dislocating redoubling is at work in plays that are less overtly self-conscious of their art, provoked by the very act of performing the city on stage before a local audience. Exploiting theatricality's irreducible differences, plays that take the city as their subject paradoxically disrupt the identification of city and stage their performances solicit. In this, these plays enact as well as represent the dislocations of urban experience, and just as their dramatic narratives trace new modes of navigating the dislocations of a changing cityscape, so too do their performances compel audiences to practice navigating another set of dislocations within the space of theatricality itself.

Yet it is not just the limits of theatrical space or urban geography that London plays challenge. They also challenge the place of the spectators themselves, repositioning audiences within a collective more along the lines of a disruptive *theatrocracy* than a unified *theatron*. The classical *theatron*, or "place of looking," was designed to allow spectators to see a performance in its entirety, from a distance, and it was this concept of a unified vision that informed the Elizabethan amphitheater, whose capacious structure generated "a system for producing, or displaying, a shared experience of seeing."[63] It is this ideal of the *theatron* that the *theatrocracy* disrupts. The term comes from a passage in Book 3 of Plato's *Laws* that criticizes the liberties of the poets, who, in mixing musical forms on stage, encouraged disorder and conceit in the multitude: "Thus our once silent audiences have found a voice, in the persuasion that they understand what is good and bad in art; the old sovereignty of the best, aristocracy, has given way to an evil 'sovereignty of the audience,' a theatrocracy."[64] Plato sees the theater in political terms and directly blames theatrical license for authorizing a dangerous political license on the part of spectators, who in speaking out refuse their proper place within established order and hierarchy. For Plato, this license overturns the aristocracy's sovereign authority, replacing it with the anarchy of a multitude that violates all bounds. Indeed, what's to be feared about the theatrocracy is that it ushers in a liberty in complete disregard for law and authority and marked by a "contempt for oaths, for the plighted word, and all religion."[65]

In its urban turn, the early modern London stage could hardly be accused of fomenting anarchy. City plays, after all, obsessively return to the problem of audiences, in prologues and epilogues that speak about the need to control spectators' behavior and shape their interpretations. Implicit in this metatheatrical commentary is the recognition that by making the local scene its subject, the stage has awakened a self-awareness on the part of playgoers, and with it a liberty reflective of the "times condition" (*EMO*, Ind. 127). As Mitis warns Asper before the start of *Every Man Out*, urging him to blunt the teeth of his satire: "take heed: / The days are dangerous, full of exception, / And men are grown impatient of reproof" (Ind. 121–23). But if playwrights took pains to contain unruly and ignorant audiences, calling instead for civility and decorum, their commentary testifies to a widening circle of participation in the stage's "reiterative openness," as playgoers took it upon themselves to work variations on the local scene. Rather than presupposing a theatrical community unified by the spectacle before them, and thus, one could argue, preconstituted by a common set of values, what city plays suggest are the possibilities for collective reflexivity within the space of performance that grants city residents a freedom to practice complex modes of urban association.

## *Overview*

The chapters that follow explore these practices by putting city plays in relation to the everyday activities of local residents as they lived and experienced metropolitan life. The plays themselves give a sense of how these residents traversed the city in networks extending from Eastcheap to Westminster, St. Martin's to Tower Hill, Crutched Friars to the Exchange, and Gray's Inn Fields to Brainford. They also give a sense of how a theater that modeled new forms of urban association at the same time provided a medium within which local residents might participate in versions of these associations. The aim of this study is obviously not a grand narrative of urban change, or a "distant reading" of patterns across the one hundred or more plays with London settings produced between 1580 and 1642. Its concern lies, rather, with charting the microdynamics of urban networks across a handful of plays in conjunction with a range of contemporaneous documents—legal texts, popular pamphlets, usury tracts, sermons, chronicles, libels, French language manuals, mortality bills, and playhouse manuscripts. More fragmentary than complete, and more suggestive than conclusive, the story this book tells is about the theater's place within the complex processes of urban plurality at a crucial turn in London's history.

Each chapter pairs a key dramatic text with non-dramatic materials. While clearly indebted to historicist methods, the decision to focus each chapter on a single play, or two in the case of the *Henry IV* plays, rests on the assumption that the formal properties of play texts, and their linguistic features especially, require and repay close reading. At the same time, I'm interested in pointing a way out of the problem of the singular, aesthetic "object" by redefining aesthetic forms such as drama as a mode of "practice" that overlaps with other cultural practices that themselves warrant careful attention. This is not to say that dramatic and non-dramatic forms operate in precisely the same way, or that they are radically separate, but rather that each form involves a distinct mode of perception and participation, and that an analysis of early modern drama can profit from reading these various practices in relation to each other. Reading is thus central to this approach, and my method throughout is to attend to the textual traces of urban experience in dramatic representations and their presentational modes in juxtaposition with cultural materials, all of which inflect the theatrical "practice" of the city. One of the aims of the pairings of individual chapters, then, is to model how reading various and diverse texts "together" is crucial to understanding both urban practice and theatrical experience and the "reiterative openness" city performances enabled.

Implicit within this focus on theatrical experience is the question of the audience, which, as Jacques Rancière reminds us, is at the heart of how we think about relations between politics and theater.[66] The question invokes a history of debate about drama, community, and political life that stretches from fifth-century Athens to today, yet its terms have particular resonance for early modern London, when the stage suddenly gave playgoers unprecedented visibility, as dramatic subjects and as spectators to be chided and cajoled by prologues and epilogues. The terms of the debate are familiar, framed by an opposition between passive and active spectators. But what complicates this question for the early modern period is the problem of evidence. Given the dearth of first-hand accounts of theatrical experience, the evidentiary burden rests largely with the play texts themselves, with metatheatrical commentary as well as the non-mimetic features of performance, the codes, conventions, and techniques shared by playwrights and playgoers.[67] Seeking to open up the politics of city plays in relation to local audiences, my approach gestures toward what Henry Turner has referred to as an "'exploded view' of early modern theatricality, a blueprint that isolates functional parts, magnifies them for analysis and then reintegrates them into the theatrical apparatus."[68] *Practicing the City* does not present a schematic of the "full 'event' of theater" that Turner envisions. But what it does offer is evidence of the extent to which the early modern London theater was at once a decidedly local event and a powerful medium for shared practice that enabled city residents to engage in the politics of urbanization.

The chapters that follow begin with history plays. Despite their London settings, these plays may seem an unusual way into the category of city plays more conventionally associated with comedy, and it could be argued that these particular history plays engage the contemporary city only indirectly, as a backdrop to larger stories of dynastic conflict and individual confrontations with state power.[69] But my interest here is precisely with this indirection, particularly with the ways in which the contemporary city intrudes upon these larger stories, interrupting or disturbing established boundaries, between past and present, most obviously, but also between state and city authority and the categories of subject and citizen, in movements that speak directly to the questions of differences at the heart of this study. The book's second half shifts to city comedies and to urban scenes ruled by merchants rather than monarchs. These plays render contemporary London with vivid and sometimes claustrophobic immediacy, but my concern here is less with realistic representations of city life than it is with the forms of practice and performance that traverse them. My aim in putting histories together with comedies is not to set them in opposition, nor is it to trace the city's increasing prominence on stage. It is, rather, to explore how the conjunctions of history and comedy might deepen and complicate our understanding of the local resonance of both dramatic forms, so that we might, for example, be more attuned to the local particularities of history plays with city settings even as we attend more closely to the formal experiments disrupting the mimetic surfaces of city comedies. It is also to adduce a common set of operations by which the London stage may be said to "practice" the city.

The first chapter, "Extending Credit and the *Henry IV* Plays," begins at the intersections of dynastic history and contemporary credit relations, mapping the anachronistic commerce between the nation's feudal past and London's commercial present. The need for credit is pervasive in these plays, extending from princes to apprentices in far-reaching networks of indebtedness. And just as this economy traverses the distance between Westminster and Eastcheap, and between past and present, so too does it bring court politics into close proximity with the legal language of debt and contract. Rather than understanding commerce and credit in these plays simply as offering a critique of the Lancastrian "purchase" of the crown, as is often argued, this chapter considers what's at stake in the credit economy for commoners as well as kings. This constitutes a crucial shift in critical perspective that takes the plays' London scenes on their own terms in order to examine credit not simply as a kind of moral shorthand for corrupt politics but as an actual practice, whose activities in early modern London were subject to debate and litigation. What this shift opens up, I argue, is a new understanding of credit networks as complex structures for securing economic and political relations across distance and difference, within Shakespeare's histories and within contemporary London. These networks also extend to theatrical practice, and I close this chapter by turning to *2 Henry IV*'s epilogue, whose banter with the audience joins playwright and spectators to the economic realm of playhouse and city.

Chapter 2, "Differentiating Collaboration: Protest and Playwriting and *Sir Thomas More*," turns from dynastic to urban history, to a play that conjoins scenes of citizen protest with the story of the rise and fall of one of London's most prominent citizens. As is much remarked, the play's traffic between past and present follows a well-traveled route, linking the infamous May Day riots of 1517 to the anti-alien outbreaks of the 1590s, and it is presumably this incendiary topicality that prompted the Master of the Revels to censor the play. But even as *Sir Thomas More* retails a familiar trope of citizen identity, based on excluding those outside the community, it simultaneously proposes an alternative structure for practicing the city in what I am calling networks of collaboration. This chapter explores the possibilities for collaboration not only within the play, in scenes of protest that culminate in the citizens' change of heart as they imagine themselves as strangers, but also in relation to the play text's own production. One of the few surviving playscripts from the period, the manuscript of *Sir Thomas More* is a remarkable document of the processes of collaborative playwriting, and much of the criticism on the play has been devoted to textual questions and debates about authorship. What interests me here, however, are the ways in which this record of playwriting informs the collaborative practices staged in the play itself, inviting us to read the collective labor of dramatists writing for the commercial stage in relation to the common cause of citizens, and thus to adduce a more fully articulated account of reciprocal practices that might counter the institutional exclusions of early modern London, including those staged in the play's opening scene.

Returning to the city's perennial confrontations with strangers, Chapter 3, "Trading in Tongues: Language Lessons and *Englishmen for My Money*," explores the linguistic circulations of the commercial city in a play that has the distinction of being the earliest surviving comedy of contemporary London, first performed in 1598. Marked by a self-conscious delight in the urban topography, the play ranges across London, from Paul's Walk to the Royal Exchange to the maze of streets and alleys around Tower Hill, a movement that reconstructs the city as a labyrinth protective of locals and inaccessible to foreigners. As recent criticism attests, language operates in *Englishmen* much like the city's topography, as a site on which the play separates native from foreign. Complicating this view, this chapter explores how language is a mode of exchange as well as exclusion, offering a structure within which distinctions might be rearticulated. As evidence of linguistic exchange, I turn to the French language manuals popular in late-sixteenth-century London. Outlining a performative practice for mediating national as well as linguistic differences, early modern language pedagogy invites new understandings not only of the cross-linguistic impersonations of *Englishmen for My Money* but also of the circulations of the play's own performances within the city's linguistic economy.

The book's final chapter, "The Place of the Present: Making Time and *The Roaring Girl*," steps back from the stage's representations of urban practice in order to concentrate on theatrical experience itself as a form of local practice. Concerned with the specific question of how the stage's local turn might inflect playgoers' experience of the here-and-now, this chapter explores the possibilities for new modes of temporal experience within metropolitan London. I approach this question of urban time through an unlikely pairing, putting Middleton and Dekker's presentation of *The Roaring Girl* together with the temporal measures of the city's newly instituted mortality bills, whose weekly appearance subjected London residents to new ways of understanding themselves within time. As the city's first "periodical," the bills dominated city life during the early seventeenth century, a period coincidental with the rise of city comedy. This is not to argue for a causal relationship between mortality bills and city plays but rather to consider the possible interplay between these two seemingly divergent modes of perceiving time. This chapter demonstrates how the theater not only figures centrally in the city's shared engagements with urban contemporaneity, but how it does so in ways that grant local audiences a freedom to participate in these engagements. This feature comes to life, as it were, in the documented circulations of the actual Mary Frith, whose performances extended from Paul's Cross to the Fortune's own stage in an ongoing "practice" of the city.

The book concludes with an epilogue that extends consideration of these experiential theatrics to the place of the spectator. Reflecting on the broader politics of the stage's urban turn, the epilogue raises the possibility of a theatrocracy constituted by what Rancière refers to as the "emancipated spectator." Rancière's work on the distribution of the sensible offers us a way to think about a city stage that licenses its spectators even as it attempts to keep them in their place. Jonson's *The Staple of News* raises similar questions about the place of the audience, writing spectators into the play with a quartet of outspoken gossips who insist on voicing their opinions. What both Jonson and Rancière recognize, for all their differences, is the theater's capacity to enact, even as it represents, the disruptive encounters of urban plurality.

Without proposing a definitive narrative of the stage's urban turn, these chapters consider the possibilities for practicing this new urban plurality on the London stage, and it's with the conditions and working out of those possibilities that this study is most concerned. It's probably not coincidental, however, that most of the plays I examine are at the forefront of the stage's urban turn, written or performed in the 1590s just when playwrights were beginning to experiment with London settings, and well before the protocols of urban mimesis were fully in place. Even *The Roaring Girl*, coming after the explosion of city comedies in the first decade of the new century, continues to traffic in innovation, pushing the limits of theatrical practice by being the first to portray a recognizable local personage onstage. Yet if I hesitate to hold up these plays as definitive or even broadly representative, I still want to claim a certain exemplarity in their local engagements that could be extended to other London plays in the period, so that it's possible to extrapolate from the readings set out in these chapters new understandings not only of the sophisticated satiric comedies of Jonson and Middleton but also of the so-called citizen plays and chronicle comedies of Dekker and Heywood. All of these plays provoked local audiences to "presuppose" the stage and city, even those plays that worked to bring those suppositions in line with a prescribed city view, and all provoked, at some level, a play of location, a "taking place," within which the local population might begin to practice the city.

# 1. *Extending Credit and the* Henry IV *Plays*

Shakespeare's *Henry IV* plays may seem an unlikely starting point for exploring theatrical mediations of urban experience. Announced by the king's promise to unite his divided kingdom with a heroic crusade to Jerusalem, "[a]s far as to the sepulchre of Christ" (1.1.19), the plays' geographic ambitions are global rather than local, in striking contrast to Shakespeare's main dramatic source, *The Famous Victories of Henry V*, which opens with the Prince, "now about a mile off London" (1.13), making his way to "the old tavern in Eastcheap" (1.74).[1] Popularized by the Queen's Men in the 1580s, *The Famous Victories* centers on London and a colorful cast of city elites and local artisans. Shakespeare's version, by contrast, appears to signal a change in direction, in a move that subordinates citizens and apprentices to princes and monarchs. It is true that there is a vitality to the Eastcheap scenes, which for some has the effect of rendering chronicle history "little more than a tapestried hanging, dimly wrought," as E. K. Chambers put it.[2] Even so, critical work on the *Henry IV* plays has tended to relegate the city scenes to functionary roles of "local color" or comic parody, counterpoint to the plays' primary concern with affairs of state.[3]

But if London doesn't take center stage in the *Henry IV* plays, contemporary urban interests nonetheless make their entrance onto the historical scene, circulated by a credit economy that extends from late-sixteenth-century London to the medieval court of the Lancastrians. Credit terms are habitual among the royal family, associated with both the king, who, as Hotspur puts it, "Knows at what time to promise, when to pay" (4.3.53), and the prince, who cryptically assures the audience at the start of *1 Henry IV* that he will eventually "pay the debt I never promised" (1.2.199). Yet the need for credit involves far more than the king's moral and political debts or his son's tarnished reputation. Cutting across boundaries of space and time, credit also comes into play with the everyday exchanges of currency and goods—the marks and angels, sugar and satin, and "little tiny kickshaws" (*2 Henry IV*, 5.1.26)—that tie princes to urban denizens within economic networks that ultimately reach, in a metadramatic sleight-of-hand at the play's end, from the past into the present to include the playwright and his audience.[4] That late-sixteenth-century London was becoming increasingly dependent on a credit economy no doubt encouraged Shakespeare's audience to identify with the events on stage and thus to see the past in relation to the present. But it is also the case that topicality in the *Henry IV* plays works much as it does in the other plays of this study, as a means of exploring new modes of urban activity and association within present-day London. My aim in this chapter is with tracing the multiple and dislocating effects of this traffic between past and present, and between the stage and contemporary London, a traffic that, I suggest, allowed ordinary Londoners a freedom to explore possibilities for mobility and change within the established hierarchies of the commercial city.

Economic questions have figured centrally in New Historicist work on the *Henry IV* plays, but they have not necessarily prompted an interest in the contemporary city or its entrepreneurial residents. Shifting attention away from the Eastcheap tavern, so often sentimentalized by earlier generations of critics, recent historicist work has instead concentrated on the monarchy and its supposed fall into commercialism.[5] The Lancastrian "purchase" of the Crown, the argument goes, results in a new society governed by "economic determinism," where characters "compete with each other ruthlessly in a world drained of intrinsic value."[6] The sacred trust of feudal rule is replaced by a modern state founded on an ethic of self-interest, calculation, and betrayal. Concerned with the production of royal power, these accounts give close attention to political discourse, particularly the Lancastrian reliance on metaphors of credit and exchange, which has the effect of equating "human relations with economic transactions."[7] What tends to disappear in this focus on a discursive moral economy, however, are the actual economic practices that connect the promises and payments of the Lancastrians to the daily reckonings of those outside the court, to Falstaff's debts or Hostess Quickly's lawsuit, for example, or to the accounting practices of artisans and tradesmen in Shakespeare's audiences.[8] The effect is to reduce London's role on history's stage so that, rather than constituting a vital economy in its own right, the city functions simply as a symbolic measure of the moral decline of Lancastrian authority. It is also to reduce the role of local audiences so as to foreclose the experiential theatrics of practicing the city on stage.

Turning attention to the contemporary city, and to local audiences, this chapter approaches Lancastrian debts from the vantage point of credit practices that in late-sixteenth-century London were linked to, but also separate from, royal power. The commercial city in this period was already enmeshed in what Craig Muldrew has called "a culture of credit," characterized by the increasingly dense webs of economic dependence that were also reshaping the social and political terrain.[9] As the recent explosion of work on early modern credit persuasively documents, this new culture of credit supplied a means as well as a measure of social mobility within a rapidly expanding economy, linking a diverse population within networks of obligation that increasingly operated across rank and distance, radiating out from England's commercial center.[10] In this sense, credit relations illustrate an urban network *par excellence*, comprising an interconnecting structure within which Londoners navigated distance and difference within the city and beyond. This is not to suggest that expanding networks of credit resulted in a utopian leveling of society or that rising debt levels didn't strain social and economic relations. But insofar as indebtedness brought strangers into contact and confrontation, the consequences of credit were far-reaching, extending from the commercial and social realms to politics and the law, defining new forms of contractual relations and political obligation.

Shakespeare was not the first, of course, to bring dynastic history together with the contemporary city. Medievalism was a hallmark of civic pageantry, and the annual Lord Mayor's shows regularly invoked legends about citizen heroes, epitomized by the celebrated fishmonger-mayor William Walworth, who bravely defended Richard II from the rebellious Jack Straw.[11] It has been argued of this pageantry that Londoners, still without "a set of values peculiarly their own," were simply emulating the neochivalric displays of the Tudor court.[12] Even so, as Lawrence Manley observes, the feudal mythology was well suited to London's interests, "accommodating the ambitious and acquisitive practices of citizens to aristocratic values, even as it masked the mobility of entrepreneurs as a manifestation of nobility."[13] As the "preferred civic style" of Londoners, the chivalric decor ennobled merchants as heroic warriors defending king and commonwealth and, at the same time, strategically underplayed the city's status as an economic power, thereby minimizing the fact of the

Crown's increasing dependence on the wealth of city merchants.[14] But even as the *Henry IV* plays invoke the trappings of civic pageantry, their temporal traffic is radically at odds with the city's accommodating fictions. For what joins the disparate spaces of past and present, court and city, and aristocrat and commoner, on Shakespeare's stage is not an idealized chivalric past but the pressing realities of the urban commerce. Delineating an economy far closer to the proto-capitalism of late-sixteenth-century London than the feudal relations of Lancastrian England, the *Henry IV* plays feature precisely the kinds of exchanges and obligations that remain hidden by the chivalric decor of civic ceremony.[15]

One effect of Shakespeare's interpolation of the commercial city into medieval history is to call attention to a changing urban economy. The pronounced temporal dislocations of this approach invite audiences to experience London from a double perspective, encouraging them both to identify with and distance themselves from the events on stage so as to reflect on the complexities of their own mobility within the urban economy. Nowhere is this more apparent than in the pronounced anachronisms of the Eastcheap scenes. As many suggest, the play's tavern is a likely reference to the Boar's Head Inn of Shakespeare's day, a popular drinking establishment on the south side of Eastcheap.[16] But as antiquarian John Stow pointed out, during Henry IV's reign, "there was no taverne then in Eastcheape"; instead, friends "disposed to be merrie" frequented Eastcheap's cooks' stalls, "where they called for meate what them liked, which they alwayes found ready dressed at a reasonable rate."[17] Unlike Stow, however, the *Henry IV* plays conspicuously refuse such historical distinctions, choosing instead to transport a Lancastrian prince into the familiar workaday world of early modern London, a world of clinking pewter, inflated prices, and unpaid bills. Shakespeare history thus offers playgoers what we might call a "presentist" version of England's past, mediating fifteenth-century dynastic struggles within the frame of the everyday concerns of late-sixteenth-century London. In the process, the plays mark off a recognizable city space for encounters not only between princes and apprentices, but between the fixed structures of feudal rule and the more fluid and contingent relations of early modern credit.

Implicit in these encounters is a political question that centers on the possibilities credit might hold for a more equitable model of urban sociability. This chapter explores this question as it extends from the play to the playhouse and beyond, looking closely at the city's credit practices in relation to the shifting economies represented on stage. While my interest here is with credit's potential to structure encounters across difference, this is not to reduce credit to a politics of consent or to suggest that the *Henry IV* plays present an unmediated celebration of credit that links commerce to community in a kind of proto-democratic politics or free-market capitalism. Nor is it to ignore the very real effects of power and privilege on credit relations. Commoners do not trade with the same freedom as kings, and the plays are filled with instances of failed credit, bad faith, and corrupt judgment. But if credit is not a panacea for social inequities, either on Shakespeare's stage or in early modern London, it does provide a crucial framework for mediating the increasingly complex reciprocities of urban life. This chapter explores the mediating effects of credit on urban sociability and politics, as represented on history's stage and as enacted within a commercial theater that is itself engaged in credit relations.

## *A Culture of Credit*

"[T]here is nothing in the world so ordinarie, and naturall vnto men, as to contract, truck, merchandise, and trafficque one with an other," John Wheeler declared in *A Treatise of Commerce* (1601), "so that it is almost vnpossible for three persons to converse together two houres, but they wil fall into talke of one bargaine or another, chopping, changing, or some other kinde of contract."[18] A great merchant and former secretary to the Merchants Adventurers, Wheeler's interests, and those of his company, were no doubt served by an argument that naturalizes trade as a social and economic practice, but his praise of commerce nonetheless points to the importance of credit and contract within the city's economy. In the absence of a public banking system, and with gold and silver currency in short supply, the economy was becoming increasingly dependent on borrowing as all ranks—noble men and women, merchants, retailers, playwrights, farmers, and even housewives—entered into credit arrangements, whether in the form of sealed bonds, tradesmen's bills, or the verbal agreements that secured the exchanges of everyday life. As Thomas Tusser put it, most simply, in his best-selling *Fiue hundreth pointes of good husbandrie*: "Who liveth but lends: and be lent to they must, else buieng and selling, might lie in the dust."[19] The popularity of Tusser's homespun advice—his pamphlet was reprinted more than twenty times in the next fifty years—tells us something about credit's place in the lives of ordinary people. His advice also bears witness to the widespread acceptance of borrowing and lending by the end of the sixteenth century.

But if credit was becoming increasingly ubiquitous, its use continued to be debated. As might be expected, anti-usury tracts viewed lending at interest as a religious issue as much as an economic one, castigating moneylenders as uncharitable and anti-Christian.[20] Creditors were "worse than Iewes," went the common refrain, and posed a threat to the urban community that should not go unpunished.[21] Criticism of lending was not limited to moral concerns, however, or to the specific problem of charity. Even more to the point in this period was the fact that credit, together with the expanding economy, was rapidly changing social relations. Central to these changes was credit's reliance on contract, which as Muldrew puts it, "led to the development of a highly legalistic language of social description which elevated the legalism of contract to a privileged position."[22] Recent scholarship on this "new discourse of contract" has done much to trace the social and political effects of this juridical turn over the seventeenth century, particularly as questions about obligation came to be adjudicated in the period's debates about common law, natural law, and covenant theology.[23] My interest here is more localized, concentrated on issues that may have been particularly pressing for London audiences in the late sixteenth century when the *Henry IV* plays were first performed. Even at the start of the credit explosion, connections between social, political, and economic obligations were already apparent and subject to discussion and debate.

One measure of the economy's potential to alter social position may be found in the shifting definitions of credit itself. By the late sixteenth century, the term had acquired a double meaning, referring to reputation, or character, as defined not only by social standing but also by wealth or financial solvency.[24] It is this doubleness that Shakespeare plays on in Shylock's assertion that "Antonio is a good man," by which the moneylender means Antonio's ability to pay, but which Bassanio takes to mean character. As this slippage suggests, in early modern London, as in Shakespeare's Venice, credit relations not only involved all ranks but, more significantly, had the potential to cut across hierarchies of rank and status. And just as the spendthrift aristocrat turns to the merchant to raise money for his Belmont venture, and the merchant, short of cash, in turn tries his credit with the Jew, borrowing in England often extended downward from the Crown and the aristocracy, who turned to London's powerful financiers and merchants for ready money, as well as horizontally among tradesmen, artisans, and neighbors. For many, credit's ability to traverse social boundaries represented a dangerous threat to moral order, and conservative critics began to speak of the need to protect the aristocracy as well as the poor from wealthy urban creditors who would "eate our English Gentrie out of house and home."[25] Even members of the clergy began to speak on behalf of the upper ranks, as illustrated by Roger Hacket's 1591 sermon warning that the usurer "gnaweth and teareth out his gaine, out of the lands and lively-hoodes not onely of the commonalty, but gentry, yea nobilitye of this land."[26]

Yet these views were by no means universal, especially within the city of London, where clergymen complained of parishioners who protested against anti-usury sermons by withholding their tithes.[27] The discrepancy between religious discourse and economic practices was especially visible at St. Paul's, where outside at Paul's Cross preachers railed against lending while inside, at the font, creditors and debtors met regularly for the "tendering and making of payment."[28] By the 1590s, some London clergymen were beginning to defend lending under certain conditions. Speaking out in the same year as Hacket, Charles Gibbon went so far as to sanction interest solely on the basis of social status—"Lend to thy better for a benefite, but to the poore for a blessing,"[29] he counseled—and Miles Mosse, in a series of influential sermons, justified lending to the upper ranks as a business venture, profitable to all parties involved.[30] Still others pointed to the unfairness of allowing profits from land but not from money.[31] By the beginning of the seventeenth century, defenses of credit and commerce began to appear in print, as London merchants and tradesmen attempted to justify their place within the changing economy. Countering objections that private gain was always at the expense of the common welfare, these defenses shrewdly linked the individual's profit with that of the community. "What else makes a Common-wealth," Edward Misselden wrote in *The Circle of Commerce* (1623), "but the private-wealth . . . of the members thereof in the exercise of commerce."[32] For Misselden and other defenders of trade, what was good for the individual was good for London.[33]

As lending expanded, and involved extending larger sums, often to strangers, credit relations became more dependent on formal credit instruments and contracts. Contracts were themselves the subject of much debate in the period.[34] Defined as early as the fifteenth century by Johannes Nider in a commentary on Roman law, transfers of goods and money must be transacted "'in accordance with an agreement'" involving mutual consent. "[I]n the giver be both the will to give, or consent, and similarly the power, and in the receiver the will to receive and the power so to do," Nider writes, his balanced terms implying equality on both sides.[35] Within the context of English common law, Christopher St. Germain's *Doctor and Student* (1531) explicitly defines a contract as a bargain or sale "made by assent of the partyes uppon agrement betwene theym."[36] In *The Boke Named the Governour* (1531), Thomas Elyot further elevates the importance of mutual consent by identifying it with justice: "Trewely in every covenaunt, bargayne, or promise aught to be a simplicitie, that is to saye, one playne understandinge or meaning betwene the parties. And that simplicitie is properly justice."[37] The anonymous author of *A Godlie Treatice Concerning The lawfull use of ritches* (1578) similarly emphasizes the imperative of equality in contractual arrangements, explaining that if a contract is to have "plainnes, and excludeth double dealyng: so it requireth equalitie betweene those whiche bargayne."[38] By definition, then, a contract necessitated mutual agreement, and, as William West's *Symbolaeographia* plainly asserts, "bare promises by worde without mutuall consent are nothing worth."[39]

Despite the insistence on the principle of mutuality, however, the bargaining power of consenting parties was frequently unequal, and popular literature and court records—like the *Henry IV* plays—document the pervasiveness of failed credit and bad faith. Indeed, as the Doctor in Wilson's *Discourse on Usury* rightly argues, "what equalytye is in bargaynynge, I praye you, when the one partie is famished, and the other is hoggesty fed? Iustice is none other thinge then a certeine evenhode or equalitie, and therefore they that do not in their dealings use an equal property, do not use Iustice."[40] Urban literature from the period trades on the inequities of credit, as illustrated in the popular tales of the London prodigal who, in the attempt to clear himself of one debt, takes on additional debt until he is finally coerced into signing away his lands.[41] Henslowe's account books suggest the reality of this pattern of spiraling debt, coercion, and ruin for the lower orders as well, detailing the degree to which credit enabled the entrepreneur to control the playwrights and actors in his pay. As Henslowe himself was said to admit, "'Should these fellowes come out of my debt, I should have noe rule with them.'"[42]

But if the evidence does not justify an idealization of credit practices, neither does it support a conclusion that mutual agreements were simply a means of justifying what were in effect coercive practices. According to C. W. Brooks's study of central court records, the number of debt cases rose significantly in the latter half of the sixteenth century, with the plaintiffs coming from a wide social spectrum, many bringing suit against their social betters.[43] While the increase in litigation may reflect both the expansion of credit as well as the extent to which credit relations broke down, it also, and perhaps more accurately, points to the expanding role of the courts in enabling the recovery of debts and, we might assume, thereby enforcing a degree of equality and trust within a wider community.[44] The figures suggest that as credit extended across social boundaries, self-interest might function as an incentive to trust in the mediation of difference across ranks, even though that trust might sometimes fail. To engage in credit was to risk loss and betrayal, but credit relations grounded in the processes of mutual consent and mutual gain also afforded opportunities for economic and political agency.

In allowing for the possibility of social equality and mobility, early modern credit practices offer a useful framework for thinking about intersections of economics and politics in the *Henry IV* plays. For not only do these practices elucidate the politics of Lancastrian economic discourse, they also direct attention to an alternative form of obligation, centered not in the monarch's authority but in the fluid economic networks of commercial London. In their movement between the court and the city, between Westminster and Eastcheap, the plays could be said to trace the sixteenth-century shift from a lineage society to a civil society, and from status to contract. As Muldrew explains the argument, in a lineage society, stability within the community depends on bonds of obligation based on "extended kinship and loyalties to great aristocratic households, and where contracts [are] subordinated to clientage"; in a civil society, stability rests more on contractual obligations, "on the equality of bargaining and contract, and on access to the courts to maintain the right of such equality."[45] One way to understand this movement within the *Henry IV* plays has been to focus on the Crown's appropriation of economic practices, and to read this turn to commercialism as necessitated by the Lancastrian violation of lineage society in usurping Richard II's throne. While this is clearly part of the story, it fails to give attention to the way in which the political advantages of a credit economy move in two directions, downward as well as upward on the social scale. For in borrowing their political strategies from the urban economy, the Lancastrians effectively endorse the principles of that economy and, by extension, the possibilities for ever-widening networks of mobility and exchange. In this case, what serves the interests of the Crown has the potential to change economic and political structures for commoners as well. It is this dialectical relationship between economics and politics, played out between past and present within the urban spaces of the *Henry IV* plays, that early modern credit relations make available.

## *Reckonings*

| | |
|---|---|
| *Item: a capon* | *2s.2d.* |
| *Item: sauce* | *4d.* |
| *Item: sack, two gallons* | *5s.8d.* |
| *Item: anchovies and sack after supper* | *2s.6d.* |
| *Item: bread* | *ob.* |

(*1 Henry IV*, 2.4.522–26)

A reckoning, discovered by the Prince and Peto when they pick Falstaff's pockets in the tavern after the Gadshill robbery, supplies the only material evidence of credit in *1 Henry IV*, a play that turns on problems of debt and obligation. In addition to what the accounting tells the local audience about Falstaff's taste for luxury imports (this passage contains the earliest reference to anchovies cited in the *Oxford English Dictionary*), it enables the Prince to continue his sport at Falstaff's expense. "O monstrous! But one halfpennyworth of bread to this intolerable deal of sack!" (527–28), the Prince sermonizes, announcing his newfound patriotism with the promise that the money they have stolen from the King's exchequer "shall be paid back again with advantage" (533–34). The Prince makes good on his promise, but Falstaff's debt to the Hostess is never paid—at least not in *1 Henry IV*. "I'll not pay a denier," Falstaff later boasts, insisting that to clear the debt is to become a too-trusting prodigal, victimized by a grasping creditor: "What, will you make a younker of me? Shall I not take mine ease in mine inn, but I shall have my pocket picked?" (3.3.79–81), he counters, reversing the charges on his hostess. The sum of his appetites, Falstaff's debts increase exponentially over the course of *1* and *2 Henry IV* until at the end, with Henry V's coronation, the old knight is hauled off to Fleet prison, for bad debts we may assume. More than simply a running gag in the *Henry IV* plays, Falstaff's indebtedness connects the economic and political worlds of Eastcheap and Westminster, bringing material obligations into play with the moral and political debts of the Lancasters. As a particular instance of material culture, the tavern reckoning also supplies a resonant point of reference for the world outside the play, in relation to London audiences in the habit of calculating their own appetites for both business and pleasure, including their place within the theater, in terms of shillings, pence, and the itemized accounts of everyday exchange.

That the play identifies credit with a tavern reckoning, and not with a merchant's bond, say, considerably extends the reach of economic networks to include society's middling and lower ranks. The identification is also important in establishing an alternative authority within the plays, one governed less by fixed hierarchies of dynastic power than by flexible credit relations. A place of exchange and change, where princes drink with tinkers and fat knights take the part of kings, the Eastcheap tavern has been profitably understood in terms of carnival festivity as a world of "celebration and critique" that stages the uncrowning of royal authority that constitutes the official world of these plays.[46] But Eastcheap may also be understood in terms of everyday as well as holiday, for if we think of the tavern as a place of both business and pleasure, then the holiday world in which some take their leisure overlaps with the everyday world in which others, like the Hostess and Francis, work for their living.[47] The tavern thus delineates a world whose ethics are rooted as much in the business practices of London's middling sort as the holiday festivities of popular culture or the reckless spending of those who desire to be men "of good reckoning," as Dekker describes the fashionable gallants who haunt taverns in *The Gull's Hornbook*.[48] Within this world, normative values require not only that credit be extended to commoners as well as to kings, but also that debts be paid and contracts honored. And it is in this sense that the economic relations of Eastcheap can be said to provide a model for political relations in Westminster, a model potentially available to all who engage in credit.

It could be objected, of course, that Falstaff's unpaid bill is hardly evidence of credit's potential to generate economic or social equality. In Falstaff's case, the need for credit seems to result in a hardening of rank and privilege. A stage version of the grasping men of business railed against by preachers and moralists during the period, Falstaff takes pride in his bad faith, pointing to his unpaid debts as a mark of gentlemanly distinction: "paid money that I borrowed—three or four times" (3.3.18), he gloats. To be sure, there is much humor in Falstaff's outrageous flouting of commercial expectation. But in the world outside the tavern, and outside the theater, his borrowing provides a grim reminder of the cost of self-interest and bad faith to the community's welfare, a reminder with particular resonance in the late 1590s when the play was first produced. Falstaff's appetite for luxury foodstuffs would, in fact, have bordered on the criminal in the dearth years of 1596–97 when, under orders from the Privy Council, London citizens were instructed to curb their "excessive dyet" and "be contented with fewer dishes" so that the excess could be distributed to the poor.[49] Other signs of the dearth, which many at the time blamed on engrossers manipulating the market (see Figure 1), are to be found in the image of poor Robin Ostler, who "never joyed since the price of oats rose; it was the death of him" (2.1.12–13), and in Falstaff's "tattered prodigals" (4.2.33–34) and "trade-fallen" ostlers, "food for powder" (65) simply because they are too poor to buy their way out of service.[50] Rather than reinforcing reciprocity and equality across ranks, these examples suggest, the circulation of credit only increases the potential for exploitation, especially when bargaining takes place between parties of unequal status.[51]

But Falstaff's bill for sack and anchovies is not the only instance of reckoning in *1 Henry IV*, nor is his bad faith its only ethics of credit. The first reference to reckoning occurs, tellingly, in a scene of verbal sparring, of give-and-take across ranks, when, in response to the Prince's question—"Why, what a pox have I to do with my hostess of the tavern?"—Falstaff

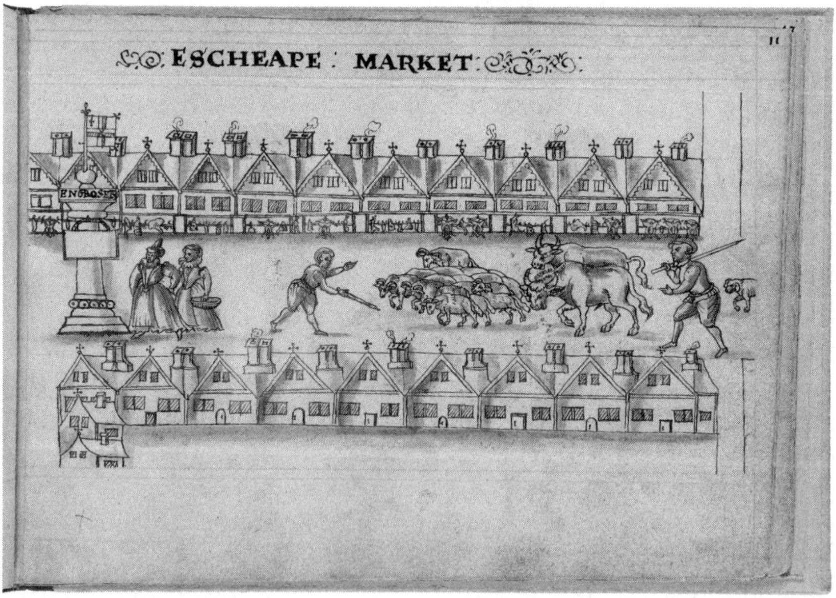


Figure 1. Hugh Alley, *A caveatt for the citty of London, or, A forewarninge of offences against penall lawes* (by permission of the Folger Shakespeare Library).

replies, "Well, thou hast called her to a reckoning many a time and oft" (1.2.45–48). The ensuing wordplay depends on credit's multivalence in early modern London and puts into play its potential to promote both self-interest and trust, all the while blurring traditional distinctions within social and political hierarchies. The term slips, for example, between the material and the moral, between what can be counted and what can only be divined, depending on whether the reckoning is interpreted as a financial accounting—in this case another tavern bill—or a moral accounting—as Williams employs the term in *Henry V*, "if the cause be not good, the King himself hath a heavy reckoning to make" (4.1.134–35). With this punning comes a slippage in power and privilege as the fixed categories of prince and subject, reconstituted as customer and hostess, dissolve into the contingent, and exchangeable, positions of debtor and creditor. Falstaff's retort—"thou hast called her to a reckoning"—may at first suggest that the Hostess is indebted to the Prince, either morally or financially, but their positions shift when Falstaff admits that it is the Prince who has been the debtor, though he has "paid all there" (*1 Henry IV*, 1.2.50–51), including paying the knight's part. As one who pays his debts, the Prince might appear to offer a counter example to Falstaff, and in many ways he does. Most important, he knows that "to pay" is not to become a "younker" but to gain power. But if the Prince prides himself on his credit here and elsewhere in the play, his payments are anything but straightforward. In this instance, the Prince finesses his debt to the Hostess by shifting from economic to erotic currency, claiming to have paid, "Yea, and elsewhere, so far as my coin would stretch, and where it would not I have used my credit" (52–53).

Linked to the Prince's credit, the play on "reckoning" in this scene initiates a pattern of exchange between economics and politics that turns on the slippage between material and metaphorical obligation. The Prince's credit, especially as it depends on his position as "heir apparent" (55), as Falstaff reminds him, is not without problems, of course. Royal credit may work to Hal's advantage in the taverns of Eastcheap, but within the political realm, its powers are less assured. Compromised by his father's moral and political debts, Hal might well lament, with Falstaff, "I would to God thou and I knew where a commodity of good names were to be bought" (79–80). And it is, in fact, to the economic realm and not to his noble lineage that the Prince turns to redeem his name, renegotiating a troubled inheritance within the flexible structures of credit and commerce. While the shift to commercialism may be construed negatively, as evidence of

Hal's "steely sense of opportunism,"[52] its political implications go beyond the interests of the Lancastrians. Hal may adapt market practices for his own gain, but in translating these practices back into court politics, he opens up the possibility for a new mode of political obligations within the city as well as the court.

Evidence of the Prince's commercial practices comes early in *1 Henry IV*, in his promise to restore his credit by casting off his tavern mates, a promise that ties trust to betrayal and community to self-interest in ways that have long troubled commentators. Here, as elsewhere in the play, the idea of credit complicates these contradictions even as it offers a means of resolving them. Reimagining his succession as a kind of contract, the Prince opens up a line of credit with the audience that rests on his implicit promise that at some time in the future, "when he please again to be himself" (190), he will "throw off" his "loose behaviour" and "pay the debt [he] never promised" (198–99). What is especially troubling about Hal's contract, of course, is the fact that his good-faith promise depends on multiple acts of betrayal. The Prince calculates his reformation as a double deception, one practiced against his friends and the other against his enemies, falsifying "men's hopes" for his continued "loose behavior," hopes that he himself falsely created by playing the prodigal. Like Falstaff's reckonings, Hal's contract appears to use credit simply as a mask for self-interest, and to exploit rather than mediate differences within the community. Given the taint surrounding his father's acquisition of the throne, however, Hal's use of contract is also crucial to ensuring a stable succession: it allows him to renegotiate his responsibilities as Henry IV's inheritor, to pay his father's moral debts without accepting them as his own—"the debt I never promised"—and at the same time to translate passive inheritance into active consent—"to be himself" in majesty.

This is not to argue that, in rewriting his reformation and eventual succession in contractual terms, Hal resolves the contradictions of this soliloquy or of early modern credit. As this passage famously illustrates, the need for credit does not guarantee trust. Credit does, however, require a mechanism whereby trust can be negotiated. And as Hal's turn to contract suggests, this mechanism has political as well as economic implications, however much it is abused. In engaging in, and thereby endorsing, common credit practices, even as he exploits those practices, the Prince's commercialism thus complicates the recent analysis of the play's Machiavellian politics, in which, as Stephen Greenblatt has pointed out, "the founding of the modern state, like the self-fashioning of the modern prince, is shown to be based upon acts of calculation, intimidation, and deceit."[53] For Shakespeare's London audience, the Prince's turn to credit and exchange may well represent a descent from "sacramental to commercial premises,"[54] but in relocating authority to the everyday affairs of city business, it also constitutes a significant widening of the political community. For if contractual arrangements allow Hal a means of renegotiating his credit, these same strategies of power were also available to London citizens, whose livelihoods depended on negotiating credit and contracts on a daily basis. To be sure, the Prince is hardly on the same level as the earnest Francis, who will swear "upon all the books in England" (2.4.48–49) to honor the terms of his indenture. But just because the drawer, whose "eloquence" is "the parcel of a reckoning" (98–99), cannot imagine running out on his master does not mean that a local audience would have seen an apprenticeship of clinking pewter as an "oppressive order," as Greenblatt contends.[55] Some perhaps might have recognized an economic protection and even a freedom in the contractual terms of the indenture.[56]

The Prince returns to the language of contract and exchange when he again promises to reform and be "more myself" (3.2.93), this time in response to the King's accusation that his son fights against him "under Percy's pay" (126). Turning his father's commercial terms to advantage, Hal here transforms himself from a spendthrift prodigal into a great city merchant engaged in a circle of commerce, a move that allows him the freedom to manipulate both the market and his place within it. In Hal's account, it is Percy who is in his pay, hired as his "factor," or agent, to "engross up glorious deeds on my behalf" (148). But rather than turning the "glorious deeds" over to the Prince, Hotspur has kept them for himself, in a clear violation of their arrangement that demands redress. Within this mercantile context, the Prince renews his promise for reform, and his credit with his father, with the vow to make Percy pay what he owes:

> And I will call him to so strict account
> That he shall render every glory up,
> Yea, even the slightest worship of his time,
> Or I will tear the reckoning from his heart. (149–52)

Promising to call his factor to "strict account" or else "tear the reckoning from his heart," the Prince situates justice firmly within an economic sphere. And as it is structured by credit and contract, the shift from moral to commercial debt works to the Prince's advantage, transposing feudal obligations into material forms that are both exchangeable and recoverable. This allows him to transfer to Percy his own debt to his father, in a reversal of the changeling substitution the King had imagined at the start of the play. It also allows him to cancel his father's debt to the Percies. By demanding that Hotspur pay what he owes, Hal clears both his own name and his father's.

That the Prince first imagines his defeat of Percy not as the scene of single combat the play eventually stages but as a balancing of accounts—or a reckoning—between merchant and factor again injects everyday credit practices into affairs of state, and again the politics are mixed. One effect, clearly, is to commercialize heroic action so that honor becomes, as Lars Engle has argued, "an exchangeable commodity which, like money, can move all at once from one person's possession to another's."[57] In Hal's accounting, however, honor is more than simply a fungible commodity. It is also a commodity whose value fluctuates with the market and can, therefore, be manipulated by skillful merchants and retailers. In this sense, the economic model has the potential to confer political agency not only on the Prince, allowing him to recover his credit within the realm, but on all those who buy and sell. No longer the domain of aristocratic warriors, honor now belongs to those who have good credit within the marketplace, to those who pay what they owe or to those, like Falstaff, who can manipulate the market. In a world governed by commerce, the city's welfare depends as much, if not more, on honoring contracts as on battlefield heroics, a shift in value that ranks tradesmen alongside princes. As elsewhere in the play, however, the expansion of economic and political opportunity carries with it the potential for abuse, as suggested by Hal's use of the term "engross" to censure Hotspur's valorous acts.[58] As the Prince sees it, rewriting Percy's chivalry in economic terms that transform heroic valor into crass self-interest, Percy's holding on to the "glorious deeds" constitutes an abusive monopolistic practice that initiates a crisis in credit that threatens the kingdom as a whole. He must be forced to pay.

With the Prince's subsequent transformation to chivalric warrior, the play might appear to abandon its own promise of economic justice, exchanging the rigorous accounting practices of London merchants for the battlefield heroics of chronicle history. But even at Shrewsbury, where the Prince is mythologized as a "feathered Mercury" (4.1.105), an ethics of credit and contract continues to structure dynastic relations, as the Lancastrians persist in defining justice as a settling of accounts, a reckoning. The reformed Prince announces his new-found identity not as the god-like warrior feared by his enemies but as a man of credit, one who makes good on his promises and pays what he owes. As he proclaims to Douglas:

It is the Prince of Wales that threatens thee,
Who never promiseth but he means to pay. (5.4.41–42)

In promising the Percies payment, the Prince exploits the metaphorical resonance of commercial language. In one sense, Hal's talk of payment is highly conventional: He will become "himself" by stepping into his role as noble justicer and inflicting bodily chastisement on the wicked. At the same time, however, the language has a decidedly contemporary ring: The Prince will become "himself" and redeem his name in much the same way those in Shakespeare's audience did, by proving his ability to pay his debts and to honor contractual agreements. In casting himself not only as the divinely sanctioned ruler who dispenses punishment but also as a man who pays his reckonings, the Prince participates in a political economy bound together by the practices of everyday commerce. In contrast to his father's aristocratic fantasy of a crusade in which "mutual well-beseeming ranks / March all one way" (1.1.14–15), or his own promise in *Henry V* to "gentle" all who fight at Agincourt, the Prince's emphasis at Shrewsbury works in the opposite direction, making all merchants and retailers.[59]

## *Promises*

If the Prince's movement from prodigal to chivalric merchant in *1 Henry IV* celebrates the benefits of turning economic practices to political use, the betrayals and bad faith of *2 Henry IV* warn of the dangers, especially when credit is extended solely on the basis of a gentleman's, or a prince's, word. Reputation conferred by social status proves unreliable at the start of the play when the rebels mistakenly credit Lord Bardolph's "certain news" of Hotspur's victory at Shrewsbury because it comes from "A gentleman well bred, and of good name" (*2 Henry IV*, 1.1.26). The actual report of Percy's death comes minutes later, from a servant who, despite Bardolph's claim that "he is furnish'd with no certainties / More than he haply may retail from me" (31–32), has better credit in this instance than his social superior. The earl of Northumberland's absence from Shrewsbury, attributed to illness in *1 Henry IV*, is now exposed for what it is. "[Y]ou broke your word" (2.3.10), Hotspur's widow bluntly tells him. And Falstaff, new graced with the gilded lie of his "good service" (1.2.61–62) at

Shrewsbury, attempts to borrow against his borrowed name. The most disturbing display of failed credit, of course, comes with Prince John's triumph at Gaultree Forest, a victory that, in contrast to Shrewsbury, replaces heroic action with a "horrible violation of faith," as Samuel Johnson characterized it.[60] The supposed agreement between the Crown and the rebelling lords, which Prince John backs "by the honour of [his] blood" (4.2.55) and the rebels mistakenly accept on the basis of his "princely word" (66), epitomizes the dangers of trusting "the word of the noble" (4.3.53) and thus goes far in undermining the optimistic conjunction of chivalry and contract, of princes and merchants, at the conclusion of the earlier play. In *2 Henry IV*, only Master Dommelton, the "smooth-pate[s]" (1.2.38) London tradesman, appears to possess enough business acumen not to take gentlemen at their word: He refuses Falstaff's request for twenty-two yards of satin on credit because he dislikes the knight's "security" (1.2.33).

In its almost obsessive concern with promises, with oral rather than written contracts, *2 Henry IV* might seem to appeal more to medieval than early modern credit practices, to an idealized past in which a man's word was his bond and an ethical standard that, by some accounts, was more exploited than honored in the expanding economy of Shakespeare's day. But while the use of bonds increased with the expansion of credit in the sixteenth century, most loans, including those within London, continued to be secured by verbal agreements founded on the promise of future payment.[61] Promises also had strong contemporary resonance in the late 1590s as debate about the status of oral contracts involving debt culminated with the hearing of Slade's Case, a case that rested on the question of an implied promise. Argued on the basis of "breach of contract," rather than simple debt, Slade's Case forms the basis of modern contract law, clarifying over a century of litigation involving the status of promises in debt recovery.[62] As a result of its historical position, Slade's Case is also useful in adjudicating credit relations in the *Henry IV* plays, offering a model for economic and political relations centered on contractual arrangements.

Slade's Case was argued under the general category of *assumpsit*, a legal action that rested on the understanding that the defendant promised to undertake—or "assume"—the performance of a particular action or payment. *Assumpsit* thus offered a broad means of redress in cases involving breach of contract and was applied during the sixteenth century to promises involving the performance of acts or services, the conveyance of lands, and, with increasing frequency, the payment of debt. Whether a case was actionable under the category of debt or *assumpsit* depended on how the obligation was defined. The action in debt cases, for example, rested on the notion of *quid pro quo*, and defendants were charged with failing to live up to their end of the bargain. Legal redress in these cases meant simply that one paid what one owed, either money or property. The action in *assumpsit*, by contrast, rested not on the exchange of goods or property but on the process by which the exchange was negotiated, specifically, on the promise itself and on its motivating circumstances, known as "consideration."[63]

As a watershed case upholding the action of *assumpsit* in matters of debt, Slade's Case was important in changing the early modern understanding of debt and its recovery.[64] It was also important in defining the responsibilities of contracting parties. First heard in the Devon Assizes in 1595, Slade's Case made its way into the Exchequer Chamber in 1597 and over the next five years was argued in both the Exchequer Chamber and the King's Bench. Initially a dispute over a grain transaction between John Slade and Humphrey Morley, the case turned on the question of whether an oral agreement, in this case the agreement to purchase grain, also included the promise to pay for it, even if that promise was not explicitly stated.[65] The court's final decision was that a bargain, even in the absence of an explicitly stated promise, constituted a legally binding contract for performance or payment and, as such, was allowable under the action of *assumpsit*. As Edward Coke wrote in his decision, "every contract executory imports in itself an *assumpsit*, for when one agrees to pay money, or to deliver any thing, thereby he assumes or promises to pay."[66]

Coke's decision in the Slade Case rests on two related assumptions: that an individual enters into an agreement knowingly and that his failure to carry through on the agreement constitutes deceit.[67] For Coke, intentions may be probative, but they do have a material basis in the actions or non-actions of the consenting parties as defined by the rule of consideration. As Coke reputedly wrote in a report on the case in 1598, "if some benefit leave the plaintiff, be it to the defendant or to a stranger, this suffices; for it shall be intended at the request of the defendant," a conclusion that goes against the earlier decision in the Exeter assize by Justice Walmsley that failure to fulfill an obligation did not necessarily involve deceit.[68] It is "'plain dealing,'" Walmsley wrote, for a man not to pay if he has no money.[69] Coke's argument, by contrast, assumes that individuals knowingly enter into bargains and that their responsibility to honor their word lies, in principle at least, outside either social or economic status. Thus a ruling that is potentially coercive in assuming intention on the part of the defendant is at the same time potentially liberating in ascribing choice and responsibility to the individuals making the transaction.[70] As recent work on Slade's case contends, the ruling significantly altered the understanding of obligation, including political obligation, by shifting it from a moral to a legal sphere, partly in response to the exigencies of commercial practices.[71]

Like early modern actions of *assumpsit*, economic relations in these plays, and in *2 Henry IV* especially, turn on the promise of payment, or performance, implicit within an agreement or undertaking. And with the notable exception of Prince John—who precisely construes his "word" to the rebels and gets away with it—the plays anticipate the outcome of Slade's Case by enforcing the promises implicit within understandings between parties that range from lowly servants to the crown prince and to the "author" himself. At one end is the case of Shallow's servant, William, whose wages are to be stopped because of the "sack he lost the other day at Hinckley fair" (*2 Henry IV*, 5.1.22–23). The assumption in this case, we may conjecture, is that William had promised either to transport or sell the sack but instead lost it, or drank it. Hostess Quickly's suit against Falstaff, which appears to be simply a case of debt—he owes her "A hundred mark" (2.1.30–31), she first claims—might also be actionable under the category of *assumpsit*, especially in the way matters of debt become intertwined with her claim that the knight had promised to marry her. When asked what "gross sum" Falstaff owes her, Quickly replies, "thyself and the money too" (82–84), her unwitting joke accurately acknowledging the interplay between erotic and monetary debt that Falstaff continually exploits. Because there is no gift of a ring and no witness (goodwife Keech, the butcher's wife, comes into her testimony not as a witness, as we might expect, but "to borrow a mess of vinegar"), Quickly's charges probably would not have stood up in the ecclesiastical court, but they might have been allowed under an action of *assumpsit*.[72] Her lengthy testimony before the Chief Justice places the emphasis on Falstaff's promise of marriage, for which she supplies a form of consideration in an outrageously detailed account of the material circumstances in which the promise took place, circumstances that supposedly give authority and authenticity to her claim:

> Thou didst swear to me upon a parcel-gilt goblet, sitting in my Dolphin chamber, at the round table, by a sea-coal fire, upon Wednesday in Wheeson week, when the Prince broke thy head for liking his father to a singing-man of Windsor—thou didst swear to me then, as I was washing thy wound, to marry me, and make me my lady thy wife. Canst thou

> deny it? . . . And didst thou not, when [goodwife Keech] was gone downstairs, desire me to be no more so familiarity with such poor people, saying that ere long they should call me madam? And didst thou not kiss me, and bid me fetch thee thirty shillings? I put thee now to thy book oath, deny it if thou canst. (2.1.84–101)

Even though Falstaff attempts to discredit the Hostess, claiming she is a "poor mad soul" (102), "distracted" (105) by poverty, the Chief Justice, like Coke, finds for the plaintiff, concluding that Falstaff has used her "both in purse and in person"(114–15) and instructing him to "Pay her the debt you owe her, and unpay the villainy you have done with her" (117–18). The unreformed Falstaff slips out of this accounting by once again parleying his erotic credit into coin. "Come . . . dost not know me?" (148–49), he asks the Hostess, assuming an intimacy that invites reciprocity.[73] This strategy works as well with Justice Shallow, who lends Falstaff a thousand pounds, on the assumption that this will further the justice's advancement at court when Hal becomes king. In this instance, the promise again appears to be upheld when, at the play's close, after Henry V destroys Falstaff's credit by publicly refusing to acknowledge any debt to his former companion, Falstaff is taken off to the Fleet. For the first time, Falstaff admits a debt, confessing, "Master Shallow, I owe you a thousand pound" (5.5.72), though not without once again attempting to regain his credit, and retain the sum, by renewing his promise to Shallow: "Fear not your advancements; I will be the man yet that shall make you great. . . . Sir, I will be as good as my word" (78–80, 85).

In its concern for the processes of exchange, the action of *assumpsit* is especially useful in charting the movement between economic and political credit in the play. As in *1 Henry IV*, the Lancastrians again adopt economic practices for political gain. As a consequence, the play invites its audience to judge princes by the same standard they apply to commoners. The most unsettling conjunction of politics and credit practices comes with Prince John's resolution of rebellion at Gaultree Forest, which exploits contractual language and its assumption of mutuality only to reassert royal power and send the rebels to "the block." Even if one justifies John's behavior on the basis of national security—he is after all negotiating with rebels who have themselves broken faith with their monarch—his arrest of the leaders for treason nonetheless might be construed as a breach of promise by the standards of *assumpsit*. The rebels' grievances, put forth in a series of written articles, constitute the required consideration, or motivating circumstances, for John's promise of speedy redress, which he makes upon his "princely word" (4.2.66). Prince John asks the rebels to show their agreement to his offer by engaging in a series of mutual displays of trust and friendship, including drinking together so "That all their eyes may bear those tokens home / Of our restored love and amity" (64–65). After the rebels have made good on their side of the bargain and dismissed their army, John then arrests the leaders of high treason. "Will you thus break your faith?" (112), the Archbishop asks. John's reply is that he promised only "redress of these same grievances" (113), nothing more. That Prince John succeeds with his exploitation of contractual expectation, while others in the play do not, underscores—but does not necessarily condone—differences between princes and commoners, or between any parties of unequal status, in a credit economy in which all are theoretically subject to the terms of their agreements.

Prince Hal also uses credit and contract to political advantage in this play, and although he, unlike his brother, honors his debts, his strategies continue to generate an ambivalent politics that heightens as much as minimizes differences in rank, especially as he comes closer to the crown. As in *1 Henry IV*, the emphasis on contract again allows Hal to translate passive inheritance into active consent and, in the process, to remove the taint of his father's own violent succession by paying "the debt [he] never promised." When the Prince, believing his father dead, takes the crown from his pillow, his speech overlays the "lineal honour" (4.5.45) of inheritance from father to son with the strict logic of a commercial transaction:

> Thy due from me
> Is tears and heavy sorrows of the blood,
> Which nature, love, and filial tenderness
> Shall, O dear father, pay thee plenteously.
> My due from thee is this imperial crown,
> Which, as immediate from thy place and blood,
> Derives itself to me. (36–42)

One effect of the Prince's turn to contract at this moment is to civilize the parricidal violence of the Lancastrian succession by transforming it into an exchange in which a son "pays" for his father's crown with the tears of "filial tenderness" rather than with blood. The Prince's balanced sentences, moreover, signal his readiness to rule by insisting on an equality between father and son, monarch and prince, that if the king were alive—which he is—would be parricidal and treasonous.[74] At the same time, however, Hal's terms set up a tension between late-sixteenth-century credit practices and fifteenth-century dynastic succession. Even as the Prince actively takes the crown from his father's deathbed and invokes the mutuality of contract, he simultaneously avoids responsibility for his actions by representing himself as the object and not the subject of this exchange—"The crown derives itself to *me*"—the recipient in a process that appears to be independent of his intentions or will. Similarly, as he here rehearses his acceptance of the crown by asserting his personal agency in a way that honors the promises implied by the contract of kinship, he simultaneously distances himself from that responsibility by making "nature, love, and filial tenderness" his agents, or factors, in paying his father "his due." Reinforcing this tension between mutuality and distance, and between equality and hierarchy, the newly crowned king's last words in the play make good on his initial promise in *1 Henry IV* by banishing Falstaff with the order "[t]o see perform'd the tenor of my word" (5.5.71). Refusing to acknowledge an intimacy with the old man, Henry V's "I know thee not" (47) cancels all debt and obligation.[75] If to know is to owe in Falstaff's account book—"A million. Thy love is worth a million. Thou owest me thy love" (*1 Henry IV*, 3.3.135–36), the knight insists to Hal in *1 Henry IV*—Henry V, in contrast to his father, begins his reign owing nothing to his former companions.

## *Performances*

With the installation of the "true inheritor" (*2 Henry IV*, 4.5.168), the *Henry IV* plays close by insisting on lineal succession rather than commercial practices. "[W]hat in me was purchas'd / Falls upon thee in a more fairer sort; / So thou the garland wear'st successively" (199–201), Henry IV pronounces to his son with his dying breath. And with the return to dynastic stability comes the remystification of monarchical power. Authority no longer resides in "divers motions of the mind," to borrow from William West's definition of contractual arrangements, but within the singular motion of the sovereign himself.[76] As if to reiterate this movement, Eastcheap's community of economic exchange is discredited, punished, and expelled from the realm. The entrepreneurial women are suddenly criminalized, as Hostess Quickly, in a startling inversion of her initial entrance in *2 Henry IV* as plaintiff in a lawsuit, is now, together with Doll Tearsheet, dragged offstage by officers to be incarcerated for allegedly having beaten a man to death. Falstaff and his company are likewise escorted to prison, denied access not only to the monarch's "person," as the banishment requires, but to the social and economic sphere as well. Rather than mediating social difference within the city's economic networks, the succession insists on traditional hierarchies founded on difference and distinction.[77] Again, the political implications of Lancastrian power are mixed. Henry V is, after all, fulfilling the promises he made in *1 Henry IV*, but as more than two centuries of criticism document, the price is high and the politics sinister. Indeed, it could be argued that the notion of credit, based in consent and mutuality, is merely a fiction, in politics as well as economics, connected in this play to a comic plot that has no basis in reality. But, in light of the play's Epilogue, it may be the closing celebration of sovereignty that is the fiction, and not the diverse web of credit and exchange.

While the conclusion to *2 Henry IV* marks the return of Lancastrian legitimacy by dismantling the credit economy, the Epilogue reinstitutes it, stepping out of the dramatic and historical frame of the play to present yet another variation on credit relations. If, as Robert Weimann has argued, Shakespeare's epilogues help to "assimilate the represented 'matter' to the actual cultural purpose of its performance," the Epilogue to *2 Henry IV* is no exception.[78] Returning to the business of credit and contract, it joins both playwright and audience with the economic world of the play, connecting contemporary London to Eastcheap in a way that reaffirms the efficacy of credit relations alongside the play's closing restoration of the "true inheritor." In the Epilogue's liminal space, the speaker, perhaps the "humble author" (27) himself, delineates the complex network that links the play's performance as well as its "matter" to the commercial exchanges of everyday London. Deferentially curtsying to the audience and begging their pardons, the Epilogue begins by proposing a "venture" that turns on a contractual relation of credit between the author and his audience. Casting himself in the role of the debtor and his audience as his creditors, the speaker offers up his play as payment or recompense for an earlier "displeasing" play:

> Be it known to you, as it is very well, I was lately here in the end of a displeasing play, to pray your patience for it, and to promise you a better. I meant indeed to pay you with this; which if like an ill venture it come unluckily home, I break, and you, my gentle creditors, lose. Here I promised you I would be, and here I commit my body to your mercies. Bate me some, and I will pay you some, and, as most debtors do, promise

you infinitely: and so I kneel down before you—but, indeed, to pray for the Queen. (7–17)

In contrast to the restrictive "Articles of Agreement" Jonson's scrivener forces on the audience at the start of *Bartholomew Fair*, drawing up a contract that limits spectators' censure to the price of their seats, Shakespeare's terms are far more flexible and equitable. Like the fluid relations of early modern credit, the contract in *2 Henry IV* plays on a give-and-take between debtor and creditor from which everyone seems to profit.

The contractual language is not merely metaphorical. As Luke Wilson reminds us, the primary use of the term "perform" in this period was in its legal sense, meaning to carry out, execute, or fulfill an action predicated on a prior promise or obligation, and theatrical appropriations of the term by Shakespeare and his contemporaries import this quasi-contractual understanding.[79] "We promis't you and we'll perform a play," Heywood declares in the prologue to *Four Prentices of London*. What Shakespeare's Epilogue suggests here, though, is more complicated than Heywood's quid pro quo. In paying admission to the theater, *2 Henry IV*'s audience has contracted for a pleasing play, which the playwright has implicitly promised to deliver. When the playwright fails to make good on this contract, as he did in this case by delivering a "displeasing play," he then incurs a second debt by promising "a better." Like Bassanio, Shakespeare undertakes this new "venture" in order to recover losses from a previous "ill venture." Understood within the economy of credit, the performance of *2 Henry IV*, if it is good, fulfills the contract implicit in the earlier promise. Conversely, if it is bad, the "venture" will "break" or bankrupt the author and cause losses for his "gentle creditors." The most likely outcome, it seems, is that the indebtedness will continue into the future (and that is part of the joke here) with the audience forgiving a portion of the debt—to "bate me some"—and the playwright promising yet more payment, which in this case means that he is bound to produce more plays just as the audience is bound to attend and, in a playful turn on credit relations, to pay. Within the space of the epilogue, in stark contrast to the plight of many Henslowe dramatists, even sharp practices have happy outcomes by conjoining playwright and audience in a relationship of credit that supports the continuation of theatrical production itself.

Capitalizing on the stage's place as a site of both holiday pleasure and commercial exchange, the Epilogue marks out a space for collective experience within the theater that stands outside the fixed relations of patronage and privilege.[80] And here, as in the Eastcheap tavern, pleasure and commerce are not necessarily antithetical but instead come together, allowing for exchange and ludic freedom. The Epilogue puts these exchanges into play in part by making the audience party to the performance. With theatrical exchange, as with early modern contractual relations, authority resides neither with the players alone nor with the audience, but with the mediating processes that underwrite the exchange, processes that, as Weimann describes it, circulate the movement of authority within the theater among the text, the performance, and the audience. "[T]he theater's readiness 'to please,'" Weimann writes, "is neither servile nor passive; the arts of performance achieve their final authority in the *exchange* of cultural signs with the audience, either through clapping hands or further talking after the play has ended."[81] More commercial than communal, this talking serves as a kind of advertising for future performances, "an extradramatic circuit of pleasurable exchanges, further engagements with, and distributions of news about, the play's events and figurations."[82] Constituted by a playful give-and-take between audience and actor, the theatrical public at the close of *2 Henry IV* is grounded in commerce, though there is mention of the queen.

As with the play itself, the Epilogue's economic discourse locates alternatives to the monarch's authority in the mediating processes of credit relations, processes that allow for the possibility of both equality and exploitation. Playing the debtor and promising "infinitely," the Epilogue brings his appeal to a close not with a call for applause, but with an extravagant display of submission—kneeling down before his audience of "gentle creditors"—a gesture that he then playfully recasts as a prayer "for the Queen." Just as the references to credit and contract suggest a profitable circle of obligation between the Epilogue and audience, the terms also hold the possibility that, for a moment at least, the speaker, his "creditors," and even the "queen," are equivalent and exchangeable. The actor may adopt a posture of deference, submitting his "body" as well as his play to the mercy of his "gentle creditors" and his queen, but in refiguring these relations in economic terms, he also gestures toward the fluid relations enacted by early modern performance.

In place of a "single fixed location of authority," Weimann asserts, the material space of the Elizabethan stage promoted a bifold authority, located in the "reciprocity and division" between the "representation of textual meaning" and the "circumstances of performing practice."[83] Yet the *Henry*

*IV* plays engage this bifold authority rather differently from its promised sequel, *Henry V*, whose choric machinery calls on audiences to use their "imaginary forces" to translate common actors into monarchs and the stage into the "vasty fields of France." The *Henry IV* plays make no claims on the audience's geographical imagination, except to ask that they stay at home and think of the past in relation to contemporary London and the everyday practices of their own lives. The localization is at once alienating and familiarizing, inviting playgoers to imagine princes together with themselves as subject to a shared set of economic and political relations even as it asks them to reconsider the hazards and gains of those obligations from the distance of the past, as it were. At the same time, this localization reminds them that performance, in all its meanings, theatrical as well as legal, is the medium within which the city's population makes good on its credit, binding itself in networks of obligation that extend from the past into the present and future.

# 2. *Differentiating Collaboration*

## Protest and Playwriting and *Sir Thomas More*

*Sir Thomas More* takes its subject directly from the annals of urban history, tracing the arc of Thomas More's career from his rise to London's sheriff and England's Lord Chancellor to his final moments on the scaffold. The play celebrates More as an exemplary citizen, renowned not so much for his national prominence, or for his treason, but for setting "a gloss on London's fame" (9.100).[1] More's story is a London story, bounded by a local geography that extends from Cheapside and St. Martins Le Grand to the Guildhall and More's residence in Chelsea. Again, as in the *Henry IV* plays, the cityscape gives history contemporary purchase by invoking the neighborhoods, buildings, and experiences of late-sixteenth-century London. The play renders the local topography in unusual detail—the Arden edition counts references to at least twenty different city locations—offering an insider's guide to the city's streets and taverns.[2] The play also takes care to keep its citizens center stage: Artisans, apprentices, servingmen, the Lord Mayor, London recorder, aldermen, local magistrates, sheriffs, and More's own household, all have a part in the city's history. In marked contrast to the *Henry IV* plays, there is no mingling of commoners and kings on *Sir Thomas More*'s stage. Deciding events from a distance, Henry VIII remains offstage and unnamed, his words delivered by the earls of Shrewsbury and Surrey, instruments of royal authority.

Compared to the nuanced topicality of the *Henry IV* plays, *Sir Thomas More*'s historical trafficking is far more overt and, in its inflammatory displays of xenophobia, far more invidious.[3] The play provocatively returns to the ground zero of sixteenth-century London's exclusionary politics, the May Day riots of 1517, when hundreds of citizens and apprentices took to the streets in violent attacks on the city's foreign population. As the play accurately recounts, this action put citizens into confrontation not only with the city's so-called "strangers" but with royal authority. The play begins by staging the citizens' grievances in a sympathetic light, with a scene incendiary enough to elicit a strong censure from the Master of the Revels—"*Leave out the insurrection wholly and the cause thereof*"—written in the upper-left margin of the manuscript's first page and signed "E. Tilney."[4] What makes the play so dangerous is its local resonance, and it is the potential to stir up trouble in contemporary London that Edmund Tilney no doubt feared when he emphatically struck out Lincoln's xenophobic lines: "It is hard when Englishmen's patience must be thus jetted on by strangers, and they not dare to revenge their own wrongs" (1.26–29).[5] This explicit example of state censorship acknowledges the possibility that plays that take the city as their subject might indeed license the "sovereignty of the audience," as Plato put it.

To the extent that *Sir Thomas More*'s staging of anti-alien sentiment reasserts the city's entrenched practices of defining itself against outsiders, the play seems hardly exemplary of new modes of urban association. But what complicates the play's exclusionary politics are the contradictory connections between the citizens' insurrection and More's own story, which widen the scope of resistance within the play even as they fracture it. The common denominator here is protest. Linking More to the rebellious citizens, protest operates on multiple levels, most obviously to assert London's privileges against foreign and sovereign pressures but also to articulate an alternative authority in the dynamic mode of collective action that brings "poor artificers" (3.76) together with city elites in what I am calling networks of collaboration. This is not to exonerate the violent riot at the play's center, as the citizens descend into the stereotypical image of a rude multitude. But it is to assume, following recent work on popular protest in the period, that collective action was not necessarily or always anarchic or disorderly. As Paul Slack observes, protests tended to reflect the shape of the local populace, embodying and molding "popular social and political aspirations, and the ties of deference, obligation and community which bound people together."[6] My concern in this chapter lies in part, then, with mapping protest in relation to ties of deference, obligation, and other forms of collective association.

Like credit in the *Henry IV* plays, protest in *Sir Thomas More* offers a structure within which Londoners might practice new forms of association. It is true that the shape of protest in *Sir Thomas More* is far more fluid and ad hoc than credit relations within the *Henry IV* plays, which reflect the structure of an adjudicating legal framework. It is also true that protest's capacity for immediate harm appears to exceed that of credit, especially when the citizens' articulation of legitimate grievances spills over into destructive violence against strangers and the torching of houses and neighborhoods. What aligns protest with credit, however, is that both entail relations across difference within the metropolis. As shown in Chapter 1, credit networks mediate differences across social and geographic distance, linking commoners and aristocrats in dense webs of obligation that extend outward from the city's commercial center. By contrast, protest in *Sir Thomas More* moves in the opposite direction, coalescing at the city's center in ways that end up mediating encounters at the heart of the commonality itself. The protesters may be like-minded, united by common grievances and a common enemy, yet the play is careful to record their debates and disagreements. As *Sir Thomas More* so powerfully demonstrates, the citizens' collaborative deliberation stands in marked contrast not only to the singularity of the monarch's authority but to the notion of an equally singular or unified "voice of the people." Through its novel staging of collaborative protest, the play begins to open up an exploration of differences not just at the city's borders but at its very center. It is probably not coincidental that in exploring the shifting terrain of citizen practice, *Sir Thomas More* returns to the May Day riots of 1517. Nor is it coincidental, I suggest, that the play's models for collaborative practices extend from its revisionary history to the even more complicated story of its own literary production.

This chapter reads the story of the play's production together with its scenes of citizen protest. As current scholarship makes persuasively evident, dramatic production in early modern London was a collective enterprise, dependent on actors, playwrights, and audiences, as well as networks of financiers, patrons, and playhouse functionaries.[7] Plays themselves were frequently written in collaboration: According to Gerald Eades Bentley's oft-cited guess, "as many as half of the plays by professional dramatists in the period incorporated the writing at some date of more than one man," and at amphitheaters like the Rose, these figures were even higher.[8] If recognizing the extent of collaboration in this period invites us to attend to a much wider canon, including plays such as *Sir Thomas More*, it also urges us to reassess our editorial and critical practices and the kinds of narratives they generate. My concern here is to consider the urban experience within the context of this more complicated view of dramatic practice. It is also to make a wider claim for collaborative practices themselves, one that extends the dismantling of individual authorship currently revolutionizing the field of textual studies to consider the ways in which dramatic production both represented and materialized the collective struggle to organize lived experience within early modern London.

The manuscript of *Sir Thomas More* is a remarkable document of early modern playwriting, one of a dozen or so surviving dramatic manuscripts.[9] It is also the period's most complex record of theatrical collaboration.[10] The manuscript consists of an original text, written by Anthony Munday (Hand S), marked up by Tilney, and then at a later date added to, revised, and annotated by five other hands—labeled A, B, C, D, and E by W. W. Greg in his 1911 edition.[11] Until very recently, scholarship has focused primarily on questions about attribution, following an editorial practice that in its search to identify individual authors has all but ignored the play's collaborative processes.[12] The names of Dekker (Hand E), Heywood (Hand B), Thomas Chettle (Hand A), and a playhouse scribe (Hand C) have all been put forward. But for most of the last century, the focus has been on Hand D and the 147 lines in Addition II thought by many to be Shakespeare's.[13] The hand is sometimes difficult to read, and the lines are not without alterations and corrections, and if these pages were indeed penned by Shakespeare, they constitute the only extant record of the author's hand apart from a few signatures. That the one surviving example of Shakespeare's actual playwriting should confirm not the singularity of his authorship but his participation in collective labor is an irony not lost on the vanguard of textual scholars today. But for most of the twentieth century, this document failed to generate interest in Shakespeare's collaborative practices.[14]

In dividing collaborative texts into stylistically discrete parts, attribution studies have tended to reinforce longstanding prejudices against coauthorship. Because shared writing is usually "only visible at the points where it fails to produce a harmonious meshing of the playwrights' contributions," as John Jowett observes of Shakespeare's printed plays, "the marks of collaboration are easily translated as the marks of failure."[15] *Sir Thomas More*'s "marks of collaboration," so plainly visible in the manuscript's patchwork of hands and revisions, have been especially easy to perceive as "marks of failure" by editors characterizing the play as "unfinished and chaotic," "a shambles," and "a welter of excisions and revisions" in "wild disarray."[16] Exacerbating these prejudices, I would add, is *Sir Thomas More*'s serious treatment of civic themes. London may be "the protagonist" of the play's first act, as the Revels edition emphasizes, but to earlier generations of scholars, the city subject seemed only to confirm the identification between citizen taste and hack writing so often satirized in city comedy.[17] For many, it seems, *Sir Thomas More*'s combination of collaborative writing and "bourgeois sympathies" has been something of an embarrassment, bearing the taint of commercial interests and middle-class taste.[18] But maybe this convergence of collaborative form and civic content is part of the point. Critical appraisal of the play is now changing. Scott McMillin has persuasively shown the manuscript to be a "coherent theatrical document," sophisticated in its design and stagecraft, and, most recently, the play's status has been endorsed by Jowett's Arden Shakespeare edition, which masterfully succeeds in giving us a play that is at once accessible and complex.[19]

It is within the context of this recent work that I return to the play's striking convergence of collaborative form and civic content. Taking this convergence seriously—as a basis for considering homologies between theatrical practices and networks of urban practice—this chapter explores *Sir Thomas More*'s collaborative writing alongside its staging of city protest. Jeffrey Masten's astute analysis of joint writing as "conversant" with other material practices and discourses in the period offers a useful point of departure.[20] Although Masten's concern lies not with bourgeois sympathies but with the "textual intercourse" of shared writing and living arrangements, his emphasis on cultural exchange can be extended to the conjunction of playwriting and local politics. What makes *Sir Thomas More* an especially resonant example of collaborative exchange, I suggest, is that the possibilities for collaborative labor play out in both form *and* content, as shared writing comes together with a staging of civic unrest to open up multiple levels of engagement—between playwriting and protest, authorship and authority, theater and politics, and citizens and aliens. But the play does not idealize collaboration as a rational sphere of unanimous consent, or as a form of utopian longing. In this, I would argue, *Sir Thomas More* enacts, even as it is constituted by, an ongoing circulation of collaborative practices marked by conflicts, confusions, and the messiness of actual labor, all of which begin to suggest a model for collective belonging that is not so much about consolidating identity as it is about acknowledging and mediating the plurality of metropolitan life.

### *Authors, Favorers, and Abetters*

Although *Sir Thomas More* opens with the May Day rising, the central subject is the rise and fall of its singular hero, which the play structures in three parts. The first part concludes with More's overnight elevation from

London's Sheriff to England's Lord Chancellor, a promotion earned by his (unhistorical) success in quelling the citizens' uprising; the second part recounts humorous anecdotes from More's private life, including the interlude with "[f]our men and a boy" (9.72); the third part concerns his refusal to sign the king's articles, his imprisonment in the Tower, and his final moments on the scaffold. The play thus moves from collective grievance to the inwardness of individual conscience, from a public to a private sphere that works to heighten More's achievement, to "set him apart from ordinary men."[21] But the proximity of More's disobedience and the May Day rising also registers a common bond between the Lord Chancellor and the ordinary men and women of the opening scenes. Those who read the play as an orthodox exploration of the "limits of obedience" typically locate this commonality in the shared position of the royal *subject*, whose duty it is to "patiently submit . . . to the law" (7.60), as the repentant rebel Lincoln instructs from the scaffold.[22] But in its concern with resistance as well as submission, the play marks out a competing, and more radical, commonality in the position of *citizen*, what Étienne Balibar has defined as the "subject who rises up."[23] The category of citizen is admittedly slippery in *Sir Thomas More*. In some cases, this category depends on traditional bonds of civic fraternity, as in More's affirmation of brotherhood with the Lord Mayor: "I was your brother, / And so am still in heart. It is not state, / That can our love from London separate" (9.93–95). Elsewhere, citizenship is constituted by deliberate acts of disobedience—by the commons who would not be "bridled by law" (1.74–75) and by More himself, who refuses "[t]he duty that the law of God bequeaths / Unto the king" (10.106–7).[24] The protest that opens the play could be said, then, to supply more than just a context for More's appointment to high office; it also models the pattern for his own resistance and his civic fellowship. Like the May Day protesters who reject the bonds of "strict obedience" (1.85), More shifts the ground of obedience away from the monarch, reconstituting the law in relation to the citizen, as well as to the subject.

As Tilney's censure recognized, the solidarity of citizen protest could easily extend beyond More and the confines of the playhouse, particularly as these scenes take their meaning from London's routine practice of using anti-alien sentiment in the service of civic and commercial consolidation. In its legal or institutional sense, citizenship depended on being admitted into the "freedom" of a company, usually by way of apprenticeship, and carried numerous privileges, most notably the right to trade within the city. Citizenship was also defined negatively, in opposition to the city's alien population, the "strangers" or outsiders perceived as threatening the livelihoods and privileges of the citizenry within.[25] As far back as Edward I's reign, in fact, the city had sought to control competition from "strangers" who, the refrain went, threatened "to take the bread out of our mouths."[26] But trade protection and xenophobia were not all that was at stake in these hostilities; as *Sir Thomas More* demonstrates, disputes over aliens often served as flashpoints in city-Crown relations, evidenced by the frequency with which anti-alien complaints became an occasion to speak out against the Crown and a ruling aristocracy.[27] Threats of bloodshed were commonplace, and while actual attacks were less frequent than we might have expected, violence did erupt, most notoriously in the spring of 1517 on what came to be known as Ill May Day. On this occasion, hostilities spilled into the streets when more than seven hundred rioters attacked aliens and pillaged their shops in the liberty of St. Martins Le Grand. City officials, including undersheriff Thomas More, attempted unsuccessfully to quell the riot, which ended only when noblemen rode into the city in force, with armed retinues. Thirteen "conspirators" were executed for treason; some four hundred more received royal pardons. Discontent continued, however, and a few months later, when the plague reduced policing within London, rumors began to circulate about making "as good a skirmish with strangers as was on May Day last."[28] "Ill May Day" had entered the lexicon as a watchword for city solidarity, and for the rest of the century it would continue to function as a means of constructing civic consensus against both "strangers" and the Crown.[29]

As most editors note, it is precisely these associations that would have made *Sir Thomas More* so dangerous to the authorities in the early 1590s when tensions in London again flared, with shopkeepers complaining about retail violations by the Flemings and French. Petitions and threatening libels followed, among them the infamous Dutch Church libel, surreptitiously posted on the wall of the Dutch churchyard in the city's Broadstreet Ward on May 5, 1593.[30] Written in verse couplets and signed "Tamberlaine," the libel rehearsed the full litany of charges against aliens, along with a glancing critique at nobles who "wound their Countries brest, for lucres sake." It also delivered a grisly message: "Weele cutt your throtes, in your temples praying / Not paris massacre so much blood did spill / As we will doe iust vengeance on you all."[31] The striking parallels between the 1593 unrest and *Sir Thomas More* suggest that the play was designed to exploit current tensions. It is the play's confrontational staging of Ill May Day, after all, rather than More's challenge to the king, that most provoked Tilney to mark out passages for omission and that causes scholars to assign the original, unrevised version of the play to the early 1590s.[32] But if this evidence has figured importantly in editorial work, it has prompted surprisingly little interest in the play's local politics, except as they relate to the ongoing debate about the manuscript's authors and revisions.

I take this evidence, and Tilney's comments especially, as a provocation for critical and textual practice. Some of Tilney's censorship speaks to the topicality of the play's content: His substitution of "Lombards" for "Frenchmen" or "strangers," for example, probably defers to the large numbers of Huguenots then living in London and reflects the paucity of Lombards.[33] What is most striking about Tilney's injunctions, though, is his concern not with the particulars of protest but with its mode of presentation. Twice in the terse instructions he penned for the opening scene, he calls for replacing the actual staging of the May Day "insurrection" with "a report":

> *Leave out the insurrection wholly and the cause thereof, and begin with Sir Thomas More at the Mayor's sessions, with a report afterwards of his good service done being Sheriff of London upon a mutiny against the Lombards—only by a short report, and not otherwise, at your own perils. E. Tilney.*[34]

What Tilney requests is as much a revision of form as substance, and the effect of this change would be to shift *More*'s locus of authority from the city to the Crown, and from the collective to the singular, reducing the play to a conservative *de casibus* drama focused on More. The emendation would drain the content from Ill May Day by reducing it to an occasion for More's "good service" to the Crown, thus suppressing the citizens and, at the same time, the network of cross-references connecting their protest to More's act of conscience. In substituting narrative for dramatic form, the change to a "short report" would further suppress the citizens' practices by replacing their multivoiced protest with the singular authority of an official account. In its sensitivity to modes of presentation, Tilney's reading practice invites us not only to set plays in relation to protest but to attend to homologies of collaborative form. This is not to assert that popular protest was a form of theater, and so to risk collapsing politics back into theatrical practice.[35] But it is, rather, to explore formal correspondences between plays *and* protest and to explicate each in terms of the other, in a way that recognizes their simultaneous independence and mutuality.[36]

Political libels, like the Dutch Church libel, provide a useful starting point for thinking about collaborative networks in the period and in relation to *Sir Thomas More.* A fluid and highly collaborative sub-genre of protest, libels circulated orally and in manuscript, were posted in public places, repeated aloud, sung, copied into commonplace books, and shared among friends and neighbors. Their political power depended on their circulation, as what mattered was not so much their original articulation as the subsequent repetitions that brought confederates together in broad cooperative networks—networks that generated solidarity but posed difficulties for the authorities.[37] Indeed, in the weeks prior to the Dutch Church libel, London had witnessed a spate of anti-alien libels, which the Privy Council tried unsuccessfully to suppress by tracking down "the authors, favorers and abetters of the libells and libellours, and to dyscover theire intencions and purposes."[38] The defiant posting of the Dutch Church libel two weeks later, deemed to "excead the rest in lewdnes," provoked immediate and extreme measures. Fearing a conspiracy, the council directed the mayor and aldermen to cast a wide net. Officers were "to make search and aprehend everie person so to be suspected, and for that purpoze to enter into al houses and places . . . to make like search in anie the chambers, studies, chestes or other like places for al manner of writings or papers that may geve you light for the discoverie of the libellers"; confessions were to be extracted by means of torture, so that the authors "maie be known and they punished."[39] By the next day, as we know, the authorities had searched the rooms of Thomas Kyd, who was then imprisoned and subjected, in his words, to "vndeserved tortures."[40] What the authorities found—the three-page fragment of "vile hereticall Conceiptes / denyinge the deity of Jhesus / Christ *our* Savio*ur*"—is a story well known in the annals of literary history for its connection to Marlowe.[41] What is less well known is that, like *Sir Thomas More*, it is a story that links the bourgeois sympathies of citizen protest with collaborative writing.

Kyd's defense, in fact, turns on collaboration; more precisely, it plays one form of collaboration against another by replacing charges of political collusion with a story about shared writing practices. As he explains in a letter to Sir John Puckering written several months later, after Marlowe's death, the fragment was Marlowe's and must have gotten mixed with Kyd's papers when the two playwrights shared a chamber some years before:

> When J was first suspected for that / Libell that concern'd the state, amongst those waste and idle papers (w*h*ich J carde / not for) & w*h*ich

> vnaskt J did deliver vp, were founde some fragmentes of a / disputation toching that opinion affirmd by Marlowe to be his, and shufled / with some of myne (vnknown to me) by some occasion of our wrytinge in one / chamber twoe yeares synce.[42]

As if to comply with the Privy Council's order to bring "light for the discoverie" into the closed spaces of chamber and study, Kyd's confession aptly discovers a scene of writing. And what his words reveal is not the "bending author" (*Henry V*, Epilogue, 2) in a solitary act of composition, but rather the messy remains of shared writing practices.[43] Kyd's defense may show the extent to which collaborative writing was considered normative.[44] It may also point to an assumed or expected slippage between literary and political practice. Yet Kyd's far-from-ideal alibi puts him in the awkward position of having to insist that their collaboration was actually accidental, "unknown to me," the result not of collusion but of bad housekeeping. The playwrights may have shared a chamber, but this doesn't mean they shared the same mind, as Kyd bluntly puts it, speaking of Marlowe's atheism. Attempting to shift the blame to others, Kyd advises Puckering to inquire with those Marlowe "conversd withall, that is (as J am / geven to vnderstand) with Harriot, Warner, Royden, and some stationers / in Paules churchyard, whom J in no sort can accuse nor will excuse / by reson of his companie, of whose consent if J had been, no question but / J also shold haue been of their consort."[45] Perhaps Kyd seeks to alleviate the malice of his insinuations, perhaps he says more than he means to, but his ambidextrous qualifications nonetheless isolate a central crux of collaboration. To consort (or even to converse) is not automatically to consent, Kyd avers. Involving more than "shufled" papers, collaboration suggests an individuated practice (i.e., Harriot, Warner, Royden, and some stationers) founded on shared "intencions and purposes," to use the Privy Council's language—intentions that in this case involve a "damnable offence to / the awefull Majestie of god or of that other mutinous sedition towrd the state."[46]

What seems readily evident from the events surrounding the Dutch Church libel is an acknowledgment by both Kyd and the authorities that apart from the ostensible message (in this case, anti-alien or atheistic stirrings), there is a content, and a politics, to collaborative form. The politics here are suggestively complex, particularly as they demarcate a struggle between authorities and suspected "authors" with differences among themselves. The directive that netted Kyd could be said, of course, to offer powerful evidence for Foucault's claim that authorship was first assigned not as an assertion of textual ownership but as a punishment for transgressive discourse: It is the authorities and not the collaborators who are most concerned with identifying "authors."[47] But the incident itself does not support the related claim that collaborative anonymity represents an originary mode of communal production *prior* to authorship. The fact that the Dutch Church libel is designed to thwart the Privy Council's directives for discovery invites us to understand collaborative anonymity, together with the search for authorship, as a strategy of resisting and even refusing an authority imposed from above.[48] At the same time, the libel's circulation demonstrates that these practices may have functioned not only negatively, as resistance to the panopticon of surveillance, but also positively, as a mode of collective activity that enacts a persuasive alternative to the Crown's singular authority. Indeed, the libel itself, with its "Tamberlaine" signature, materializes a practice that refuses to locate authority in individual authors, its fictive authorship at once a taunting strategy of evasion and an imaginative assertion of collective identification.[49] In this, the libel would seem to corroborate Masten's contention that joint writing is "a dispersal of author/ity, rather than a simple doubling of it; to revise the aphorism, two heads are different from one."[50]

But if the Dutch Church libel appears to reinforce the oppositions of current critical discourse—between authority and popular culture, or between authorship and collaboration—it complicates the idealized notions about anonymity and communal production that tend to accompany this discourse. For the libel's authors, anonymity, whatever else it might mean, functions as a protective mask or disguise. As a strategy of concealment, then, it is decidedly *not* transparent, signifying a utopian state of preauthorial "namelessness," say, "informed by differing mechanisms of textual property and control, different conceptions of imitation, originality, and the 'individual.'"[51] As Marcy North cautions, anonymity functions as a "flexible convention" in this period: "It can represent an accident of text transmission, an act of modesty, or an act of self-protection. It can point to a writing process that locates authority in a source other than that of the author, or it can suggest a very active author, one just below the surface of namelessness."[52] In an anonymous collaborative work such as the *Mirror for Magistrates*, writers might "argue among themselves and seem involved in distinct tasks," exemplifying "early modern authorship ideals and oppositions."[53] Both the *Mirror for Magistrates* and the Dutch Church libel suggest that the unity of the anonymous collective—so commonly represented as undifferentiated and homogenous, whether demonized as a faceless mob or idealized as a self-effacing equality—may actually look different from within, constituted not by a preauthorial namelessness but by the reciprocities of plurality. For what Kyd's defense implies (albeit in the negative form of betrayal)—and what *Sir Thomas More*'s scenes of protest confirm, more positively—is that collaborative networks are neither anonymous nor representative of an idealized and uniform community, but instead form a community constituted by difference.

The widely circulating accounts of May Day 1517 in the chronicles of Hall and Holinshed—primary sources for *Sir Thomas More*'s scenes of citizen protest—similarly affirm the complicated reciprocities of these collaborative networks. Borrowed from numerous sources, including eyewitness accounts and official reports, the chronicles are themselves "shufled" texts, and in their multilayered, multivocal narratives we can glimpse struggles among authorities and authors over forms of collective representation. As in the documents surrounding the Dutch Church libel, the authorities tend to focus on the rioters' identities. And so, in the marginal note in Holinshed, the broker John Lincoln is named as "the author of the insurrection."[54] At the same time, the chronicle accounts show the protesters concentrating on what is being said, on causes rather than agents, on questions of justice and legality, and on the collective power of their voices. Decidedly sympathetic to the city, Hall's account fully airs the citizens' complaints, citing the recent thefts in which victims were denied redress by a legal system that was then turned against them. It is this "mocke," Hall writes, together with "many other oppressions," that prompts John Lincoln to write the bill of grievances that Doctor Bele then agrees to read from the pulpit in Easter Week.[55] Repeated verbatim in the play's manuscript, Lincoln's bill sounds a theme of commonality, insisting that "redresse must be *of the commons, knyt and unite to one parte*, and as the hurt and dammage greueth *all men*, so muste *all men* set to their willyng power for remedy."[56]

Their strength, however, lies as much in the medium as the message, as much in the circulating rumors and murmurings as in the grievances listed in Lincoln's bill. Illustrating this common circulation, Hall's chronicle attributes the riot's outbreak not to Bele's Easter Week sermon but rather to a sudden "commen secret rumour, & no man could tell how it began, that on May daye next, the citie would rebell & slaye all Aliens."[57] That the rumor is paradoxically "secret" and "commen" reflects a narrative doubleness that registers, on the one hand, the difficulties faced by the authorities who stood outside the collaborative circle and, on the other, the solidifying reach of "commen" discourse. As with the Dutch Church libel, the secrecy is strategic. It thwarts the authorities' attempts to quell the disturbance, since "they coulde not tell who woulde take their parte"; it also makes prosecution difficult, for "it could neuer be proued of any metyng, gathering, talking or conventicle at any daye or tyme before y[t] day."[58] But the secrecy and anonymity also suggest that the uprising takes its shape not so much from the "author" Lincoln as from a collective participation that extends from the disenfranchised to the city elite. As Ethan Shagan argues, rumors emerge from "a morass of commonly circulating ideas," and it was "exactly this freedom of movement that made rumours 'political,' since every person spreading them was implicated in the creation of their meaning."[59] According to Hall, women were suspected of conveying secret rumors when they came "together to bable & talke."[60] City leaders, too, came under suspicion, accused of "concentyng to thesame." In the words of the king, "you neuer moued to let [i.e., stop] theim, nor sturred once to fight with theim, whiche you saye were so small a numbre of light persones, wherefore we must thynke, and you cannot deny, but you dyd wyncke at the matter."[61]

If we turn from these documents to *Sir Thomas More*'s staging of Ill May Day, following the lead of the playwrights themselves, we notice that the play borrows heavily from the chronicles and from contemporary contexts, particularly as it adopts a double perspective, detailing the nobles' fears as well as the populace's demands. But what also becomes apparent is that, as Tilney feared, the form of presentation matters. The chronicle narratives look back on the events from a distance and, while recording multiple perspectives, seem to endorse none. *Sir Thomas More*'s performance, by contrast, would reduce that distance with a volatile presentation designed to rile contemporary audiences. The play casts its "strangers" not as refugee artisans but as imperious courtiers gleefully helping themselves to the citizens' property and wives. Francis de Barde opens the play by abducting Doll Williamson, a carpenter's wife, claiming her as his "prize" to take "[w]hither I please" (1.2), while Cavaler seizes a pair of doves from Doll's husband, a theft the "Lombard" justifies with an elitist sneer: "Are pigeons meat for a coarse carpenter?" (1.24–25). That the stranger wears a strangely familiar face gives disturbing currency to city legend, caricaturing the Crown's care for aliens as a form of collusion across national boundaries.[62] Forced to witness these egregious insults against the city, the play's audience is urged to identify with Lincoln and the two Betts brothers as they bear silent witness to this abuse at the hands of strangers, "bridled by law, and forced to bear your wrongs" (1.74–75).

The form of presentation matters most in the representations of the citizens themselves, in that the play embodies, quite literally, what was "commen" and "secret" in its sources. The effect is an intimate history from below that gives a flesh-and-blood particularity to the generic "commons" of official histories. Such particularity garners sympathy for their cause; moreover, it has a politics. When told from within, the citizens' story no longer requires protective anonymity but can instead reveal an individuated collaborative practice. In the manuscript's opening scene, for example, the speech prefixes insist on distinctions among the citizens by identifying them by name, rather than by number as, for example, in *Coriolanus*. And in performance, *Sir Thomas More*'s citizens would possess both names and visibility, to be shared with the audience if not with the ruling elite within the play, who continue to see them as a faceless crowd—"this frowning vulgar brow" (3.4) of "the displeased commons of the City" (3.8), as Shrewsbury refers to them. Perhaps it is this differentiation that first attracted the attention of the censor, whose response was to strike out the first half-dozen speech prefixes, as if to restore anonymity—and invisibility—to the commons. In performing rather than reporting the May Day "insurrection," *Sir Thomas More* thus manages to rewrite the faceless multitude of chronicle history as an individuated commonality identified not only by social status but, more importantly, by participation in shared activity, by the joint labor of their protest. Again, Tilney's markings offer interpretive direction, for it is at this moment—when the citizens on stage form a collective, when they coalesce in their cries for justice against the crimes they are forced to endure—that Tilney begins striking out whole speeches until eventually the entire scene has been cut.

*Sir Thomas More*'s opening protest is remarkable for its grounding in literate culture. Compared with Jack Cade's rebels, who sentence the clerk Emmanuel to be hanged "with his pen and inkhorn about his neck" simply because he can write his name (*2 Henry VI*, 4.2.109–10), *More*'s citizens seem positively bookish. They launch their protest not with threats of violence backed by a staff-wielding rabble but with the "publication" of Lincoln's bill underwritten by the fastidious records of George Betts, who transcribes the names of their confederates, "friends enough, whose names we will closely keep in writing" (1.140–41). Still, despite these glimpses of a literate, deliberative public sphere, this is hardly an idealized collective. The rebellious citizenry may be open to women—witness Doll Williamson's unhistorical part—but it is nonetheless based, in part at least, on the exclusion of strangers. Nor is Lincoln "representative" in any modern sense of the term; no election, contract, or acclamation validates his authority. His leadership instead rests, much like More's later in the play, on his ability to articulate the "vile enormities" (1.91–92) and his willingness to "remedy" them with "loss of [his] own life" (1.93–94). *Sir Thomas More* takes care to particularize both the cityscape and its inhabitants, to restore distinction, as it were, to the fantastic city of undifferentiated and nameless citizens celebrated in More's own *Utopia*. In its emphasis on an individuated collective network, the play perhaps looks less to the past than to the future, anticipating what Balibar characterizes as the "'double relationship'" of the modern citizen, who "properly speaking is *neither* the individual *nor* the collective." "The citizen is unthinkable as an 'isolated' individual," he writes, "for it is his active participation in politics that makes him exist. But he cannot on that account be merged into a 'total' collectivity."[63] In its representation of the collaborative practices of citizen protest and in its own collaborative playwriting, *Sir Thomas More* registers the complex relations between individual citizens and the urban collective, relations that depend as much on differentiation as on consent.

## *A Common Strangeness*

Dramatic collaboration has long been understood in terms of differentiation, but the emphasis has been on the contributions of individual authors, rather than on how those contributions converge. For nearly two centuries, collaborative plays have been assumed to be the aggregate of supposedly discrete parts, of scenes and speeches parceled out to various playwrights and then compiled by a master author or playhouse functionary. Accordingly, editors devoted themselves to identifying the parts and the playwrights on the basis of individual styles and writing habits. This author-centered approach has also dominated critical assessments, providing the normative standard against which collaborative projects are found wanting. Devalued as fragmented rather than unified, belabored rather than inspired, or "mechanic" rather than "organic," collaborative writing suffers in comparison to romantic idealizations of individual genius.[64] Even unity itself becomes suspect in collaborative texts, disparaged as "the deadness of compromise" or mourned as a loss of individual style and even a loss of selfhood.[65]

More recent accounts take issue with these assumptions. The desire to recover individual styles and identities, Masten contends, is anachronistically at odds with early modern notions of textual production and individual identity. Masten delineates an "undifferentiated collaboration," epitomized by the partnership of Beaumont and Fletcher, whose "intersubjective indiscernibility" thwarts authorial paradigms that would police "the borders of personhood."[66] Beaumont and Fletcher live and write together, united by "a wonderfull consimility of phansey," as John Aubrey described them, sharing their clothes, their bed, and "one wench in the house between them."[67] Drawing on Renaissance friendship texts such as Florio's Montaigne, Masten derives a model of "consenting consort" that harks back to Aristotle's description of friends sharing "one soule in two bodies."[68] Whatever possibilities friendship might hold for collaborative difference closes here in "an erotics of similitude."[69] Early modern collaboration may be said to disperse authors and authority—"two heads are different from one"—but the idea of the "intersubjective indiscernibility" of collaborative coupling pushing in the opposite direction risks replacing one model of singularity with another. Masten's model, moreover, seems more attuned to partnered writing than to playwriting syndicates, to plays like *The Two Noble Kinsmen* rather than *Sir Thomas More.* I would suggest, however, that the limitations lie not with the notion of collaboration as friendship but with its definitional constraints, and that rather than discounting Masten's model we might instead open it up to the play of difference.[70]

Difference figures centrally in many accounts of friendship, political friendship especially. Derrida begins his *Politics of Friendship*, for example, by asking us to "dream of a friendship that goes beyond this proximity of the congeneric double . . . . 'beyond the principle of fraternity.' "[71] For Derrida, friendship may suppose symmetry and equality but is at heart contradictory, in its "distance" and "respectful separation," its recognition of "the transcendent alterity of the Other who can only ever be heterogeneous and singular."[72] But how does this interplay of likeness and difference translate into the political domain? The classical interlocutor in these discussions is Aristotle, whose oft-repeated statement—"Friendship seems too to hold polities together, and lawgivers to care more for it than for justice"—places friendship at the center of politics.[73] Political friendship, according to Aristotle, is the association of self-interested parties for the purpose of mutual gain; as such, it both preserves and bridges difference.

Because of its grounding in *mutual* gain, it also comprises more than the sum of individual interests and involves more than mere calculation. Political friendship can be said, then, to model an individuated community unified by shared practices and benefits—by the agreement or "meeting of minds" and by what Aristotle refers to as "the thing," the mutual benefit or shared interest constituting the community. It is this notion that informs Sir Thomas Smith's influential account of commonwealth in *De Republica Anglorum* as "a society or common doing of a multitude of free men collected together and united by common accord and covenauntes among themselves, for the conservation of themselves aswell in peace as in warre."[74] Political friendship does not model a perfect concord—indeed, as commentators note, it is marked by conflict—but in placing attention on that which represents the "common wealth," it supplies the necessary ground for deliberation and resolution, for the "pleading betwixt thone and thother."[75]

This notion of political friendship thus complicates standard accounts of collaborative exchange—first by assuming, if not requiring, individual differences or interests, and then by looking to "the thing," whose wholeness depends on but is not reducible to differentiation (to the performed or written play, for instance, or in the example of citizen protest, to the resolution of grievances). *Sir Thomas More* exemplifies this collaborative give-and-take. Written in various hands, the manuscript directs attention to individual parts and writers and to the labors of composition. In that these hands constitute a theatrical text, however, the manuscript shows *Sir Thomas More* to be more than the sum of its parts, not simply "a collection of 'foul papers,'" but rather "a coherent and actable play," sophisticated in its dramaturgy and close to being ready for performance.[76] The play's representation of city protest illustrates a similarly differentiated whole, one constituted and authorized by individual participants. Spoken on behalf of those "*that inhabit within this city and suburbs of the same*" (1.122–23) and insisting that "*redress must be of the commons knit and united to one part*" (1.129–30), Lincoln's bill of wrongs invokes the power of a unified collective. Yet the protesters recognize, as does Thomas Kyd, that consort does not automatically confer consent: The "commons" may live together within the city and share their grievances, but they may not be of the same mind (as would subjects identified in the sovereign will, say). The citizens indeed take care to solicit and verify consent by collecting signatures of "friends" (1.140). Like the play's manuscript, this stage property document of names possesses a power that far exceeds the aggregate signatures or hands; at the same time, individual differences among hands and persons don't simply disappear into seamless unity or collective unanimity. As the uprising itself demonstrates, particularly as it descends into contentious violence, the collective is precariously complex. In this, *Sir Thomas More* affords an unusual record of collaborative practice, not as an idealized success or an abject failure but rather as a mutual undertaking marked by contradiction, compromise, and sacrifice, and by the "pleading betwixt thone and thother."

The three folio leaves (7, 8, and 9ʳ) of Addition II, which by some accounts include "the most famous—or notorious—manuscript pages in the whole of English literature,"[77] powerfully witness these instabilities in scenes that bring increasingly violent protesters into confrontation with the humanist More, who acts as peacemaker on behalf of the nobles. Written in three different hands (identified as B, C, and D), these pages represent one of the most collaborative portions of the play; they are also the most reproduced and closely analyzed. The collaborative record has been largely occluded, however, by the ongoing speculation about the "Shakespearian flavour"[78] in the scene detailing More's quelling of the riot. Basing their arguments on the "expression of ideas—particularly political ideas," scholars have found in More's words a Shakespearean position on unruly mobs consistent with plays like *2 Henry VI* and *Coriolanus*.[79] One effect of this attribution is to shape the reading or misreading of the play's protest by replacing the citizens' collective voices with the single, authoritative voice of More, who resolves conflicting positions with the transcendent, universalizing discourse of the "wise and learned gentleman" (3.86) that we can take to be Shakespeare's. The canonical ghost similarly skews textual study of the play, encouraging editors to theorize a division of labor between the author and playhouse functionaries. Beginning with Greg, editors have identified Hand C as that of the scribe who corrects, edits, and adds to Hand D's work. Hand D, by contrast, is thought to display "the working of an individual mind" and the writing habits associated with authorial genius.[80] "This hand is obviously that of the author," R. W. Chambers pronounces, "for we see the writer occasionally pausing, cancelling a word or phrase, and then finishing the line according to his second thoughts. However, for an author composing as he writes, he seems to show great fluency. Shakespeare, we know, worked in this way. 'His mind and hand went together.'"[81]

But what Addition II actually shows is that minds and hands don't always work together (some of Hand D's lines are so altered and interlined and without punctuation, as Greg confessed, that "it becomes impossible to follow his intention"[82]); nor do these pages support clear distinctions between authors and scribes. As Paul Werstine points out, many of *Sir Thomas More*'s authors did not themselves honor these distinctions but instead acted in multiple capacities, Chettle as a compositor and editor, Munday as a printer's apprentice, pamphleteer, and actor. Further eroding distinctions is the continuing debate about the identity of Hand B, whose contenders include an author (Heywood) and an actor/playhouse functionary (a bookkeeper recording an actor's clowning improvisations).[83] Even the evidence of the supposedly scribal Hand C, who worked in Addition II and elsewhere to bring coherence and consistency to the manuscript, threatens to undo assumed hierarchies of theatrical labor. While Hand C "freely" overwrites Hand D, adding speech prefixes, stage directions, and clearing up omissions, the two hands are so similar that, as Greg noted, they are "sometimes confused."[84] His observation prompted McMillin's provocative suggestion that Hand D might actually be Hand C—overwriting *himself.*[85] McMillin's point is not to solve the mystery of Hand D but rather to undo the genius/scribe binary by describing a writing practice that resists the distinctions imposed by the search for authorial identity. Looking not to the identity of hands but to the work that hands do, McMillin asks us to understand Hands C and D as "belonging to one intention."[86] McMillin's hypothesis undermines assumptions about the seamless writing of the canonical author by making *all* writing collaborative. The effect is to acknowledge the work of each hand but at the same time to look to the shared intention of the play which, like both the self-divided writer and "the thing" of political friendship, comprises collaborative difference.

If we turn from a consideration of Hand D's identity to analysis of the scene itself, these insights suggest a template for critical as well as editorial practice, one that fragments the unified front of the More-Shakespeare intervention. Like McMillin's self-divided authorial hand, More occupies conflicting positions in this scene. His office as London's sheriff aligns him with his fellow citizens and earns the trust that allows his message to be heard: "'a made my brother, Arthur Watchins, Sergeant Safe's yeoman. Let's hear Shrieve More!" (Addition II, 6.52–53), Doll shouts to the crowd on his behalf. But More's role as negotiator, the play reminds us, comes at the behest of the nobles, who select him because he is "a wise and learned gentleman" and, more cynically, because he is "in especial favour with the people" (3.86–87). More's doubleness as exemplary citizen and royal subject gives him credit with both the May Day protesters and the nobles. Yet such doubleness, I would argue, also complicates his message. His appeal to the populace in this scene is twofold, combining familiar Elizabethan arguments about order and obedience with an impassioned plea for a shared humanity with aliens. The speech has been much praised for its Shakespearean echoes, and critics have characterized the owner of Hand D as both a Tillyardian conservative and an enlightened liberal, a supporter of the Crown and a spokesman for the right of asylum. But if we step back from questions about authorial identity and look closely at the argument itself, we may find that the two strands of More's appeal sit uneasily together, and that rather than resolving the collective protest with the unified and transcendent voice of More-Shakespeare, the play instead dismantles the appeal to sovereign authority at its center.

Lauded by earlier generations for its "passionate advocacy of authority,"[87] More's call for obedience unarguably celebrates the sovereign's supremacy. The king is "a god on earth," More instructs the crowd, reminding them that in "Rising 'gainst him that God Himself installs, / [they] But rise 'gainst God" (Addition II, 6.118–20). To More, the citizens of Addition II represent the anarchy of self-interest. Unimpressed by the virtues of their collaborative authority, More seizes on the absence of a legitimate leader as a way to discredit their cause: "What rebel captain, / As mutinies are incident, by his name / Can still the rout? Who will obey a traitor?" (Addition II, 6.130–32), he warns Lincoln, the collaborator turned mock king, who now arrogantly and unhistorically threatens the city's peace with a "lawless train" of murderers and felons sprung from Newgate (Addition II, 5.22). The leaderless rioters themselves usurp royal authority, having become, in More's words, "kings in your desires" (Addition II, 6.88) and "in ruff of your opinions clothed" (Addition II, 6.90). Their willful self-assertion threatens to destroy generation itself and, in More's imagination, mirrors a past and future laid waste by other "ruffians" doing as "their fancies wrought, / With selfsame hand, self reasons, and self right" (Addition II, 6.95–96). More's warning has been taken to invoke the language of mutual benefit, and in a way it does: "The citizens must consider more deeply who and what they are. Though grossly wronged, they must nevertheless recognize that they are not simply individuals but part of a larger system of laws and obligations whose earthly authority is vested in the sovereign."[88] But in that this recognition is more coerced than voluntary, and in that it is founded in a sovereign authority that subsumes rather than preserves individual interests, More's appeal for social order sounds less like Aristotelian polity than a Hobbesian contract in which, when the multitude unites "their wills virtually in the sovereign, there the rights and demands of the particulars do cease."[89]

The argument that actually wins over the citizens is based in fellowship rather than fear, in voluntary acts of empathy rather than coerced obedience. In a broad appeal to Christian universalism, More asks the citizens to imagine themselves as "strangers":

> Would you be pleased
> To find a nation of such barbarous temper
> That, breaking out in hideous violence,
> Would not afford you an abode on earth,
> Whet their detested knives against your throats,
> Spurn you like dogs. . . .
> . . . What would you think
> To be thus used? This is the strangers' case,
> And this your mountainish inhumanity.
>
> (Addition II, 6.146–51, 154–56)

In some sense, the citizens are already acutely aware of their connections with aliens. They live together, after all, in a proximity that fosters economic rivalry and competition even as it thwarts the attempt at rough justice, as witnessed by the citizens' reluctance to set fire to strangers' houses for fear that it "would much endanger the whole City" (Addition II, 4.41). There is also a strange equivalence in the recourse to violence by which citizens enact a talion justice against strangers: "A purchase, a purchase! We have found, we ha' found" (Addition II, 4.68–69), the Clown sings, echoing Francis de Barde's violent "purchase" of Doll Williamson at the play's opening. The bond More requests, however, asks citizens to see their connection to strangers as a basis not only for conflict and competition but also for commonality and trust. He asks that they recognize that the harms they visit on strangers might come back to them, and he also urges them to confront and take responsibility for their *own* strangeness. By reminding them that they could themselves become refugees vulnerable to the violence they visit on others, More indeed succeeds in making strange the homegrown barbarism of these "free-born Englishmen" (1.80–81). The citizens need no more convincing, and they mirror More's lesson in their response, a proverbial formulation of the Sermon on the

Mount: "Faith, 'a says true. Let's do as we may be done by" (Addition II, 6.157–58).

What's crucial here, especially in conjunction with the earlier appeal to sovereign authority, is that the citizens' recognition of common strangeness depends on their disobedience or, more precisely, on the alienation from sovereign authority that disobedience entails. For it is only when More asks them to imagine themselves as banished—as no longer subjects—that the citizens are able to perceive their mutual interest with strangers. More's point is to impress upon them how tenuous their position actually is and to remind them that if they were to become refugees, no country would have them because of their offense:

Say now the King,
As he is clement if th'offender mourn,
Should so much come too short of your great trespass
As but to banish you: whither would you go?
What country, by the nature of your error,
Should give you harbour?

(Addition II, 6.138–43)

Banishment may be lenient punishment, coming "short of your great trespass," but in that it also represents a severing of relations between subject and ruler, it gives a radical spin to the humanist plea to follow. More's appeal indeed resolves the problem of the stranger not by "the removing of the strangers" (Addition II, 6.80), as the citizens had asked, but by the removal of both citizens *and* strangers. Identification here depends on the citizens' recognition of their shared status with strangers: Both are now political and religious refugees in need of safe "harbour." But it is also a status that, in releasing citizens from sovereign authority, renders them free to admit and experience difference within the reciprocities of a horizontal commonality. Henry Finch had made a similar appeal before the House of Commons in 1593, a month before the posting of the Dutch Church libel, arguing against an anti-alien bill put forth by the city; the differences between his phrasing and More's are telling. For Finch, an ardent puritan, the comparison between strangers and refugees has poignant immediacy, recalling those forced into exile by Mary Tudor: "In the days of Queen *Mary*, when our Cause was as theirs is now, those Countries [i.e., the Low Countries especially] did allow us that liberty, which now we seek to deny them. They are strangers now, we may be strangers hereafter. So let us do as we would be done unto."[90] As with More, the argument hinges on the Crown's oppression, but Finch takes care to avoid sedition by identifying the monarch as the Catholic Mary. More's iteration, by contrast, substitutes the ruling monarch, a move that—even as it appears to defend Henry VIII against the rebels—anticipates the error that will leave More himself without "harbour."

Addition II closes by appearing to resolve More's contradictory message—with his promise to "procure" pardons for the citizens in exchange for their submission—and thus to have it both ways, merging a subject's obedience with universal brotherhood. But when we read *Sir Thomas More* collaboratively—moving from Addition II back to the so-called original manuscript, written by Hand S, and from More's singular authority to the fragmented politics of city and state that follow—Hand D's call for peace seems less and less tenable. For despite More's assurances, the pardons are predictably slow to come. In the interim, Lincoln is hanged, delivering a scaffold speech that invokes the familiar script of a "theater" of punishment:

> I must confess I had no ill intent
> But against such as wronged us overmuch.
> And now I can perceive it was not fit
> That private men should carve out their redress
> Which way they list.
>
> (7.53–57)

But Lincoln's words seem a bit too studied, and the peace compromised by bad faith. When "mercy" (7.59) does finally arrive, the nobles are quick to blame the injustice on the city's "haste" (7.137) to execute. The city defensively fires back: "would we so much had known! / The Council's warrant hastened our dispatch. / It had not else been done so suddenly" (7.141–42). Amid the finger-pointing, the rebels receive their pardons, and More is made "Lord High Chancellor of England" (7.147), ushering in a resolution to citizen protest that, within the shared intentions of the play's multiple hands, is tentative at best.

More's own disobedience a few scenes later (written in Hand S, with numerous passages struck by Tilney) further exposes the contradictions at the heart of this brokered peace. It also opens up another axis for collaborative exchange in More's shared status with the May Day rioters, all identified now as "subjects who rise up," a realignment that once again links universal brotherhood not with obedience but with resistance and political alienation. The nature of More's "error" remains vague—represented in the play simply as his refusal of the king's request to "subscribe" to the "articles"—and might be read in part as the playwrights' wish to avoid the censor's hand. The absence of specificity has the effect, however, of universalizing More's offense so that it more easily recalls the earlier scenes of citizen protest. One could argue that More's measured response—"Subscribe these articles? Stay, let us pause. / Our conscience first shall parley with our laws" (10.72–73)—is far from the taunts of the citizen rabble in Addition II. But in its recourse to a standard of judgment outside the king's authority, the response clearly recalls the thinking of the protesters at the start of the play that, contrary to Lincoln's scaffold speech, "private men" should indeed "carve out their redress" (7.56). The king's attempt to force More's signature, moreover, pointedly contrasts with the May Day collection of signatures of "friends" (1.140), setting coerced obedience to the monarch alongside the voluntary collaboration of London's citizenry. The collaborative bond between the city's famed Lord Chancellor and its protesting citizens is not without its differences, most obviously marked by rank, but more profoundly by the religious and legal particularities of More's unnamed offense. Yet the fact that the playwrights quietly sidestep the religious question in order to celebrate More as the citizen who "set a gloss on London's fame" (9.100) in itself offers persuasive testimony to the power of the civic commonality.

The playwrights indeed collude with both the historical record and each other to secure a bond between the Lord Chancellor and the citizens that extends from the opening scene of protest to More's execution at the play's close. The stagecraft itself insists on the connection, because More's final appearance on the scaffold recalls not only his earlier appeal to the May Day rioters (perhaps delivered from the same raised playing space) but also, and even more pointedly, the spectacle of Lincoln's execution, a repetition that speaks to "an intentional and coherent design."[91] And just as the play's stagecraft refigures differences between More and the citizens by identifying More's fate with Lincoln's, the collaborative hands of Addition II document a similar give-and-take in the working out of this design. Hand D, for example, famously assigns generic speech prefixes to the protesters, often identifying them simply as "other" or "oth" or "all," in marked contrast to the opening scenes' individualized prefixes. This includes the key speech in which the rebels capitulate to More's terms for peace—agreeing to "be ruled by you, Master More, if you'll stand our friend to procure our pardon" (Addition II, 6.159–60)—which Hand D assigns to "all." Hand C, however, reassigns the lines to Lincoln, a small but crucial emendation that alters the play's dramatic structure, deepening the irony of Lincoln's execution (he is, after all, the only citizen *not* to receive pardon), as well as his identification with More (see Figure 2).[92] The play as a whole corroborates C's revision in the formal patterning of verbal and visual cross-references, which both preserve and bridge the differences between citizen protest and More's own act of conscience. Like Lincoln, who willingly gives his life to "remedy" the "vile enormities" (1.91–92) perpetrated against London's citizens, More too casts his protest as a sacrifice, a subscription on his own terms, by which he offers up his "bones to strengthen the foundation / Of Julius Caesar's palace" (13.177–78). As the glancing reference to *Richard III* (3.1.69) suggests, More's death will memorialize him within a noble lineage sacrificed to tyrannical authority. The more radical point, however, is that Lincoln too shares this lineage, forming an association that includes London brokers together with Yorkist princes.

## *"Some Curious Citizen"*

But if *Sir Thomas More* seems to gesture toward a utopian city in which citizens come together with alien outsiders and with each other, across ranks, the play decidedly avoids celebrating, or even representing, this newfound commonality. The bond between More and Lincoln, so strikingly figured by the stagecraft, remains to be played out in the civic sphere on stage and in the audience's collective imaginings. What most disturbs the commonality, at least for us, however, is not its uncertain future but its deeply compromised past. *Sir Thomas More*'s belated acknowledgment of common strangeness seems hardly compensatory for the xenophobia that drives its protest, the play's democratic stirrings being hard to reconcile with what Richard Wilson has recently referred to as the "race-riot" at its center.[93] And there *is* cause for discomfort, especially when the initially sympathetic citizens turn violent, their legitimate grievances degenerating into xenophobic panic over "strange roots" (Addition II, 6.11), the imported pumpkins and parsnips feared to spread contagion and disease within the city.[94] But rather than confronting this discomfort, critical response to the play has tended to take refuge in a binary logic that sets the chaos of a rioting crowd against the universalizing humanism of More and

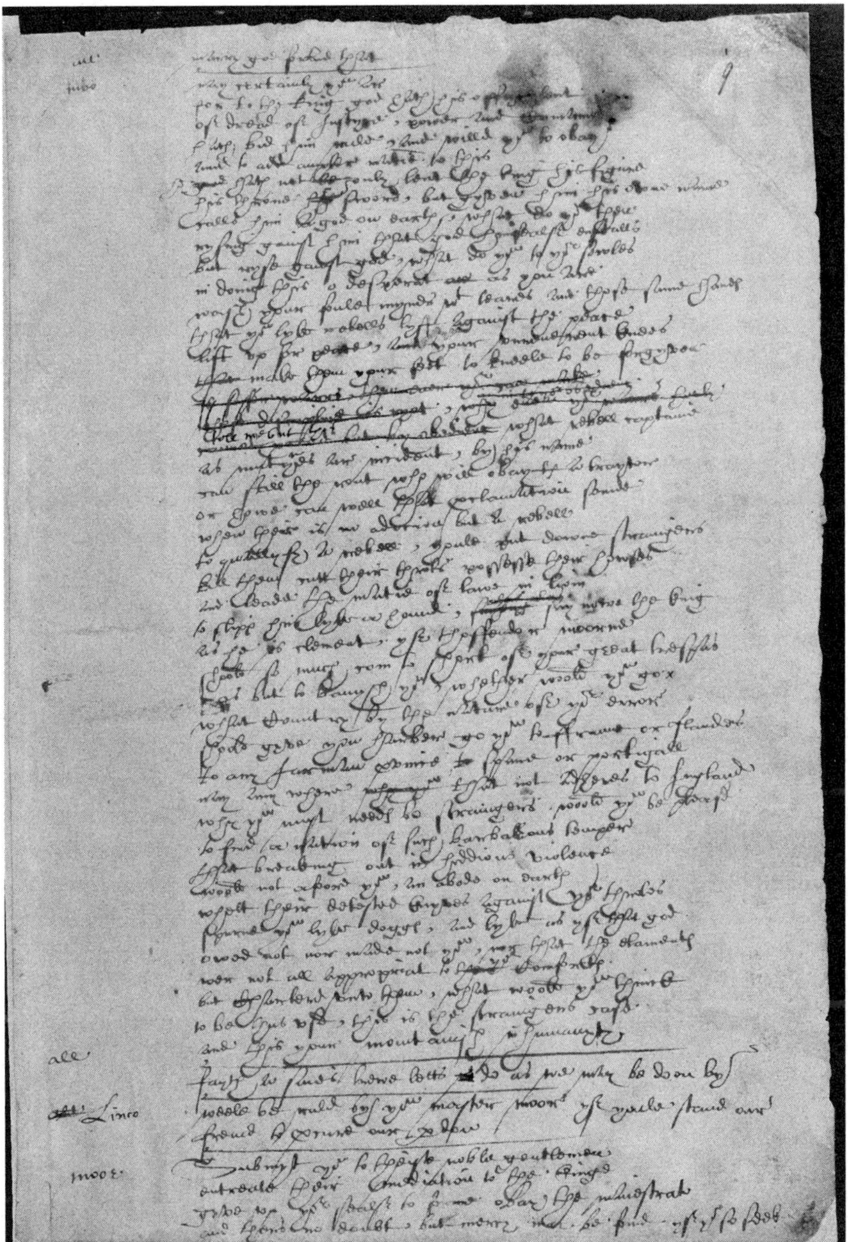

Figure 2. *Booke of Sir Thomas Moore*, Addition IV. 9a (© The British Library Board).

Shakespeare. In Wilson's formulation, the "stand-off" is between "popular exclusion" and "official inclusiveness," between the "Hobbesian world of Carnival and the Kantian one of hospitableness,"[95] an argument that, if it doesn't necessarily reinforce the singularity of the More-Shakespeare position, nonetheless reduces citizens to an undifferentiated collective. What gets left out of this binary is a recognition of the paradoxical centrality of "the stranger"—not only as a demonized outside of citizen identity, as it is usually understood, but as an unsettling figure for the differences at the heart of civic polity.

More's call for a bond between citizens and strangers lays the intellectual framework for this recognition, but it is Addition II's protest that actually materializes the paradox of the differentiated collective on stage. The ugly scapegoating of strangers, presided over by an unruly Clown (added by Hand B[96]), may call up a "Hobbesian world of Carnival," but the scene simultaneously gestures toward an individuated collective, insisting on a common strangeness or separateness among citizens at the very moment when they seem to merge into xenophobic oneness. Again, the manuscript supplies a template for critical practice, registering differentiation in both playwriting and protest, as illustrated by Hand C's corrections of D's speech prefixes in Addition II. For Greg, C's emendations are simply editorial: "indifferent to the personae," Hand D "writes 'other' and leaves it to C to assign the speech to whom he pleases," to do the scribal work of fitting D's contribution into the play as a whole.[97] But if, following McMillin, we think of Hand D and C as working collaboratively—as being both equal and "at odds"—what puts them at odds is the very question of collaborative differentiation, as C works to give the protesters names and so to restore individuation to D's representation of mob violence. When editions, notably the Revels edition and the *Norton Shakespeare*, choose to reproduce Hand D's speech prefixes in Addition II largely *without* C's emendations, the effect is, predictably, to minimize differentiation among the play's protesters and its playwrights.[98] As Walter Cohen describes the scene for the *Norton Shakespeare*, Hand D "belittles the protesters, depriving them of an individuality they possessed earlier in the play."[99] To separate Hand D from his collaborators is thus to elide Addition II's striking documentation of common strangeness located within, as well as outside, the scene of collective protest.

Collaborative difference and common strangeness are also on display in *Sir Thomas More*'s performance of *The Marriage of Wit and Wisdom*, the play within the play that holds a collaborative mirror up to theatrical practice itself. The occasion is one of civic hospitality, as More, now Lord Chancellor, opens his house to the city's ruling elite, feasting the mayor and aldermen and their wives. In this setting, the strangers at the door are not the reviled Lombards but the Lord Cardinals' Players, a traveling troupe of "[f]our men and a boy" (9.73) come "to tender" their "willing service" (9.47). Pleased by the chance for entertainment, More chooses a play title that promises a "liberal argument" (9.66), but one whose large cast requires the small company to double roles, including three parts for women. "And one boy play them all? By'r Lady, he's loaden!" (9.77), More remarks.[100] Just as *The Marriage of Wit and Wisdom* necessitates doubling, so too does *Sir Thomas More*, a play that, even in its revised state, contains an unusually large number of parts. Within the play's collaborative contexts, however, this Elizabethan stage practice itself performs a kind of doubling—functioning both as a practical solution to casting problems and as a powerful materialization of the humanist plea for shared identity across difference. Protesting artisans and tradesmen, who drop out of *Sir Thomas More* after the uprising, might return as Erasmus, or Roper, or More's hangman, doubling ranks and professions along with their roles. Even more pointedly thematic, casting demands within *The Marriage of Wit and Wisdom* suggest that both strangers and citizens from *Sir Thomas More*'s opening scenes might double as itinerant actors, as sharers in the dual labor of performance.[101] The purpose of playing in *Sir Thomas More*, one could argue, is not to solidify citizens against strangers, as Tilney had feared, but rather to model an individuated commonality, one that marries wit and wisdom at the play's center by bringing citizens and strangers together as "fellows" (9.71), bound in a theatrical venture that includes More himself.

But while it is tempting to see the stage here as a place of utopian possibility, like *Sir Thomas More* itself, performance of *The Marriage of Wit and Wisdom* stops short of idealized notions of theatrical fellowship, looking instead to the precarious complexities of collaborative practice. This holds for More's participation as well, in his extemporaneous performance in the role of Good Counsel. Again, theatrical contingency creates the opening for fellowship, when More's choice of play apparently necessitates a last-minute procurement of "a long beard for young Wit" (9.141) from Ogle, the famous theatrical wigmaker. When the actor, named Luggins, fails to return from the errand in time for his cue, More merrily steps in, improvising Good Counsel's part "almost as it is in the very book set down" (9.305–6), to the astonishment and praise of the players. Like *Sir Thomas More*'s other collaborative ventures, this performance coalesces separate interests—its purpose, as More first explains to the players, is "to pleasure me and benefit yourselves" (9.52). We are reminded of these differences when, after the play, one of More's servants delivers the monetary "reward" (Addition VI, 9.317). Like the other ventures, the performance also seems to insist on its own imperfections—the company is short on costumes and even More's brilliant improvisation is, in the end, only "almost" perfect. But what ultimately "mar[s] the play" (9.295), to the point of stopping its performance, is neither the "lack of a little good counsel" (9.261–62) nor More's extemporaneous playing, but divisions among More's guests. For, as we learn in Addition VI (Hand B), the play was dismissed. As Wit complains, at first blaming Luggins's negligence, "some curious citizen disgraced it, / And, discommending it, all is dismissed" (Addition VI, 9.323–24). Within the imperfect commonality of the collaborative, the performance is stopped not by a monarch or by the royal censor but by "some curious citizen." The difference matters.

# 3. *Trading in Tongues*

## Language Lessons and *Englishmen for My Money*

William Haughton's *Englishmen for My Money* (1598) is notable for being the earliest surviving comedy of contemporary London life.[1] Evidence for its dating comes from Henslowe's account book—a brief entry on February 18, 1598 recording the ten shillings "lent vnto Robarte shawe . . . to paye vnto harton for a comodey called a womon will have her wille"—fitting documentation for a play that is itself so fully engaged in matters of credit and exchange.[2] Centered on a Portingale merchant-usurer named Pisaro and his three clever daughters, *Englishmen for My Money* follows a tradition of "Englishing" the conventional plotting of Roman new comedy. Haughton's innovation, however, is to set his story within the walls of London, in contemporary locations that extend from Pisaro's neighborhood of Crutched Friars near Tower Hill to the Royal Exchange and Paul's Walk. Appearing the same year as John Stow's *A Survey of London*, Haughton's play revels in the urban topography, its intrigues unfolding within a matrix of geographical reference that only the locals could understand and that all others, newly arrived English provincials as well as foreign merchants and visitors, would probably need a map to follow.[3] Haughton peoples his cityscape with the usual mix of merchants, middlemen, spendthrift gentlemen, and tricky servants, into which he introduces three "stranger" merchants, rival suitors to three English gentlemen for the hands of Pisaro's three daughters. It is this competition between Englishmen and strangers that drives much of the comedy.

*Englishmen for My Money* is also notable for its exuberant xenophobia, and in capitalizing on the city's longstanding anti-alien sentiments, Haughton appears to look back to the crudely drawn caricatures of moral interludes like *Wealth and Health* rather than ahead to the more sophisticated city comedies of Jonson and Middleton.[4] Launched by clown Frisco's gleeful riff on foreign accents—"pigs and Frenchmen speak one language, 'awee

awee'" (1.1.173–74)—*Englishmen for My Money*'s jokes turn on an unapologetic mimicry of national stereotypes and vernaculars.[5] Foreign merchants fill the theater with a comical babble of stage Dutch, French, and Italian, a linguistic hodge-podge that provokes derision as well as misprision. Predictably, Pisaro's daughters will have none of it, mocking the "dogbolt eloquence" (2.3.4) of their foreign suitors as reason enough to reject them. Indeed, as one outspoken daughter parries to her Dutch admirer:

> If needs you marry with an English lass,
> Woo her in English, or she'll call you an ass. (2.3.159–60)

It is no surprise that critics have chafed against these sentiments, echoing Sir Philip Sidney's criticism in *The Defense of Poesy*: "For what is it . . . against law of hospitality, to jest at strangers, because they speak not English so well as we do? What do we learn?"[6] What we learn, Haughton's play seems to say, is that we should put our money on the English and come together in a ritual mockery of foreigners that, for a moment at least, seems to elide class differences within a chauvinistic celebration of civic and national pride.

Without exonerating Haughton from charges of jingoism, recent studies have begun to complicate this story of stranger relations by looking to the play's fault lines—to Pisaro's denizen status and the mixed blood of his daughters, for example, and to the conflict between the city's economic interests and its celebration of an explicitly English identity. As Jean Howard succinctly puts it, *Englishmen for My Money*'s main "problem" is to negotiate "the alien presence at the heart of London's merchant world."[7] Interestingly, the play conspicuously avoids an outright rejection of foreign trade, preferring to maintain a stance of neutrality or even acceptance. Nor does it resort to demonizing alien merchants as blood-sucking parasites who, in the common parlance, "eat by trade the bread out of our mouths."[8] The play attempts instead to separate questions about the need for foreign merchants from those about their suitability as husbands for London maids. These questions are not so easily disaggregated, however, especially in a play that insists on conjoining its marriage plot, whose resolution requires the exclusion of strangers, with a money or exchange plot, which depends on commerce with these same strangers to underwrite the marriage plot's happy outcome. Haughton thus comes up against a familiar dilemma in early modern London: how to accommodate the costs of international trade, and the problem of the alien, within a commercial city whose prosperity depends on the "commodity" of strangers.[9] The play's resolution is at once resolutely comic and evasive. Rather than confronting the dilemma, it imagines a fantasy economy in which the prodigal English gentlemen—gaining marriage, money, and land—become the beneficiaries, if not the inheritors, of a global traffic that continues to be supported by the capital of Pisaro and the stranger merchants who, now that "the storms are passed" (5.1.307), hope to reap the profits of unimpeded trade.

*Englishmen for My Money*'s persistent mockery of foreign tongues is central to this strategy of containing the threat of the alien without sacrificing the city's commercial investments. What makes the foreign merchants unsuitable husbands, after all, is not their trade or even their rude manners but rather their broken English, the indelible marker of alien status said to remain like "a watch-word vpon his [a stranger's] tong to descrie him by," as Richard Carew declared in "The Excellencie of the English tongue."[10] Not surprising in a play that boasts its sympathies in its title, Englishness is securely aligned with the "mother tongue" and fiercely protected by Pisaro's daughters, who prove their patriotism by outwitting their foreign suitors and thereby refusing to allow "a litter of languages to spring up amongst us" (1.2.105). Women will have their wills, the play's subtitle instructs us, and these half-English daughters of a Portingale money-lender shrewdly opt for English husbands with whom they may breed good English sons. But, as critics rightly point out, within the context of late-sixteenth-century London, this version of assimilation is magical thinking, a fantasy belied by the city's ongoing legislative battles over alien trade and denizen status.[11] Equally fantastic, I would add, is the play's celebration of linguistic purity. For even as the comedy denigrates strange accents and broken English, city residents were themselves conversing in foreign tongues in unprecedented numbers. Not only did Londoners have occasion to hear a "confusion of languages" in the daily congress of Paul's Walk or the cosmopolitan Royal Exchange, as Thomas Dekker observed, but they contributed to that confusion, practicing outlandish accents by investing in the increasingly popular study of foreign vernaculars.[12]

By all accounts, modern language study was in demand in late-sixteenth-century London. Proficiency in languages, and French especially, was now considered indispensible for an expanding merchant class increasingly dependent on foreign trade. Languages were also gaining currency as a requisite form of cultural capital among the city's middling ranks eager for access to the privileges of aristocratic households. With the influx of Huguenot refugees in the latter half of the century, the city saw an expansion of language instruction across ranks. No longer the exclusive domain of private tutors, instruction was now available in newly established language schools within the city and supported by an explosion of printed materials in the form of cheap instruction manuals and phrase books geared to ordinary citizens and their families. What this growing industry in language study documents is an urban population increasingly engaged in linguistic encounters with strangers. Within the context of these encounters, the broad comedy of *Englishmen for My Money*—where the jokes turn on the "dog-bolt eloquence" of both English and foreign speakers—seems more than just xenophobic mockery, suggesting a fascination as well as amusement in the cross-cultural exchanges of urban commerce. This is not to dismiss claims that language lessons were instrumental in England's colonialist ambitions, consonant with "the activities of a culture in the process of extending its boundaries and reformulating itself," as Steven Mullaney and others have argued.[13] But it is to turn attention to the ways in which this new fashion for trading in tongues might have operated within London itself, offering residents yet another means of working out new forms of sociability by practicing encounters with strangers within a city whose institutional identity was founded on the exclusion of strangers.

"*[I]t is always the practical confrontation with different modalities of exclusion . . . that constitutes the founding moment of citizenship*, and thus of its periodic test of truth," Étienne Balibar observes, putting into question the inside/outside opposition that typically structures thinking about citizenship.[14] This opposition is a founding principle within political communities defined by exclusions, but as Balibar points out, it also operates within inclusive communities that aim to dismantle exclusions by extending rights and privileges in a spirit of normalizing "solidarity."[15] Balibar's point is that "emancipation" is never natural or spontaneous but instead requires active and on-going struggles across difference. Attempting to think "difference" together with "sharing," and "conflict" together with "general interest," Balibar proposes not so much a solution to debates about political exclusion and inclusion but rather a recognition that citizenship involves "a contradictory process, fed by permanent conflicts between several types of subjectifications or identities."[16] While Balibar's interest is in the contemporary question of transnational citizenship, his exploration of the possibilities for "citizenship without community" is useful for thinking about problems of identity and belonging within early modern London, a city whose communal traditions, like those of modern nations, were coming under pressure. That citizenship, broadly construed, might be understood not as a fixed and permanent condition or status but rather as an ongoing activity, founded on the "practical confrontation with different modalities of exclusion," is especially valuable in shifting attention to the processes at stake not only in linguistic encounters but in the urban activities taken up throughout this study.

As we have seen in Chapter 2, it is precisely the confrontation with "modalities of exclusion" that constitutes what might be called the "founding moment of citizenship" in *Sir Thomas More*. Once the rioting commons are banished from the realm, they come to understand their commonality with strangers—both are now excluded, for example—and it is at this point that the commoners' status shifts from subject to citizen within a newly formed polity that acknowledges the constitutive outside at the heart of the civic collective. Rather than appealing to a "common good" imposed from above, the play instead registers the complex and fractured processes of collaborative politics. Haughton's play confronts many of the same exclusions as *Sir Thomas More*, linking foreigners with a threatening traffic in women and goods even as it relocates these confrontations within a comic realm. *Englishmen for My Money*'s politics may seem to be less explicit and less radical than *Sir Thomas More*'s. There is no spokesman to articulate citizen grievances in Haughton's comedy, and the play's ostensible heroes, the prodigal Englishmen, may be street-wise city residents, but their goal is to recover their lands and livings and return to a traditional economy free of the demands of strangers and of the "extortion" and "simony" (4.1.137) of the credit economy. The play indeed models a hybrid strategy that would pair the city's institutionalized policies of excluding strangers with an equally coercive fantasy of assimilation that would impose Englishness on desirable outsiders, in the form of Pisaro's half-English daughters. But if Haughton's plotting appears to reinforce a version of the city's exclusionary politics, the play's staging of linguistic confrontations and confusions nonetheless offers resistance to any simplified choice between inclusion and exclusion.

As most recent work on the play contends, language is the "key site" for distinguishing native from foreign, marked out by the repetitive jests at the strangers' broken English.[17] But if language is a primary location for staging distinction, it is also a medium within which these distinctions might be confronted and rearticulated in ways that open up rather than resolve the city's so-called alien problem. It is this possibility of simultaneously invoking and reconstituting traditional differentiations that this chapter explores. I begin outside the theater, with the popular French language handbooks that could be said to give literal purchase to the linguistic and commercial transactions at stake in Haughton's play. These books not only supplied readers with lessons in foreign tongues, but they also outlined a practice for confronting differences in eminently practical terms. As such, the language manuals supply material evidence of the ways in which Londoners in their daily pursuits of economic and cultural capital were actively involved in confronting exclusions. Within this context, Haughton's play seems more than just another staging of contemporary anxieties about foreigners within London, although this is surely part of the story. With its plots and counterplots turning on possibilities for linguistic as well as commercial exchange, as Englishmen impersonate foreigners and foreigners Englishmen, the play performs a comic version of the pedagogical constructs recommended by the language books. This is not to reduce Haughton's comedy to a parody of London's fashion for language lessons. It is, rather, to look to the lessons as a way of understanding the cultural work of theatrical performance within the city, not only within the specific context of a linguistically self-conscious play like *Englishmen for My Money* but also within the wider contexts of an urban theater that itself modeled practical confrontations of inside and outside, here and elsewhere, location and dislocation, within the medium of practicing the city on stage.

## *A Linguistic Marketplace*

By some accounts, Londoners in the late 1590s did not need to take up the study of foreign languages to encounter alien tongues, nor did they need to frequent Paul's Walk or to embark on walking tours of neighborhoods like Crutched Friars. They had to look no further than the English language itself. By the close of the sixteenth century, English had transformed from an ostensibly rude tongue into an eloquent vernacular, newly enriched by a massive influx of foreign words and neologisms; between 1580 and 1619 alone more than 10,000 words entered the language.[18] These changes did not go uncontested, and many, while acknowledging the need for an expanded and standardized vernacular, condemned the fashion for neologisms as vain affectation. As Thomas Wilson put it, in an oft-repeated passage in *The Arte of Rhetorique* (1553): "Some seeke so far for outlandish English, that they forget altogether their mothers language. And I dare sweare this, if some of their mothers were aliue, thei were not able to tell what they say."[19] The sixteenth-century debate over England's vernacular project has been much discussed, notably in Richard Foster Jones's extensive study of the "triumph" of the English language and Paula Blank's more recent work on literary dialects.[20] What bears mention here, however, is the debate's metaphorical purchase on questions about Englishness, language, and foreign trade within a rhetoric of exclusion, the very same conjunctions that sit together so uneasily in sixteenth-century language books and in *Englishmen for My Money.*

The discourse of nationhood, Richard Helgerson argues, is constituted by a double alienation—from a nation's "former self or selves" and from other, so-called foreign, nations and communities.[21] In its vexed relationship both to the vulgar language of the past and to the more refined tongues of its linguistic neighbors, England's vernacular enrichment offered instruction in how these double exclusions might operate in tandem; for not only did the expanding vernacular civilize the barbarous mother tongue, subduing the alien within, as it were, but it did so in part by translating, or "Englishing," the alien without. Foreign words were deemed "strangers" and thought to require control and even alteration in a process akin to England's colonialist ventures abroad. The vernacular debates also tapped into strategies for dealing with alien problems at home, borrowing from London's highly charged rhetoric about its own stranger population. Some, for example, objected that foreign words constituted a kind of illegal immigration, acting as dangerous "Free-denizens" outside local regulations and parliamentary consent.[22] Others, like Richard Mulcaster, were confident that these "stranger denisons," once subject to "the lawes of our cuntrie," could be fully assimilated into the English language.[23] An outspoken proponent of an expanded and reformed vernacular, Mulcaster reassured students of English in the closing arguments of *The Elementarie* (1582) that, "tho it were an enemies word, yet good is worth the getting. . . . And when the foren word hath yeilded it self, & is receiued into fauor, it is no more foren, tho of foren race, the propertie being altered."[24]

Economic metaphors were pervasive in these debates. Words that could be "coined," "minted," and even "clipped" were understood as a kind of property, to be exchanged and traded for profit. Carew, for example, defended English "borrowing" in explicitly mercantile terms: "For our own partes, we employ the borrowed ware so farre to our aduantage that we raise a profit of new words from the same stocke, which yet in their owne countrey are not merchantable."[25] Others, less sanguine, worried about the catastrophic cost of this borrowing in the form of trade imbalances and national bankruptcy when England was required "to repay our borrowed speech back again."[26] Language in these accounts comprises a national treasury or storehouse, one that might be increased, borrowed, exchanged, or stolen. Yet for all the talk of enrichment and trade, this new economy was hardly a linguistic land of Cockayne, equally open to all. New words might be "coined" and "stranger denizens" brought under English control, but, as some feared, vernacular expansion could also be counterproductive in that rather than leading to greater literacy it might instead exacerbate exclusions and divisions within the nation itself. Roger Ascham urged writers to eschew the example of those who "vsinge straunge wordes as latin, french and Italian, do make all thinges darke and harde," directing them instead to follow Aristotle's counsel and "speake as the common people do, to thinke as wise men do: and so shoulde euery man vnderstande hym, and the iudgement of wyse men alowe hym."[27] Rather than leading directly to increased access to a common language, the enriched and increasingly regulated English vernacular was fostering what we now think of as a linguistic market—a competitive "system of specifically linguistic relations of power based on the unequal distribution of linguistic capital," to use Pierre Bourdieu's well-known formulation.[28] Indeed, as Blank has persuasively argued, by the century's end, writers were themselves competing for linguistic privilege and possession and, in the process, raising questions about "who had the prerogative to 'gain' words, to 'mint' words, to discriminate among 'base' words and the genuine article. And who, finally, stood to profit from the trade."[29]

That the late-sixteenth-century vogue for foreign language study should raise many of the same questions as the vernacular debate is perhaps to be expected; it was the rising interest in modern vernaculars, after all, that helped drive the growth of English in this period. But in its close association with London's increasing involvement in global traffic, this new push for foreign languages complicated these questions in immediate and practical ways, not least that it offered a strikingly literal example of a linguistic market that both Bourdieu and Blank understand primarily as metaphoric. Asserting the connection between languages and profitable commerce, Robert Robinson argued in *The Art of Pronuntiation* (1617) that "the true pronuntiation" of languages was vital "for the commodity and aduantage it may beget to the common-wealth as well at home, as in commerce and traffique had in forraine parts."[30] As the popular language books themselves attest, foreign trade required a facility with foreign tongues, and French especially. English was said to be "woorth nothing" past Dover, and as John Eliot confided to readers of his French language manual, "to trafficke with the stranger, the French is the only trading tongue in Europe."[31] Following the practice of aristocratic households, city merchants hired refugee teachers to instruct their children in the language of commercial and cultural capital. For the middling ranks, enterprising refugees such as Claudius Hollyband set up language schools around Paul's churchyard, educating citizens' sons in Latin and serviceable French for a shilling a week.[32] Those wishing to learn "priuatly in their owne study or houses" might purchase one of the many French-English manuals available from the nearby bookshops, and as the proliferation of language books and schools within London suggests, language study had itself become a profitable business, tied to the city's increasing dependence on trade and traffic.[33]

Language instruction and printed books were hardly new, of course: witness John Palsgrave's massive and expensive folio dedicated to the "puissant king" Henry VIII, or the elegant quarto Giles Duwes designed for Mary Tudor, or even the cheap phrase books long used by English traders.[34] What was new was a program of language study repurposed for London's citizen households and supported by the widescale reproduction of do-it-yourself instruction books, to be used "without any helpe of Maister or teacher," as Hollyband advertised on the title page of his perennially popular textbook, *The French Schoolmaster* (1573).[35] In contrast to language books for the nobility, which featured grammar instruction supplemented by dialogues on elevated subjects like love, the nature of the soul, and receiving foreign ambassadors, the popular French handbooks printed in London in the 1570s reduced grammar to a minimum and focused instead on dialogues related to trade in the style of the fifteenth-century *manières de language*, written for merchants and travelers. Set up in facing pages of French and English, the books were small, affordable, and portable so that they "might be easier to be caried by any man about him."[36] Their instruction typically aimed at practical language use. The anonymous *A plaine pathway to the French tongue* (1575), for example, advertised as "profitable for Marchants" and "good to all men, learned, and unlearned, Gentilmen, Merchauntes, and all others," opens with a dialogue about fabrics and credit set in a draper's shop.[37] The text also includes boiler-plate letters of exchange, obligations, and indentures needed by apprentices and factors traveling abroad. The emphasis, as in so many of these manuals, is on use and profit. Though this book is "small," the author explains in his preface, it is highly valuable, like the goldsmith's "finer siluer," measured "not as it seemeth in greatnes, but as it is worth in price and estimation."[38]

The city's economic interests thus authorized its population to take up what had traditionally been a courtly curriculum associated with diplomacy and law. Yet the courtly associations no doubt contributed to the remarkable currency of these little books, affording city residents access to cultural capital previously reserved for the elite. The social value of language instruction may even have received a boost from the unusual status of the refugee teacher himself whose livelihood depended in part on his success in exploiting a patronage system within a market economy. Hollyband, for example, probably served for a time as private tutor to the young heir to whom he dedicates his two manuals, Robert Sackville, son to Lord Buckhurst. Aristocratic patronage offered refugee teachers protection and publicity, as well as the credentials necessary to set up schools and to shop their texts in London's book market. And it may also have increased the books' value among the citizenry by explicitly linking common purchasers with noble patrons, a strategy Hollyband reiterates in the dedication to *The French Littelton* when he voices his surprise that his earlier manual was "liked of, both by the nobilitie and meane estate" (sig. ii). For a small price the aspiring tradesman and his wife could emulate their social superiors by studying the lessons dedicated to an aristocrat who, like themselves, was "new to learne" the language (*French Schoolmaster*, sig. A3$^{v}$).[39]

It is not surprising, then, that concerns about the popularity of language lessons spoke of social as well as economic dangers. There were the usual warnings against foreign trade, linking imported tongues with luxury goods and condemning both as a drain on the English economy; as Robert Cawdrey put it in *A Table Alphabeticall* (1604), recycling Thomas Wilson's earlier critique of linguistic affectations, "as they loue to go in forraine apparrell, so they will pouder their talke with ouer-sea language."[40] But there were also fears about the social and political costs of making foreign language study too widely available. Even Mulcaster, who believed strongly that children should be taught to read and write, recommended restricting access to Latin and other languages unless they were required by the necessities of trade. Some of Mulcaster's concerns were economic: An overly educated "multitude" would not find preferment commensurate with its training and would drain trades of their labor force. But he also worried that opening up access to language instruction "disquieteth the whole state."[41] When country "clounes" and city "artificers" learn languages, he complained, they fail to understand that it is "not the toungue, but the treasure of learning and knowledge, which is laid up in the toungue whereunto they never came, which giveth the toungue credit, and the speaker authoritie." These would-be scholars, Mulcaster warned, "will not be content with the state which is for them."[42]

Yet the demand for foreign languages continued to increase, and by the early 1590s, at least according to John Eliot's claim, there were some in London who spoke tongues "volubly and very fluently," and "many others who would be very glad to learne, if ther were any learned teachers to instruct them."[43] As one of the city's few native-English language teachers,

Eliot's observations, set forth in his own French language book, have the ring of self-promotion.[44] Even so, as he jockeys for advantage among his foreign-born competition, Eliot offers an unusually vivid picture of the booming market for language instruction, catered to by "so many famous teachers and professors of noble languages, who are very busie dayly in deuising and setting forth new bookes, and instructing our English gentlemen in this honorable cittie of London."[45] The facts support Eliot's claims. Hollyband's textbooks continued to be in demand in the 1590s: *The French Littelton* went through multiple printings (1591, 1593, 1597, and 1602), *The French Schoolmaster* was twice reprinted (1596, 1602), along with *A Treatise for Declining Verbes* (1590, 1599, 1604), *A Dictionarie French and English* (1593), and *The Italian Schoolmaster* (1597). Both John Florio's *Second Fruits* and William Stepney's *The Spanish Schoolmaster* appeared in 1591 and Eliot's own *Orthoepia Gallica: Eliot's Fruits for the French* in 1593.

How then does the city's clamor for languages square with the ongoing criticism about foreign trade and foreign tongues? Or, to put it differently, what practical ways did these popular language books offer for negotiating conflicting attitudes toward London's increasing investments in trading in tongues? Eliot's solution is to "buy local," promoting English over native French and Italian schoolmasters, who "are a little too high minded, and doe not fit themselues long to the nature of us English."[46] But how did the foreign-born schoolmasters like Hollyband manage so well? I want to explore these questions by turning briefly to Hollyband's popular handbooks. Not only were these texts in wide circulation, reprinted well into the seventeenth century, but they set the standard for early modern language pedagogy.[47] Like other language books from the period, Hollyband's volumes contain the usual mix of dialogues, grammar, vocabularies, and proverbs. What makes them innovative is his close attention to pedagogy and his inventive handling of the standard dialogue format. In what follows, I want to take these influential texts as models not only of language acquisition but of practical ways of addressing entrenched practices of excluding foreign tongues and foreign trade.

## *Language Lessons*

Claudius Hollyband's name appears in the May 1571 return of aliens for St. Olave's Parish in Southwark, identified as "Glood Holebrand, Frenchman, scolemaster, denizen, haith byne here vij yeres."[48] Anti-alien sentiments ran high in the early 1570s, as they would again in the 1590s, and 1571 was an especially difficult year. Following the discovery of the Ridolfi plot, the

Privy Council had ramped up its surveillance of the alien population by ordering an unprecedented series of detailed returns, listing every alien in each of the city's wards by name, along with his nationality, occupation, and dependents. The May 1571 return tallied 4,287 aliens living in and around London (about four percent of the population), and by December the number had risen to 6,513.[49] That same year, London citizens, concerned about "the great numbers of strangers in and about this cytty," published a list of grievances against alien merchants and craftsmen.[50] Most seriously, and in what was to persist as a major point of contention for the rest of the century, the citizens accused alien merchants of transporting their profits out of the realm to England's detriment, claiming that "whereas they have halfe the trade of this Kingdome in importe they imploy not a twentieth part thereof, but transport the money or make it over by Exchange, and keepe the Exchange within their own handes."[51] In 1572 the Privy Council instituted orders for the city to make secret searches for strangers who "'cannot yeld good reason of there comynge here'" and to subject Thames' boat traffic to search.[52] Later that year the St. Bartholomew's Day massacre would bring even more refugees to London, further exacerbating tensions within the city, and by 1573 the Council's orders included dispersing the large concentrations of strangers who "'dwelt pestred up in one place.'"[53]

With his denizen status, Hollyband would have enjoyed a certain protection from the government crackdowns. After taking a loyalty oath and paying fees for a royal letter patent—Hollyband's cost ten shillings in 1565/6—denizens were allowed to ply a trade or craft, keep a shop, lease property, and even initiate lawsuits.[54] Still, they did not enjoy full economic and political rights, particularly in matters of trade and inheritance: The status of a denizen's children and their right to inherit would remain in question well into the next century.[55] London companies did admit both denizens and strangers "to use their trade," but records show that relations were far more competitive than cooperative, and over the next decade numerous companies directly petitioned the crown for permission to exclude stranger artisans.[56] Denizen privileges could also be long in coming; Hollyband's name remained on the parish rolls for alien poll taxes as late as 1593, nearly thirty years after his denization.[57] Most telling, perhaps, denizens and their English-born children continued to be counted among the city's strangers in various returns and records, as if to underscore their permanent status as outsiders.

Yet, for all its considerable limitations, denizen status nonetheless offered important accommodations to the city's customary exclusions. It marked out a category between "free" and "unfree," English-born and alien, inside and outside, and, rather than reconciling these defining oppositions of citizen identity, the designation instead kept them in precarious tension, epitomized by the commonly used term "denizen stranger."[58] Denization probably did not put the categories of citizens and subjects themselves into question, at least not directly. But as a legal category in its own right, it did offer a useful mechanism for authorizing exceptions to the status quo in the interests of the city and state, interests often framed in economic terms with an eye to manufacture and export. Denization also offered a potent metaphor for understanding other forms of traffic with strangers in early modern England—in the vernacular debates, for example, where the category served as a way of defending borrowed or imported words, or in relation to horticulture and the importation of foreign plants.[59]

In what follows, I want to consider ways in which Hollyband's innovative language lessons, launched by *The French Schoolmaster* in 1573, may themselves have profited by advocating a pedagogical version of denization for their London readers and thereby assuring a place for the French tongue within England's rapidly expanding *entrepôt.* The title itself perhaps argues against such a claim. Borrowed from Robert Ascham's *The Schoolmaster* (1570), *The French Schoolmaster* would appear to reverse the direction of denization in that rather than translating a foreign text into English, it adapts into French a popular English text on teaching and learning Latin. What Hollyband actually delivers, though, is a curiously bifurcated model of language acquisition that enacts the unresolved tensions or contradictions of denizen status—at once domesticating the foreign tongue *and* reasserting its strangeness.

When it first appeared in 1573, *The French Schoolmaster* no doubt surprised and delighted London readers with its lively dialogues of everyday urban life. The familiar phrase-book lessons of buying and selling are there, to be sure, but relegated to the back of the volume. In the place of notice, Hollyband instead offers an extended dialogue sequence set not in the foreign locales typical of the genre but in a contemporary London vividly rendered with local detail and civic pride. This is a striking innovation on Hollyband's part, one that brings the French lesson home, so to speak, as if to regulate foreign tongues within the city's jurisdiction. Strangers are conspicuously absent from Hollyband's London dialogues; there are no French merchants or travelers, no commercial exchanges, indeed, no trace of the foreigner at all except during the elaborate feast scene when the talk turns to French wine and condiments. In contrast, John Florio's more up-market Italian language book, *His Firste Fruites* (1578), although modeled

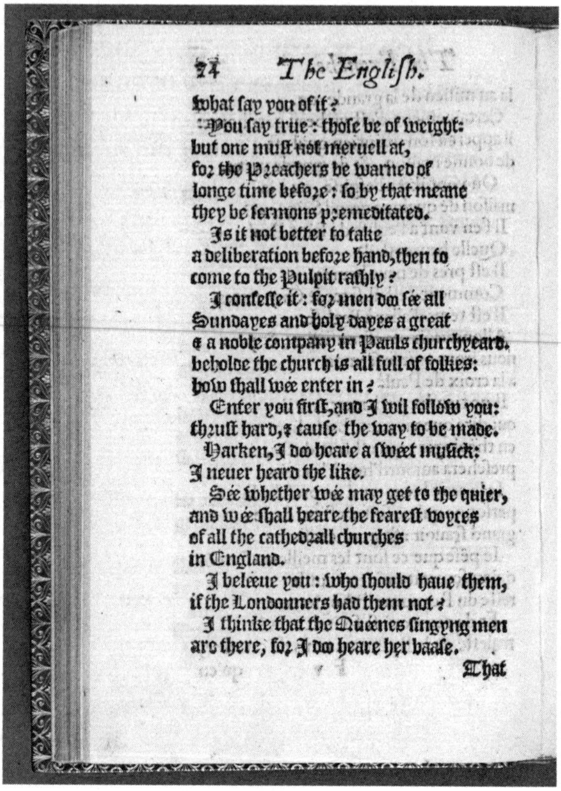

24 The English.

what say you of it?
You say true: those be of weight:
but one must not meruell at,
for the Preachers be warned of
longe time before: so by that meane
they be sermons premeditated.
Is it not better to take
a deliberation before hand, then to
come to the Pulpit rashly?
I confesse it: for men doo see all
Sundayes and holy dayes a great
& a noble company in Pauls churchyeard.
beholde the church is all full of folkes:
how shall wee enter in?
Enter you first, and I wil follow you:
thrust hard, & cause the way to be made.
Harken, I doo heare a sweet musick:
I neuer heard the like.
See whether wee may get to the quier,
and wee shall heare the fearest voyces
of all the cathedrall churches
in England.
I beleeue you: who should haue them,
if the Londonners had them not?
I thinke that the Queenes singyng men
are there, for I doo heare her baase.
That

Figure 3 (*above and opposite*). C. Hollyband, *The French Schoolemaister* (London, 1573). (This item is reproduced by permission of The Huntington Library, San Marino, California.)

on Hollyband's, directly engages cultural and social differences in its dialogues. When asked "What do you thinke of the people of England, are they louing?" Florio's Italian interlocutor replies with unguarded frankness: "I wil tel you the truth, the Nobilitie is very curteous but the commons are discorteous, & especially toward strangers, the which thing doth displease me."[60] Hollyband's dialogues politely avoid the discomforts that might come from talking with strangers, turning attention to London itself.

With the city at its center, *The French Schoolmaster* is as much a primer on contemporary London culture as it is on the French tongue. Taking its readers through a day in the life of a prosperous citizen family, the dialogues, or "familiar talkes," follow the model of Latin colloquies, with son Peter waking up and preparing for school. But as the scene opens out to

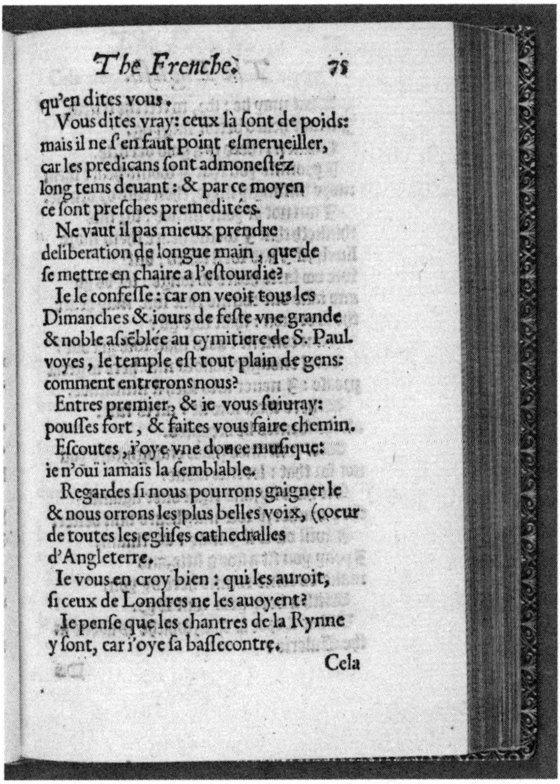

The Frenche. 75

qu'en dites vous.

Vous dites vray: ceux là ſont de poids: mais il ne ſ'en faut point eſmerueiller, car les predicans ſont admoneſtéz long tems deuant: & par ce moyen ce ſont preſches premeditées.

Ne vaut il pas mieux prendre deliberation de longue main, que de ſe mettre en chaire a l'eſtourdie?

Ie le confeſſe: car on veoit tous les Dimanches & iours de feſte vne grande & noble aſſẽblée au cymitiere de S. Paul. voyes, le temple eſt tout plain de gens: comment entrerons nous?

Entres premier, & ie vous ſuiuray: pouſſes fort, & faites vous faire chemin.

Eſcoutes, i'oye vne douce muſique: ie n'ouï iamais la ſemblable.

Regardes ſi nous pourrons gaigner le & nous orrons les plus belles voix, (cocur de toutes les egliſes cathedralles d'Angleterre.

Ie vous en croy bien: qui les auroit, ſi ceux de Londres ne les auoyent?

Ie penſe que les chantres de la Rynne y ſont, car i'oye ſa baſſecontre.

Cela

the city streets and the business of everyday London, the "familiar talkes" quickly become both less conventional and more familiar. Conversing as they walk, a city merchant and his gossip head toward Paul's Cross to hear a sermon. Their talk touches on minstrels and maypoles, the wedding of the sheriff's daughter underway at the cathedral, and the spectacle of the crowded churchyard. At noon, they head home to dine with family and friends. The interlocutors are well-educated and well-connected; one, for example, boasts of dining "touchying some businesse" (80) with the Master Chancellor of London, a former schoolfellow from Winchester. Their houses are commodious, their servants stubborn, and their tables amply furnished. The sermons at Paul's are "the best sermons that men may heare in all the rest of the Realme of England" (72). Their cathedral choir showcases the fairest voices. "[W]ho should haue them [these voices], if the Londonners had them not?" (74) they exclaim with pride (see Figure 3).

Trading on local gossip, colloquial banter, and easy humor, as if to point the way to the later city comedies, Hollyband imbues his dialogues with the cadences of the urban everyday. The topicality is striking, as is Hollyband's care for realistic detail. Local references abound, including mention of Hollyband's own family and his school; so much is the concern for accuracy, in fact, that subsequent editions update this information, adding children to the schoolmaster's family as the years pass and alerting readers to address changes for his school. There's even a theater history footnote in the bit of dialogue about poet and playwright Richard Edwards, the much-loved master of the Children of the Chapel. The reference occurs in the extended feast scene, when the host, promising singing, sends his wife to retrieve his music books, safely kept in a "little til" (126) in his closet:

| There is a good song: I do | Voila vne belle chanson: ie |
|---|---|
| maruell who hath made it. | m'esmerueille qui la faite? |
| It is the maister of the children | C'est le maistre des enfans de cueur |
| of the Queenes chapell. | de la chappelle de la Rynne. |
| What is his name? | Quel est son nom? comment s'appelle il? comment l'appelle-on? |
| Maister Edwards. Is he a liue? | Maistre Edouard. Est-il en vie? |
| I heard saie that he was dead. | i'auoye oui dire qu'il estoit mort. |
| It is alreadi a good while a go: ther are at | Il y a ia long tems: il y a pour |
| the least five yeers and a half. | le moins cinq ans & demy. |
| Truelie it is pitie: he was a man | Certes c'est dommage: c'estoit vn home |
| of a good wit, and a good poete: | de bon esprit, & vn bon poete: |
| and a great player of playes. | & vn gran ioueur de farses. |

(132–35)

Edwards had died in 1566, seven years before the first printing of *The French Schoolmaster*, and the reference lends the manual a contemporary currency that authenticates Hollyband's portrait of an urbane citizen culture that values songs as well as sermons, plays as much as prayers.

Keeping foreigners and even talk of trade at a distance, discretely behind the scenes, *The French Schoolmaster* looks instead to the fruits of that trade, to the prosperous lifestyles and material splendor of the merchant class, and to the promise of social emulation. There's an intimacy to these "familiar talkes" that is at once exclusive and beckoning, as if to invite readers to sit at the table of city elites, to share their pastimes and their tastes. And just as the dialogues model social as well as linguistic behaviors, it is not hard to imagine Hollyband's books doing double-duty as courtesy manuals, competing in the market of improvement literature for London's expanding middling ranks. French was acquiring a certain cachet within London society, to be worn as a fashionable accoutrement by citizens and their wives. "I had my Latin tongue and a spice of the French before I came to him" (2.1.335–37), Mistress Openwork sniffs in *The Roaring Girl*, asserting her status in the face of rumors that her husband "keeps a whore i' th' suburbs" (327–28).[61] And many probably did mine the language books for "fragments of French or small parcels of Italian to fling about the table," as Dekker later charged in *The Gull's Horn-book*, although by then the fashion for linguistic ostentation had become a staple of satiric comedies, part of a more general critique of urban commodification.[62] In the face of rising anti-alien sentiment in the 1570s, however, *The French Schoolmaster*'s strategic linking of French lessons and social capital may have gone far in legitimating what was for many a suspect congress with strangers.

As if to trade on the allure of social emulation, Hollyband's vocabulary-rich dialogues display an array of commodities, much like the shop windows in the upper pawn of the recently opened Royal Exchange. But they also offer something the shops cannot: instruction in the social use of these goods. Nowhere is the invitation to emulative misbehavior more compelling than in *The French Schoolmaster*'s feast scene, an extensive sequence comprising nearly half the manual's London dialogues. Here, Hollyband's innovations turn what is a set piece in Latin school texts into an extravagant display of urban hospitality and abundance.[63] In contrast to the Latin colloquies, where the feast is an occasion less for eating than for reflection, philosophical debate, and lessons in good manners, Hollyband concentrates on food.[64] Accompanying the lavish repast are lessons in social and culinary presentation, as illustrated in this exchange between the jocularly imperious host and his silent servant: "Take away this boyld meat: now bring us the roaste: pull hither that shoulder of Veale: it is very wel larded, it prouoketh mee to eate truly: make roume to set the disshes: set that a side a litle: cut that Turkie cocke in peeces: but let it be colde, for it is better colde then hot" (104). Hardly the exotic menu of nightingale's tongues and sheep's brains conjured by Volpone, the plentiful fare of Hollyband's table caters to London appetites, serving up a banquet of salted beef, garlic stuffed mutton, sugared mustards and venison, and capons boiled with leeks. And without the qualifying moral commentary of the Latin school texts, which Hollyband studiously avoids, the pedagogical abundance, or *copia*, is seductively alluring, encouraging language learners to revel in a bounty of French words within a linguistic market that is also a showcase for material goods and social consumption.[65]

Yet the alien presence doesn't completely disappear from these seductive language lessons. Instead, it audibly returns in the imitative performances at the heart of Hollyband's pedagogy. Like the humanists who rehearsed their students in Latin colloquies and plays on a regular basis, Hollyband requires his readers to become actors in their learning, to perform dialogues that, presumably, they would later adapt to suit the occasion. Fundamental to these strategies is oral practice: "Rehearse after supper the lesson which you will learne to morrow morning: and read it six or seuen times: then hauing said your prayers, sleepe upon it: you shall see that to morrow morning you will learne it easely" (sig. C6$^{v}$), Hollyband instructs students in *The French Littelton*. More than simply a mnemonic method, these prescribed rehearsals suggest the kind of imaginative role playing John Brinsley recommends in his grammar school handbook, urging students to "vtter euery dialogue liuely, as if they themselues were the persons which did speake in that dialogue, & so in euery other speech, to imagine themselues to haue occasion to vtter the very same things."[66] But who exactly were Hollyband's students imagining themselves to be? For many, as I've been suggesting, the dialogues authorized an alluring social shape-shifting, inviting readers to take the parts of prosperous citizens and schoolboys. But to the extent that these lessons required a double set of impersonations—whereby English readers of various ranks imitated well-heeled London citizens speaking *French*—Hollyband's dialogues suggest something more complicated.[67]

In a dedicatory letter prefacing *The French Littelton*, Hollyband explains that the "yong learner, and euery other persone intending to learne the same language, forsakinge all other thornie and vnapte bookes, shall first *frame his tongue* by the reading of this worke" (sig. iii, emphasis added). The usage may appear to be metaphorical, but Hollyband takes the figure literally in order to underscore his innovative emphasis on pronunciation. In contrast to other French language textbooks that "teacheth nothinge concerninge the readinge and pronunciation," Hollyband promises "a sincere and parfecte anneringe of syllables" (*French Schoolmaster*, sig. Aiii). This is a remarkable claim, especially for books to be used without teachers, and

Hollyband takes pains to support it. In place of the schoolmaster's voice, there are pronunciation charts, phonetic marks and glosses, and a lengthy section titled "Rules for Pronunciation," including detailed instructions on how to hold the mouth and tongue. To take one example of many, Hollyband explains that in pronouncing diphthongs followed by a double "ll," as in "grenoille" or "bouillir," "one must pronounce them not with the ende, but with the flat of the tongue, touchynge the roufe of the mouth" (sig. Biii[v]). He then adds that "Englishmen ought to mark diligentlie" this particular pronunciation "for it is one of the greatest difficulties that they finde in the Frenche tongue" (sig. Biii[v]).

Hollyband was certainly not the first to elaborate a mechanics of articulation in language study. Pronunciation figured centrally in humanist pedagogy, as outlined in Erasmus's dialogue *The Right Way of Speaking Latin and Greek* (1528), a foundational work emphasizing the importance of proper speaking to a classical education. The dialogue's interlocutors, named Lion and Bear, begin by discussing the importance of the tongue itself, affirming that there "is no other part of the body so quick and so pliable and so ready to take up different shapes, nor any other on which a man's acceptability and success so much depends." Bear then works out the logic in practical terms: "The fact is that poetry is the first thing taught to children as a sort of game or exercise for reading and reciting and learning the best words for things. So the poet can be said to 'form boys' mouths.'"[68] The assumption, of course, is that framing the tongue is crucial to framing the mind. Writing nearly a century later in *The Art of Pronuntiation* (1617), Robinson makes a similar claim for modern language study. Lamenting the difficulty students face in "fram[ing] their mouthes" to other tongues, Robinson proposes a universal phonetic alphabet to enable them "speedily to learne the / Exact touch of pronuntiation of any / forraine language whatsoeuer."[69] What then might be the effects of a stranger who is not a poet or a grammarian forming the student's mouth? Erasmus's dialogue, though concerned with Greek and Latin rather than modern vernaculars, suggests one answer when Bear strongly advises against mimicking "actual voices when you are quoting a woman, a boy, an old man, a German, a Frenchman, or an Englishman. It would be undignified." "But it might be funny," Lion remarks.[70] More than simply debased mimicry or role-playing, the act of "framing the tongue" to outlandish accents risks unwelcome transformations.

For readers today, the early modern concern with "framing the tongue" may recall Bourdieu's observations on the "articulatory style" or "bodily hexis" at work in the linguistic market. "Language is a body technique," he asserts, and the means by which speakers signal social as well as linguistic competence. A speaker's "articulatory style," or "life-style 'made flesh,'" is associated with an "*overall way of using the mouth.*"[71] While Bourdieu's interest here is primarily with the symbolic capital of class, the notion of bodily hexis, when applied to foreign language acquisition, suggests that the mouth might be the marker of national distinctions as well. And it is within this context that we might understand Hollyband's double impersonations. By requiring students to adopt the words of prosperous London citizens in their everyday dealings, *The French Schoolmaster* promotes a linguistic competence that promises to translate into social as well as economic capital and, at the same time, minimizes the outsider status of an alien tongue. Still, as Bourdieu's account of articulatory style reminds us, these French lessons are hardly a model of incorporation or assimilation, along the lines of Mulcaster's vernacular program, say, by which the "foren word," once it is altered and "receiued into fauor, it is no more foren." What Hollyband's students end up imitating, and embodying, are the tensions of legal denization, as the lessons force them to use their mouths as linguistic outsiders even as they express the tastes and opinions of London's prosperous insiders. Thus, by requiring students to "frame their tongues" in emulation of native French speakers, Hollyband's pedagogy tacitly reinstates at the bodily level the very strangeness the content of the London dialogues would seem to displace.

This is not to argue that Hollyband's language lessons produced a kind of hybrid monster, a French version of Ascham's Italianated Englishman, although the attention to pronunciation and "framing the tongue" may well have exacerbated anxieties about English susceptibility to foreign manners and customs.[72] Nor is it to claim an idealized form of cultural dialogue, a mingling of French tongues and English interests in the name of a new urban prosperity or cosmopolitan commerce. It is, rather, to give a sense of the enforced estrangements or alienations solicited by Hollyband's pedagogy, alienations that disrupt the period's commonly held assumptions about language as the primary site for distinguishing native from foreign.[73] It is also to imagine that as Hollyband's students framed their tongues to perform these double impersonations with every word and phrase they uttered, they participated in the practical—and political—work of enacting the city's conflicting attitudes toward strangers in their midst.

*Performing Words*

In its fascination with foreign tongues, city locales, and linguistic performances, *Englishmen for My Money* stakes out a cultural terrain reminiscent of Hollyband's language books. Like *The French Schoolmaster,* the play choreographs a day in the life of London's merchant class with scenes that shift from Pisaro's household to the Royal Exchange to Paul's Walk and the back alleys of east London. Haughton may even offer a direct nod to the language books when Pisaro, in the play's extended Exchange sequence, proffers the requisite dinner invitation, entreating the stranger merchants, once "our business [is] done here at the Burse" (1.3.11), to come home with him and "take in worth such viands as I have" (13)—including his daughters. The effect, however, seems radically different from Hollyband's accommodating pedagogy, as signaled by the strangers' response, their first words in the play:

| | |
|---|---|
| VANDAL | Zeker Meester Pisaro, me do so groterly dank you, dat you maak me so sure of de wench, dat ik can niet dank you genough. |
| DELION | Monsier Pisaro, mon père, mon vader, O, de grande joy you give me, écoute, me sal go home to your house, sal eat your bacon, sal eat your beef, and sal tack de wench, de fine damoisella. (18–22) |

Haughton's merchants speak not in the proper phrasings of the language books but in a comical broken English, marked by heavily accented speech, "rustic phrases," and "[s]tammering half sentences" (2.3.3–4). The patois may have been a clever way to make foreigners understandable to London audiences, as some have argued, but it nonetheless supplies much of the play's humor and chauvinistic preening.[74] Rather than accommodating the presence of strangers within London, *Englishmen for My Money* seems intent on calling out their differences by drawing on a ready repertoire of national stereotypes and stage vernaculars.

There is nothing especially new about Haughton's use of broken English to underscore national differences. As G. K. Hunter long ago observed, it "may be taken as a fair example of stock attitudes."[75] What is new, however, is Haughton's decision to stage these "stock attitudes" within a strikingly contemporary London. And it is these local connections that have prompted much of the recent critical interest in the play. Taking issue with earlier dismissals of *Englishmen for My Money* as a "run-of-the-mill comedy," scholars have reopened the play's questions about Englishness in relation to the city's expanding commercial investments and on-going debates about denizens and resident aliens.[76] What this recent work suggests is that even as *Englishmen for My Money* trades in national stereotypes, it also troubles that trade by confounding normative distinctions between English and aliens. This confusion is clearly on display in the marriage plot, in the central, and highly unstable, opposition between the stranger merchants and Pisaro's half-English daughters, who emerge as the unlikely champions of English language and Englishness. The marriage plot frames its questions about national identity and citizenship, broadly construed, in terms of two competing models: one based on the exclusion of foreigners and the other on their assimilation, as figured by the daughters' marriage to Englishmen. But it then links the two by using the latter to enforce the former: the daughters of a bottle-nosed Portingale, who is probably a Jew, become fully assimilated only by rejecting the stranger merchants along with their own alien blood. As women who "will have their wills," the usurer's daughters are actively instrumental in the play's exclusionary practices.

I want here to explore another, and much less remarked, locus of confusion in *Englishmen for My Money* by turning a critical ear to the linguistic traffic not of foreign merchants but of the English themselves and to the language lessons and impersonations that underwrite much of the play's comic intrigue.[77] With this self-conscious linguistic turn, I suggest, the play puts pressure on its own pervasive practices of exclusion, in part by confusing linguistic and national identities but also by gesturing toward a performative practice that replays some of the constitutive tensions of Hollyband's pedagogy. Language lessons are hardly incidental to the plotting; indeed, it is the prospect of a lesson that sets the proliferating intrigues and impersonations in motion. The impetus for the lessons originates with Pisaro, who sends his servant Frisco in search of a tutor for his three daughters: "one that is expert in languages, / A good musician, and a Frenchman born" (1.1.163–64). Pisaro's plan is to outwit the English suitors by making his daughters more attractive to the stranger merchants, teaching them "the tongues, / That they may answer in their several languages" (216–17). But the plan is quickly commandeered by Anthony, the Latin schoolmaster whom Pisaro has just fired for "infect[ing] my three girls, / Urging the love of those [the Englishmen] I most abhorred" (143–44). Though he speaks no French, the "smooth-faced" (166) Anthony poses as a Frenchman with the aid of a cloak, a black beard, and a mouthful of fancy words. The disguise gives him access to Pisaro's daughters and the chance to advance his own interests as a go-between for the English suitors; it also supplies opportunities for mischief, mayhem, and linguistic hijinks.

Unsurprisingly, no formal language lessons actually take place. Not only is the French tutor a sham, but the daughters themselves stridently resist framing their quick tongues to anything but English—except in fun. Like Portia and Nerissa in *The Merchant of Venice*, Pisaro's daughters take turns parodying their suitors. The youngest, Mathea, is particularly bold in her mockery, giving bodily presence to Delio's unctuous delivery:

> My Frenchman comes upon me with the 'sa, sa, sa.
> Sweet madam pardone moy I pra'.
> And then out goes his hand, down goes his head,
> Swallows his spittle, frizzles his beard. . . . (2.3.19–22)

Tolerating neither the strangers nor their speech, the sisters pretend not to understand their amorous advances. "Pray, sir, what is all this in English?" (2.1.37), Marina coyly asks of Alvaro's "*dulce*" Italian. Her sister Mathea is more blunt: "Think you I'll learn to speak this gibberish, / Or the pig's language? Why, if I fall sick / They'll say the French *et cetera* infected me" (97–99). Pisaro may believe that the language lessons will pay off by ensuring his daughters' marriages to wealthy merchants and thereby allowing him to retain the mortgaged properties of the prodigal Englishmen. But his willful daughters have ideas of their own, and in refusing the merchants' tongues, they act to protect English assets, figured in their own "mother's tongue" and in their marriages to the prodigal English suitors. In this, the three sisters stand as shining examples of virtuous London maids, in pointed contrast to the proverbial city wives said to ape foreign speech and fashion to the detriment of England's trade balance.

Yet even as Pisaro's daughters reject language lessons, reasserting Englishness in the face of foreign trade, *Englishmen for My Money* is not without its cross-linguistic rehearsals. Indeed, impersonating strange tongues is central to the comic intrigue as Haughton capitalizes on the current vogue for outlandish accents on the city streets even as the play's linguistic hijinks fuel a fashion for trading in tongues on stage.[78] Frisco and Anthony both practice framing their tongues to European vernaculars—Frisco in his vaudeville routines, and later in his impersonation of the Dutchman Vandal, and Anthony in his extended role as the French tutor, Monsieur Mouche. Their impersonations may operate as the foreign language device does in other Elizabethan plays—to profile "the merits of the native tongue by setting it off against a variety of other or allegedly inferior modes,"[79] as A. J. Hoenselaars observes—but they also turn attention to the fumbling linguistic performances of the English themselves. Pisaro's man, Frisco, "[a] simple sot, kept only but for mirth" (1.2.57), is the first to shape his mouth to foreign speech. Tasked with finding a language "expert" when he himself has no such skills, Frisco undergoes a brief tutorial from Pisaro on stage French and Dutch. For the unschooled Frisco, foreign languages are no more than sounds to be manipulated to advantage—a hilariously reductive rendering of the humanist emphasis on pronunciation—and the clown is quick to point out to his master that he will be able to speak "perfect Dutch" if he has his "mouth full of meat first, and then you shall hear me grumble it forth full mouth, as *Haunce butterkin slowpin frokin*" (1.1.181–83). To be sure, Frisco's clowning performs yet another parody of the foreign merchants' broken English, but it is also the case that his and Anthony's botched impersonations show up the linguistic weaknesses of the native-born English, exposing an insularity that is simultaneously a measure of patriotism and vulnerability.[80]

Adding to Frisco's linguistic escapades is the matter of his own precarious command of English. By his own admission, he speaks English "so like a natural" (3.2.105)—like the "natural" or uneducated native speaker that he is, of course, but also like a "natural fool."[81] Frisco's natural abilities are soon put to the test at Paul's Walk, when he interviews Anthony in the guise of Monsieur Mouche. With no French to draw on, the Oxford trained Anthony effects his disguise by larding his speech with pretentious or "hard English words," epitomized by his mannered solicitation of Frisco: "I beseech you, Monsieur, give me audience. . . . Pardon, sir, mine uncivil and presumptuous intrusion, who endeavour nothing less than to provoke or exasperate you against me" (2.2.17, 19–21).[82] Flattered by Anthony's ornate locutions, Frisco takes the obscure diction to be French. "So by this little French that he speaks, I see he is the very man I seek for" (22–23), the simple servant exclaims, and begins to show off his own recently rehearsed phrases—"*Content pore vous Monsieur Madamo. . . . Nella slurde Curtezana? . . . Ducky de doe watt heb yee gebrought*" (28, 32–33, 35). "[Y]ou speak it like a very natural" (33), the disguised Anthony remarks.

Who is the joke on here? Elizabeth Schafer suggests that the clown's gullibility reflects on those in the audience "who also accept stagey caricature accents as indicative of national identity," an effect that, in calling out those who laugh at the broken English of foreign merchants, also subjects the play itself to "self-conscious scrutiny."[83] But even as the joke threatens to unsettle linguistic distinctions between English and aliens within the play and within the theater, as it surely does, it simultaneously opens up distinctions *among* English speakers by playing to the linguistically sophisticated audience members who hold themselves above "natural" speakers like Frisco. Yet even these linguistic hierarchies are not above scrutiny when, later in the play, Frisco turns the tables and impersonates the Dutchman, speaking "groote and broode, and toot and gib'rish" and hoping for "a fling at the wenches" (3.1.12–13). This time it is the supposedly sophisticated Englishmen who fall for the joke. So intent are these gentlemen on thwarting the foreign competition that they fail to hear the difference between the outlandish accents of the merchants and Frisco's base caricature—although on Haughton's stage, one suspects, there may have been little difference to hear.[84] Like Frisco, the Englishmen can't distinguish between imposters and card-carrying foreigners, or between servants and merchants.

By linking confusions about imposters to the performative operations of language, *Englishmen for My Money* not only gives contemporary currency to the conventional disguise plots of intrigue comedy; it also provokes an awareness of linguistic authority reminiscent of the mediating pedagogies of the language books. For all the mockery of foreign accents, in the commercial London of Haughton's play, the ability to "trade in tongues" puts speakers at a distinct advantage, and as the plotting reminds us again and again, the loss of linguistic opportunity is also the loss of economic opportunity. Yet the advantage, it seems, lies more with the skillful performers, with the tricky servants and linguistic fakes, than with the native or natural speakers. Like the tradesman who frames his tongue to Hollyband's London dialogues, Frisco gains a certain authority in his linguistic impersonation of the Dutchman, even if he doesn't succeed with his "fling," as does Anthony in his Mouche disguise. Their hijinks often threaten to self-destruct—most comically, for example, when the disguised Anthony comes face to face with the stranger merchants and gasps: "I have no French to slap them in the mouth" (2.3.70)—but their performances often have as much efficacy as the actions of legitimate authorities. Pisaro, for one, is utterly convinced by Anthony's disguise, so much so that in the play's final scene he deems Mouche "[w]orser than Anthony" (5.1.216) and sends for officers to imprison the double-crossing French teacher in Bridewell. The double-cross, of course, turns out to be executed not by Anthony himself, but by yet another impersonator—daughter Laurentia cross-dressing in the role of Mouche.

Nowhere is the performative confusion more curiously on display, however, than in the comic wooing scene of Act 4. The setting is conventional, borrowed from the so-called balcony scenes of *Romeo and Juliet* and *The Merchant of Venice*: Pisaro's daughter Mathea appears above, at her chamber window, while her suitor, Ned Walgrave, stands in the darkness of the street below, professing his love.[85] But in Haughton's version, the usually clever Mathea makes the astonishing mistake of taking her English suitor for the French Delio. Remarkably, in a play so attentive to linguistic distinction, her confusion of identity rests solely on the basis of voice and accent. Granted, Mathea is expecting Delio, having been warned by Anthony that the foreign merchants are planning to impersonate the Englishmen at the midnight assignation. Moreover, as the play continually warns the audience, it is too dark to see without a light. And so, when Walgrave first identifies himself to his love, rather modestly, as "Thy Ned, kind Ned, thine honest, trusty Ned" (4.1.38), Mathea takes him for "Monsieur motleycoat" (40) and launches into a defensive attack, rejecting both the Frenchman and her father's blood:

> Though I am Portingale by the father's side,
> And therefore should be lustful, wanton, light,
> Yet, goodman goose-cap, I will let you know
> That I have so much English by the mother,
> That no base, slavering French shall make me stoop. (42–46)

Initially rendered speechless by Mathea's drubbing, Ned responds with an equally aggressive marriage proposal, concluding with a threatening, rather than slavering, French: "Why then, *Madame* Delion, *je vous lassera a Dio, et la bon fortune*" (61–62). With these words, Mathea exclaims: "That voice assures me that is my love" (62).

The humor lies in the timing. Mathea succeeds in distinguishing between her "honest, trusty Ned" and the imposter suitor she expected, but on what basis? Maybe it is Walgrave's threatening proposal—"take me as you find me" (58) or become a "Frenchman's trull" (60)—or maybe it is the characteristically colorful rant that precedes it, but there's a delightful irony in the fact that it is only when "trusty Ned" speaks a stumbling French, impersonating Delio's broken English, that Mathea finally recognizes him. The moment recalls the parallel scene from *The Merchant of Venice*, also played in the dark, when another usurer's daughter presses her love for confirmation: "Who are you? Tell me for more certainty, / Albiet I'll swear that I do know your tongue" (2.6.27–28). Jessica's hesitation, however, is more a measure of her abiding insecurities about Lorenzo's love than confusion about his identity; she does, after all, seem to "know" his tongue. It is tempting to attribute a similar interiority to Pisaro's daughters, who seem strangely unbothered by the mercenary motives of their English suitors, or even to imagine that Mathea only pretends not to recognize Walgrave as a way to test his love. Yet however audiences hear it, Mathea's momentary confusion of the rival suitors still stands, and as French substitutes for English as the marker of Walgrave's identity, the play inverts conventional assumptions about language and national distinctions. Like *The French Schoolmaster*'s scripting of double impersonations, Haughton's cleverly turned jest, taking the audience as well as the play's speakers by surprise, has the unlooked-for effect of reinstating strangeness in the very act of asserting exclusion.

The English suitors make quick work to regain control of the wooing by securing language within its conventional contexts. As Englishman Heigham boasts, countering Marina's report of the Italian's love-protestations, "Look what he said in word, I'll act in doing" (4.1.93). "[T]he thing is quickly done" (98), Walgrave advises, urging him to "perform" his words:

> . . . Will you perform your words?
> All things are ready, and the parson stands
> To join, as hearts in hearts, our hands in hands. (95–97)

The marriage ceremony—J. L. Austin's example *par excellence* of performative speech—promises to control language by returning it to a conventional and ritually sanctioned context in which words *are* deeds and in this case irrevocable deeds. Further securing the marriages and their economic benefits is the matter of sexual performance, the equally irrevocable act by which Walgrave promises to make the sisters "mothers of six goodly boys" (101), for it is through children that the gentlemen plan to recover their assets from Pisaro, as Walgrave crows once the sisters are offstage:

> This works like wax. Now ere tomorrow day,
> If you two ply it but as well as I,
> We'll work our lands out of Pisaro's daughters,
> And cancel all our bonds in their great bellies. (112–15)

Reasserting English virility against slavering foreigners and the bottle-nosed Pisaro, Walgrave's braggadocio retakes possession of the English language along with English lands. In "performing" their words, the Englishmen will beat out the foreign competition by producing healthy English boys rather than the grotesque "litter of languages" Frisco imagines as the merchants' progeny: "O, the generation of languages that our house will bring forth! Why, every bed will have a proper speech to himself and have the founder's name written upon it in fair capital letters, 'here lay—', and so forth" (4.3.98–102).

## *Cross-Talking*

In his recent book *Aliens and Englishness in Elizabethan Drama*, Lloyd Kermode identifies two phases in Elizabethan representations of foreigners. Exemplified by Tudor morality plays such as *Wealth and Health* and *The Tide Tarrieth No Man*, the first phase defines Englishness *against* a corrupt, immoral, and dangerous foreignness. But the second, late Elizabethan, phase constructs Englishness in combination *with* the foreigner so as to incorporate otherness and thereby "extract[s] out of that fusion a reformed, expanded, revitalized, and always politically equivocal definition of the English self."[86] Shakespeare's *Henriad* illustrates this second phase in that the Welsh presence "maintains its alien status as the other that Englishness incorporates, without destroying, to enlarge itself."[87] Kermode locates a similar pattern in *Englishmen for My Money*, pointing to Pisaro's half-English daughters as the epitome of a revitalized and expansive fusion. "[T]hey are the embodiment of the alien within Englishness, and their determination is to be (re)producers of Englishness," he writes, emphasizing their desire "to incorporate themselves into the English body politic," linguistically as well as nationally.[88] Indeed, Pisaro's daughters enthusiastically offer up their father's monies, their mother's tongue, and their own bodies in an outspoken bid for assimilation that recalls Mulcaster's description of vernacular expansion in which the foreign word, seemingly of its own volition, *yields itself* and is "receiued into fauor," whereupon "it is no more foren, tho of foren race, the propertie being altered." In this account, linguistic incorporation, or "Englishing," much like the marriage of Pisaro's daughters, ostensibly effaces all trace of the foreigner and, contrary to popular suspicion, leaves no "watchword" on the stranger's tongue "to descrie him by."[89]

But if Pisaro's daughters aspire to a self-effacing Englishing through marriage, the play's comic cross-talk raises questions about the possibility of assimilation and acceptance. It is true that in the end the play advances what Kermode identifies as a strategy of incorporation, setting the Englishmen's marital and economic triumphs against the foreign merchants' humiliations. Shamed into silence, the foreigners retreat to the sidelines, the French tutor Mouche returns to his native roots as the English Anthony, and clown Frisco momentarily refrains from riffing foreign accents. But even as the stage community absorbs the alien in the name of Englishness, the play's far less predictable pattern of linguistic impersonation pushes against such tidy conclusions, leaving open the possibility that foreign tongues might again disrupt English speech, in the necessities of foreign exchange, to be sure, but also in the comic imitations of servants and in the outlandish accents that erupt on the tongues of English gentlemen like Walgrave. Like Hollyband's double-voiced language lessons, *Englishmen for My Money* models the contradictions that come from trading in tongues. For all its mockery of foreign accents, the play's cross-talk is above all a means of exchange and profit, enabling English gentlemen to change places with foreign suitors. But because this cross-talk requires that native speakers emulate foreigners, even as they attempt to displace them, the comedy ends up reinstituting strangeness within the English gentlemen themselves, and in the process disrupting distinctions between native and foreign.

Rather than resolving the problem of the alien presence in early modern London, *Englishmen for My Money* instead turns the problem into an opportunity for performative confrontations that rearticulate what it means to trade in tongues in the commercial city and on the commercial stage. The politics at work here takes its cues more from confusion than fusion as linguistic performances hilariously misfire, veering out of control to threaten linguistic rules and borders. The plotting uses impersonation as a means of consolidating Englishness, following a double strategy of driving out foreign merchants and at the same time incorporating the other "to enlarge itself," as Kermode puts it, as the English suitors marry Pisaro's daughters and his wealth. Yet as the comedy reminds its audience, these impersonations also register something closer to Hollyband's pedagogy, putting into play a linguistic practice of embodying the alien that sidesteps normative models of either inclusion or exclusion.

This practice of cross-talk is in some senses radical in that it enables an increasingly diverse local population to enact the unpredictable pluralities of daily urban life, as both Hollyband's language books and Haughton's play demonstrate. Recalling the situation of denizens such as Hollyband himself, trading in tongues in early modern London gives form to the dynamic processes of a citizenship founded by what Balibar describes as the "practical confrontation with different modalities of exclusion," the confrontations that come when English men and women "frame their tongues" to become linguistic outsiders.

# 4. *The Place of the Present*

## Making Time and *The Roaring Girl*

London city comedies catered to the moment and to an increasingly consumerist public—"fit for the times and the termers," Thomas Middleton quipped to readers of *The Roaring Girl* (1611), slyly retailing his own as well as the city's investments in the contemporary scene.[1] Famous for the notoriety of its title character, *The Roaring Girl* pushes these investments far beyond those of the other plays in this study. Not only do Middleton and Dekker track the close encounters of London's population across a vividly drawn cityscape, but they take the novel step of impersonating a recognizable local figure on stage, one Mary Frith of Bankside, known not for her civic virtue but for her colorful public appearances on the city's streets and stages. As a kind of local reporting, *The Roaring Girl* invites comparison with what we now think of as news. Much as printed news would later in the century, the play's preoccupation with the contemporary scene turns everyday London into a form of common currency that brings together local residents to experience and reflect on city life. But the play does more than this. By claiming contemporaneity itself as a subject, *The Roaring Girl* provokes a heightened awareness of the temporal rhythms of present-day London, as distinct from as well as connected to a remembered past and an anticipated future. Focusing on the collective experience of these rhythms, this chapter considers the stage's engagements with new forms of urban time, including that of playgoing itself.

London commerce offers an obvious starting point for thinking about urban temporal experience, and here one might extend the abiding critical interest in economics in city plays to include the workings of "merchant's time," the commercial time that is measurable, predictable, and thereby subject to manipulation and profit.[2] As Jacques Le Goff explains it, merchant's time "superimposed a new and measurable time . . . an oriented and predictable time, on that of the natural environment, which was a time both eternally renewed and perpetually unpredictable."[3] This opposition between merchant's time and the "eternally renewed" time of nature figures crucially in satiric city comedy, for just as the plays satirize bourgeois "acquisitiveness," in L. C. Knights's influential formulation, so too do they satirize the regularized commercial time that supports such practices.[4] Indeed, it is the very notion of a time that might be quantified and calculated into the future that city comedies hold up for critique. Yet this critique is not without contradiction. As has been much remarked, these plays are characteristically ambivalent, defined by contradictory attitudes toward the commercial city.[5] City plays may warn of the predatory dangers of commerce, but they simultaneously model new economic practices for the city's expanding population. Similar contradictions shape the plays' temporal registers, as Walter Cohen astutely observes of distinctions between satiric and romantic comedy: "Pastoral atemporality is transformed into its opposite, an urban sense of the brevity, the pressure, the contraction of time that is constraining, even claustrophobic, in effect."[6] The intrigue plotting works in part, then, to enact a version of the urban time the city plays critique. The effect is to register the conflicting temporalities of the commercial city together with the stage's own conflicted investments in commerce and calculation.

The commercial rhythms of early modern London figure centrally in this chapter as a framework for exploring the stage's explicit critiques of merchant's time. But I want to approach these rhythms by way of a new technology not usually associated with either city comedies or city commerce: the weekly death counts instituted by London's famous bills of mortality, considered by some to be an early form of printed news. During the first decade of the seventeenth century, plague constituted an extended crisis for metropolitan London, upending commerce, livelihoods, and lives. In 1603 alone 25,000 died from plague; another 15,000 or so would perish between 1604 and 1610.[7] One of the effects of this ongoing devastation was to make time painfully visible, in the scale of death and suffering, most obviously, but also in the city's strategic decision to publish this suffering in weekly bulletins. Beginning in 1603 and extending through the next eight years of plague, the bills appeared every Thursday, tallying the week's christenings and burials by parish, with a separate column for plague burials.[8] For those who followed the London bills, and many did, the numbers supplied an unparalleled quantitative measure, a public time regulated not by church calendars or law terms or sessions at court but by the weekly tabulation of life and death. Even commercial time became subject to the rise and fall of the bills' sequential rhythms. So too did the stage.

By most accounts, then and now, the relationship between London's mortality bills and its theater was oppositional if not openly hostile. Not only did the fearful statistics have little in common with the stage's flesh-and-blood performances, but from the theater's perspective, the bills supplied a powerful "document of control" that the Privy Council regularly used to suppress playing and other "like assemblyes" in the city and suburbs.[9] As Leeds Barroll's research persuasively documents, the weekly numbers quite literally regulated theaters during plague years, with periods of high mortality leaving stages dark and actors and playwrights penniless.[10] "I dwindle as a new player does at a plague bill certified forty," a character in *Ram Alley* (1611) laments, underscoring the inverse relationship between the death counts and theatrical production.[11] Yet for all their crucial differences, mortality bills and city comedy shared some striking commonalities. For one, they were contemporaneous, coming of age, as it were, in the first decade of the new century.[12] Both, moreover, registered the same innovative turn to the immediate present, finding their subjects and their audiences in the same metropolitan community. Both brought Londoners together in a social imaginary based not in traditions or customs but in a shared sense of the here-and-now. And both generated what could be called "temporal stories," practicing new ways of experiencing and understanding urban time in the intersections of commerce and crisis.[13] This does not mean, of course, that they told the same story, and one of the concerns of this chapter is to take their differences together with their commonalities as a way of opening up how city residents both experienced and created time within metropolitan London.

That the bills constituted a powerful temporal document in early modern London seems self-evident; their stark statistics, after all, directly report on matters of life and death, time and finitude. But because they publicized these statistics for all to read, morality bills engaged time in other, seemingly less obvious, ways that also worked to heighten temporal awareness among residents of the plague city. What is especially striking about early-seventeenth-century mortality bills, for example, was their regularity. Published serially, from week to week, the bills introduced an unprecedented periodicity into everyday London, and it is this periodicity *together* with the grim numbers, I suggest, that altered the city's temporal experiences. Weekly publication served, of course, as a powerful reminder of the plague's presence within the city. But it also held the promise that irregularities of human life and suffering might be reduced to scientific order, to patterns that could be understood and even predicted into the future. Marking life and death sequentially, along a trajectory that extended from one week to the next, the bills encouraged city residents to look forward as well as back, to acknowledge the dead and at the same time to hope for a future grounded in the possibility of controlling historical contingency, even at the moment when control seemed most elusive. The weekly bills thus served not only as documents of control, to be used by the city and crown in enforcing plague orders. They also provided the general population with a crucial opportunity to make use of this new technology for themselves, to interpret the past and present and to speculate about the future.

But if the weekly death counts heightened temporal awareness within London, how did this experience carry over into a theater that was itself engaging the contemporary city? For many playgoers, tracking the numbers may have made them more attuned not just to plague time but to the temporal effects of city plays that trafficked in the here-and-now. The effects of this conjunction are complex, however, and the aim of this chapter is to explore how the proximity of plague bills and playgoing allowed for multiple and even divergent temporal experiences within the city. One effect of the bills' weekly appearance, for example, may have been to complicate responses to the stage's critiques of merchant's time, inviting audiences to question, even as they longed for, the possibility of an "eternally renewed" natural time. But the more radical intervention of mortality bills within the theater may have been to complicate the temporal experience of performance itself, especially when the performance turned on the stage's contemporaneous redoubling of the city scene. Colluding with city comedy's pervasive metatheatricality, this redoubling provokes temporal encounters between the stage and local audiences. And it is within these complex encounters of performing the city for the city, I suggest, that city comedies begin to enact alternatives to the double bind of their own narrative investments as well as to the rationalized time of city commerce and plague control.

This chapter pursues these encounters largely within the context of one play, Middleton and Dekker's *The Roaring Girl*, which I take to be a kind of limit case for city comedy's temporal experiments. The play was first staged by Prince Henry's Men at the Fortune theater just outside Cripplegate on Golding Lane, probably in late April or early May 1611, a year that would finally bring respite from plague, although the city could not yet have known this.[14] Basing their unusual heroine on a real-life personage—a reputed pickpocket, transvestite performer, and later a broker of second-hand and stolen goods—the playwrights were, as Katharine Maus comments, "trying something new."[15] And it is this novelty together with the notoriety of Mary Frith herself that has driven much of the recent critical work on the play, and its gender politics especially. It is this same combination of novelty and notoriety that provokes the play's striking temporal engagements, both within the dramatic narrative and in the metatheatrics of live performance that the play delights in. In what follows, I'm interested in how the play traverses a plurality of times, as if to evade or resist the sequential unfolding of city commerce and perhaps even of death itself. In this, the comic stage could be said to fracture commerce's temporal modalities so as to open the present to the possibilities of change, to a future that is new and not exactly predictable. Not simply about the times, innovative and popular city comedies like *The Roaring Girl* could be said to be about time itself. To borrow from Paul Ricoeur's formulation, it is "the very experience of time that is at stake in [their] structural transformations."[16] The concern of this chapter is with tracing this experience. But before turning to the stage's timely and untimely engagements, I begin with the deathly measures of the mortality bills themselves.

## *Cemeteries Within Cities*

Frip, the broker-gallant in Middleton's *Your Five Gallants* (1608), "love[s] to smell safely" (1.1.55).[17] Clothing was suspected of carrying disease, and fearing infection from the pawned garments of plague victims, Frip subjects his clients to strict interrogation:

FRIP My friend, of what parish is your pawn?
FIRST FELLOW Parish? Why, St Clement's, sir. . . .
FRIP What parish is your pawn, my friend? [*Reading from the bill*]
St Bride's: five; St Dunstan's: none; St Clement's: three.
Three at Clements! Away with your pawn, sir; your parish
is infected. I will neither purchase the plague for six pence
in the pound and a groat bill-money, nor venture my small
stock into contagious parishes. You have your answer;
fare-you-well, as fast as you can, sir.

(1.1.39–50)

While the play text doesn't identify the paper Frip reads from, the Blackfriar's audiences would have recognized it at once (see Figure 4). By 1608 mortality bills had become a fixture within greater London. They had kept pace with shifts in infection and, as Frip's recitation documents, now included adjoining and outlying parishes, delineating a city that was increasingly metropolitan and increasingly segregated.[18] Local residents, along with foreign correspondents, domestic newsletter writers, city officials, even the king himself, all followed the weekly fluctuations, depending on the tallies to calculate the fine line between safety and profit. As John Graunt, the century's most famous observer of mortality statistics, later put it, Londoners looked to the bills to see "how the *Sickness* increased, or decreased, that so the *Rich* might judge of the necessity of their removal, and *Trades-men* might conjecture what doings they were like to have in their respective dealings."[19]

More than a simple chronography of death, the mortality bills imposed a rhythm on the city, marking time and livelihoods against the weekly rate of disease. Dekker's haunting account of the 1625 outbreak in *London Looke Backe* describes local residents as painfully aware of the numbers, collectively counting out the days and weeks with dreadful anticipation and increasing horror:

> Tis strange to obserue, that if a Bell be heard to Ring out, and that tis voyc'd, in such a Parish within the walls of LONDON, a man is dead of the *Plague*, O what talke it breedes! If the next Weeke it mounts to two, then the Report stickes cold to the heart of the whole *Citty*. But if (as now) it rises to 41. Trading hangs the Head, and thousands fearefully suspect, they shall bee vndone.[20]

Dekker's arithmetic captures both the scale of the catastrophe and its dehumanizing economics. In its succession of temporal markers—moving from a hypothetical present and future ( if "a man is dead," "if the next Weeke") into an immediate present ("as now") and future of fearful "undoing"—the passage also suggests the kind of "reckoning with time" Ricoeur describes as a "preoccupation" that may prompt, but is not reducible to, abstract measurement.[21] As Ricoeur sees it, temporality is inherently narrative, a plot that mediates our experience of events or incidents by drawing "a configuration out of a simple succession."[22] And it is in this sense that Dekker's passage bears witness to a new urban temporality configured by the unrelenting succession of plague deaths. But what does it mean that this time-keeping takes the form of numerical tabulation akin

ECOPIE OF ALL THE BVRIALS AND C

..ll within the City of LONDON as the Liberties thereof, as in other Pa[illegible] the City, and out of the Freedome, according to the report made to the Kings most ex[illegible] Company of Parish Clearkes of the said Citie, From the 13. of October, 1603. to [illegible] same. Whereunto is added the true Relation of the whole number of all that [illegible] of this Visitation, from the 17. of December, 1602. to the 20. of this present moneth of O[illegible] 1603. with the whole number of all that haue dyed in Westminster, in the Sauoy, in Stepney, Newington, and sundry other places, since the sicknesse began there.

| | | Buried in all | Of the Plague | | Buried in all | Of the Plague |
|---|---|---|---|---|---|---|
| London within the Walles. | Albones in Woodstreet | 3 | 2 | Margrets Pattons | 2 | 0 |
| | Alhallowes Lumberstreet | 3 | 3 | Margrets Moyses | 1 | 1 |
| | Alhallowes the great | 12 | 11 | Margrets Lothbery | 2 | 2 |
| | Alhallowes the lesse | 5 | 3 | Martins in the Vintry | 8 | 7 |
| | Alhallowes Bredstreet | 0 | 0 | Martins Orgars | 2 | 2 |
| | Alhallowes staynings | 7 | 7 | Martins Iremonger lane | 4 | 3 |
| | Alhallowes the Wall | 4 | 4 | Martins at Ludgate | 5 | 4 |
| | Alhallowes Hony-lane | 0 | 0 | Martins Outwich | 0 | 0 |
| | Alhallowes Barking | 12 | 9 | Mary le Bow | 2 | 2 |
| | Alphage at Cripplegate | 1 | 1 | Mary Bothawe | 0 | 0 |
| | Androwes by the Wardrope | 3 | 3 | Mary at the hill | 2 | 2 |
| | Androwes Eastcheape | 7 | 6 | Mary Abchurch | 6 | 6 |
| | Androwes vndershaft | 4 | 4 | Mary Woolchurch | 3 | 3 |
| | Annes at Aldersgate | 4 | 4 | Mary Colchurch | 2 | 2 |
| | Annes Blacke Fryers | 6 | 6 | Mary Woolnoth | 6 | 6 |
| | Auntlins Parish | 0 | 0 | Mary Aldermary | 4 | 4 |
| | Austines Parish | 0 | 0 | Mary Aldermanberry | 2 | 2 |
| | Barthelmew at the Exch. | 4 | 4 | Mary Staynings | 1 | 1 |
| | Bennets at Pauls-Wharf | 7 | 3 | Mary Mountawe | 1 | 1 |
| | Bennets Grace-Church | 2 | 2 | Mary Sommersets | 4 | 3 |
| | Bennets Finck | 2 | 2 | Mathew Friday-street | 1 | 1 |
| | Bennets Sherhogg | 1 | 1 | Maudlins Milke street | 3 | 3 |
| | Buttols Billingsgate | 3 | 3 | Maudlins by Olafishstreet | 1 | 1 |
| | Christ Church Parish | 11 | 9 | Mighels Bassieshawe | 1 | 1 |
| | Christophers Parish | 0 | 0 | Mighels Corne hill | 3 | 3 |
| | Clements by Eastcheape | 1 | 1 | Mighels in Woodstreet | 5 | 2 |
| | Dennis Backe-Church | 3 | 3 | Mighels in the Ryall | 6 | 5 |
| | Dunstones in the East | 6 | 4 | Mighels in the Querne | 0 | 0 |
| | Edmunds in Lumbard-st. | 9 | 8 | Mighels Queene-hithe | 6 | 4 |
| | Ethelborow within Bishopsg. | 0 | 0 | Mighels Crookedlane | 6 | 6 |
| | S. Faithes | 2 | 2 | Mildreds Poultry | 7 | 6 |
| | S. Fosters in Foster-lane | 3 | 3 | Mildreds Bredstreet | 2 | 1 |
| | Gabriel Fan-Church | 5 | 5 | Nicholas Acons | 0 | 0 |
| | George Botolph lane | 1 | 1 | Nicholas Cole-abbay | 5 | 4 |
| | Gregories by Paules | 12 | 10 | Nicholas Olanes | 5 | 4 |
| | Hellens within Bishopsg. | 1 | 1 | Olaues in the Iury | 3 | 3 |
| | Iames by Garlike-hithe | 4 | 4 | Olaues in Hartstreet | 6 | 3 |
| | Iohn Euangelist | 0 | 0 | Olaues in Siluer street | 3 | 1 |
| | Iohn Zacharie | 0 | 0 | Pancras by Soperlane | 1 | 1 |
| | Iohns in the Walbrooke | 6 | 5 | Peters in Cornehill | 2 | 0 |
| | Katherines Cree-Church | 15 | 11 | Peters in Cheape | 1 | 1 |
| | Katherine Colemans | 5 | 5 | Peters the poore in broadst. | 0 | 0 |
| | Lawrence in the Iury | 10 | 9 | Peters at Pauls wharf | 0 | 0 |
| | Lawrence Pountney | 6 | 4 | Stephens in Colemanstreet | 14 | 10 |
| | Leonards Foster-lane | 1 | 0 | Stephens in the Walbrook | 0 | 0 |
| | Leonards Eastchape | 0 | 0 | Swithins at London-stone | 3 | 1 |
| | Magnus parish by the Bridge | 3 | 2 | Thomas Apostles | 2 | 1 |
| | Margrets New fishstreete | 6 | 5 | Trinity parish | 8 | 8 |

The number buried within the Walles of London is 351. Whereof of the Plague 191

| | | Buried in all | Of the Plague | | Buried in all | Of the Plague |
|---|---|---|---|---|---|---|
| London without the Wals, and within the Liberties | Androwes in Holborne | 39 | 36 | Dunstones in the West | 13 | 9 |
| | Barthelmew the lesse Smith. | 8 | 6 | Georges in Southwarke | 10 | 7 |
| | Barthelmew the great Smith. | 2 | 2 | Giles without Cripplegate | 37 | 22 |
| | Brides parish | 23 | 17 | Olaues in Southwarke | 21 | 17 |
| | Buttols Algate | 23 | 20 | Sauiours in Southwarke | 39 | 36 |
| | [illegible] | [illegible] | [illegible] | [illegible] | [illegible] | [illegible] |
| | Buttols Bishopsg. | 7 | 4 | Thomas in Southwarke | 4 | [illegible] |
| | Buttols without Aldersg. | 21 | 19 | Trinity in the Minories | 3 | 2 |

The number buried without the wals, and within the liberties is 296. Whereof of the Plague, 255.

| | Buried in all | Of the Plague | | Buried in all | Of the Plague |
|---|---|---|---|---|---|
| Clemēts without Templeb. | 25 | 19 | Martins in the Fields | 20 | 17 |
| Giles in the fields | 21 | 19 | Mary Whitechappell | 20 | 17 |
| Iames at Clarkenwell | 9 | 7 | Magdalens in Barmondsey-streete | 5 | 4 |
| Katherines by the Tower | 4 | 3 | At the Pest-house | 1 | 1 |
| Leonards in Shordich | 14 | 9 | | | |

Buried without 119 Whereof, Of the Plague 96

Christnings—67—Parishes cleere of the Plague—19—Parishes infected—93

Buried in all, within the places aforesaid — 766

Whereof, of the Plague — 642

From the first great plague in our memory, after the losse of Newhauen, from the first of January, 1562. to December, 1563. there died of the plague twenty thousand, one hundred thirtie sixe.

And in the last visitation, from the 29. of December, 1592. to the 23. of the same moneth in the yeare 1593. died in all, 25886, of the Plague in and about London, 15003. And in the yeare before 2000.

And now in this present visitation which it pleaseth God to strike vs with, there hath died from the 17. of December 1602. to the 14. of July, 1603. the whole number in London and the Liberties, 4314. whereof, of the plague, 3120. The rest are set downe as they haue followed weekly.

From the 13. of October to the 20. of the same — 647, whereof, of the plague — 546. In the out parishes — 119, whereof, of the plague — 96.

Buried in all this weeke, 766 whereof of the plague 642

Buried in all within London and the Liberties and Suburbes, since the sicknesse began. 35267. Whereof, of the plague. 29402.

The time when it began in the City of Westminster, *and these places following.*

Buried in Westminster, from the 14 of Iuly to the 20. of October, in the whole number, 832. whereof of the plague, 723.

Buried in the Sauoy, from the first of Iune to the 20. of October, in the whole number, 18[illegible] whereof, of the plague, 171.

Buried in the parish of Stepney, from the 25. of March, to the 20. of October, in all 19[illegible] whereof, of the plague 1874.

Buried at Newington-butts from the 14. of Iune to the 20. of October, in all 636 whereof, of the plague 562.

Buried in Islington, 201. whereof, of the plague, 170

Buried in Lambeth 372. whereof, of the plague, 362.

Buried in Hackney, 192. whereof, of the plague, 169.

Buried in all, within the 7. seuerall places last aforenamed. 4378 Whereof, of the Plague. 3997.

The whole number that hath beene buried in all, both within London, and the Liberties, and the 7. other seuerall places last before mentioned is, 39380. whereof, of the number of the plague. 31609.

Printed by Iohn Windet, Printer to the Honourable City of London.

Figure 4. London Bill of Mortality, October 20, 1603 (Guildhall Library, City of London).

to the columns of merchants' account books, or that it appears weekly, with mechanized regularity?

As Paul Slack's extensive work on Tudor and Stuart plague affirms, London's systematic numbering of its dead stands as an early experiment in public data collection. And in this, one could argue, the bills register both the desire for order in the face of disaster and the need for an instrument of intervention and control. Because of the bills, both city officials and ordinary citizens were increasingly able to anticipate upturns in mortality and take precautions.[23] But it is also the case that plague control became a form of social control, particularly as the disease took hold in the over-crowded and impoverished suburbs. Produced by an elaborate apparatus that extended downward from the state to the parish, from the king and council to the elderly women consigned to search the bodies of the diseased and dead for plague "tokens," the London bills constituted an unparalleled tracking of an urban populace in its state of emergency.[24] Reducing names to numbers, the innovative technology anticipates the shift from "people" to "populations" that Michel Foucault identifies with the eighteenth century.[25] The mortality bills went a step further, however, in tracking the population over time, thereby producing a temporal equivalent of the aerial city maps printed in *Civitates orbis terrarum*, the bird's eye view or, in Michel de Certeau's more sinister phrasing, the scopic eye of the "voyeur-god" looking down on the "geometrical" space below.[26] This long view of a population over time is precisely what prompted John Graunt later in the century to mine the bills as a database for the city's first demographic study, the aptly titled *Natural and Political Observations* (1662). Graunt was especially drawn to the bills' potential for state or "statistical" thinking, and his advocacy of government record keeping is thought to have influenced Louis XIV's administration to institute plague bills in Paris in 1667.[27] But if the London bills enabled the "central registry of pathology" Foucault sees as underwriting the punitive quarantines of late-seventeenth-century France, their widespread circulation in London earlier in the century argues against categorizing them simply as forerunners of political arithmetic.[28]

For the London bills were innovative not only because they recorded empirical data in the service of the state, but because they made this information widely available to the general public. One recent estimate puts the print run of bills during the 1603 outbreak at five or six thousand copies a week, a staggering figure.[29] Graunt, for one, is surprised by the practice. "There seems to be good reason," he writes, "why the *Magistrate* should himself take notice of the numbers," but not "why the same should be made known to the People, otherwise than to please them, as with a curiosity." Compelled to speculate on the reason for public disclosure, Graunt imagines it was so "[t]hat the state of health in the City may at all times appear."[30] The politics of transparency are debatable, and one may safely argue that the weekly reports encouraged the populace to accept or at least "to bear quietly" restrictions placed on them from above.[31] Yet the government plague orders make no stipulation for public circulation; if anything, state officials seemed more interested in withholding information than exploiting its release.[32] The evidence suggests, rather, that the city's commercial interests, as much as the need for plague control, were the driving force behind the bills' publication.[33] The weekly numbers had a direct impact on the city economy. As John Donne uncharitably put it, "the number of the Plaguy Bill" was a "discourse fit" for common citizenry, guaranteed to appeal to London's tradesmen and merchants.[34] City officials and trading companies stayed on top of the figures, using the data to counter rumors and fearmongering and to plan for the future, although as the decade wore on and the plague lingered, they began to feel less confident about the salutary effects of public disclosure, fearing that the bills were damaging trade "'to the public hurt.'"[35]

In instrumentalizing life and death and even time itself, the mortality bills were unavoidably at odds with the spiritual directives of clergy who called on Londoners to "looke backe" on their sins and repent in preparation for a messianic future. Not only did the weekly accounting reinforce the much-lamented shift from "church's time" to "merchant's time," to use Le Goff's formulation, from a time that belongs "to God alone" and therefore "cannot be an object of lucre" to a time that is secular (temporal), measurable, predictable, and is itself a profitable commodity within a credit economy. But the bills reiterated this temporal shift in ways that seemed to exacerbate social inequities within the plague city.[36] It is precisely this supplanting of the spiritual by the commercial that Dekker decries in *A Rod for Run-awayes*, a pamphlet chastising wealthy residents who had fled the plague-stricken city, leaving the poor without provision. Dekker's critique moves between moral and quantitative reckonings, weighing the virtues of proper spiritual accounting, or divine reckoning, against the hard numbers of merchants' account books and plague bills. "But we that are Christians, and deale in the merchandise of our soules," he avers, "haue other bookes of account to turne ouer, then to reckon that we dye in great numbers." For Dekker, the bills not only enable a sinful traffic in the dead, they also register the city's eagerness to accommodate human loss to the exigencies of commercial time at the expense of the true and everlasting "merchandize of our soules." "[L]et no man goe about to abate the number: His Arithmetick brookes no crossing," Dekker warns, offering solace in the familiar but increasingly controversial explanation of divine providence as both cause and remedy for the visitations.[37]

Following Graunt's pioneering analysis in the 1660s, most work on the London bills—including Foucault's powerful critique of the plague's "disciplinary measures"—has concentrated on their science, an approach that privileges their statistical use in controlling death and disease within the regularized time of government and commerce.[38] Less remarked, but no less crucial, however, are the bills' unintended uses and unanticipated consequences. By anatomizing the epidemic's social and moral injustices, early-seventeenth-century pamphleteers such as Dekker suggest something of the imaginative effects of these numbers on the urban population. Recent work on the bills speculates that by listing plague deaths by parish, the weekly broadsides reshaped the population's mental maps of the city. As J. C. Robertson suggests, for example, as the scope of the bills extended to outlying parishes, the data prompted city residents to see their surroundings "in metropolitan rather than municipal terms."[39] But insofar as the bills' parish designations provoked a topographic imaginary, and a rethinking of city space, their weekly publication no doubt also provoked a temporal imaginary, one that if it didn't exactly synchronize its readers into a virtual community along an axis of "homogeneous, empty time"—as Benedict Anderson famously describes the "mass ceremonies" of modern newsreading—nonetheless began to move in that direction, counting out a regularized rhythm for collective understandings of the city in time.[40] And this rhythm, together with the pressing immediacy of the bills' fearful content, provoked a new awareness of temporal sequence and the modalities of past, present, and future.

By the end of the seventeenth century, historian Daniel Woolf asserts, printed news had "generated an extended present of duration, not instant. Or, to put it another way, it had carved out a 'detemporalized zone' between past and future, a zone that offered a space for the discussion of current events analogous to Habermas' emergent public sphere."[41] At the century's beginning, I would argue, the weekly publication of London's death bulletins similarly extended the present, instituting a periodicity based not on the natural (if pathological) cycles of the disease itself but on the artificial time of administrative procedure. At a time when translations of foreign news were subject to regulation and censorship, and local news largely limited to the occasional publications on crimes and other sensations, the weekly bills were unique in supplying a continuous report on urban life.[42] Indeed, their exact periodicity was something of a phenomenon in the early 1600s, unmatched even by London's first newsbooks, the foreign *corantos* on the Thirty Years War translated and published by Nicholas Bourne and Nathaniel Butter in the 1620s.[43] For all who charted the plague's progress from week to week—in contrast to demographers like Graunt who concentrated on the broader trends of annual death rates—the cumulative effects of periodicity no doubt heightened the experience of a protracted and urgent present. During periods of high mortality, for example, inveterate newsletter writer John Chamberlain regularly reported the weekly fluctuations in his missives to Dudley Carleton. "Our weekly bill litle abated, not past eleven in all, the whole number beeing 247, of the sicknes 124," he writes from London on October 21, 1608; the following week, "our bill was this weeke 240 in all, of the sicknes 102"; and three weeks later on November 11, "Our bill is abated (thanckes be to God) this weeke 47 in the whole number."[44] Whether this extended present was perceived as "detemporalized" or as *hyper*temporalized, as seems more likely, it nonetheless marked out a new space—a duration, as it were—for experiencing the contemporary city.

Just as the bills' periodicity contributed to an "extended present of duration," however, it may also have heightened a sense of division and distance between the immediate present and the recent present, now receding into the past.[45] For despite the unprecedented speed of dissemination, the numbers were already old news by the time they were printed. As one of the rascals in Jonson's *The Staple of News* quips, in a swipe at the fledgling news syndicate of Bourne and Butter: "when news is printed, / It leaves, sir, to be news" (1.5.48–49).[46] So even as the mortality bills prompted awareness of the lived present as a "current event," they simultaneously encouraged an awareness of time's passage from week to week, along the trajectories of expectation and memory. And to the extent that readers perceived the latest numbers as representing a time already past, the bulletins inflected the urban temporal experience with what we might call historical consciousness, encouraging city residents to look on the previous week and even on the immediate present from a distance, apart from as well as a part of the present moment. In this, the bills enacted a version of what de Certeau describes as a paradox of historiography. Like a burial rite or tomb, he writes, history both "honors and eliminates" the dead and so "liberates the present" for the living. Operating to "exorcise[s] and confess[es] a presence of death amidst the living," history's narratives thus serve as the "equivalent of cemeteries within cities"—a comparison that seems especially apt in excavating the temporal work of the London mortality bills.[47]

To read the mortality bills each week, then, was simultaneously to identify with and separate from the dead, a temporal practice that during periods of high mortality found a grim spatial analogue in London's burial practices. As Vanessa Harding's research persuasively documents, the dead and the living were "separate but interacting categories, needing to occupy the same urban space and to resolve or at least accommodate their different sets of interests and priorities."[48] Giving grotesque materiality to this claim is the city's much-decried practice of digging mass graves, or "plague-pits," in which piles of corpses were "pestred together, in one litle hole, where they lie and rot," as many as "threescore (contrary to an Act of common Councell against In-mates)," Dekker laments in *Newes from Graues-end*.[49] Expeditiously counting and covering over the dead so as to make a place for the living, the mass burials underscore the dehumanizing work of the mortality bills. For like the actual cemeteries of plague cities, the bills arranged the dead alongside the living, including numbers of births alongside deaths. One of the effects of this dreadful economy is to generate a commonality *among the living*, a commonality predicated on a temporal as well as spatial differentiation between the recent deaths, now past, and one's place in the immediate present—although as moralists like Dekker might warn, it is a differentiation predicated as well on proximity and profit and therefore not without moral cost.

The London mortality bills thus begin to put into play a doubly defined temporality that would later be associated with modern notions of history and news, retrospectively recording the events of the recent past and, at the same time, prospectively delineating a narrative that opens up the present and extends into the future. But what sort of future did these spare tables of death anticipate? As Woolf observes of news more generally, the orientation toward the future "does much more than recount events that are part of a longer story, still in play; it solicits possible resolutions to that story."[50] For the bills' less fortunate readers, the story resolved itself shortly in death; for others, resolution took the form of prayer or, for those with means, flight to the country. But as plague literature liked to emphasize, mortality bills also encouraged commercial speculation and risk-taking, and many seem to have played the weekly numbers, hoping to game the system—brokers like Frip, perhaps, trading daily in death's garments, or others, like the subtle rogues of *The Alchemist*, banking on the master's absence as long as "there died one a week, within the liberties" (4.7.116).[51] While it is difficult to know if there was truth to these tales or if they were simply urban myths circulated to discourage the wealthy from abandoning the city, the evidence suggests that for many readers, and for those in trade and retailing especially, the bills' quantitative form fostered expectations of a future that might be calculated, regulated, and even predicted. Indeed, as if to encourage probabilistic thinking, the bills often included previous mortality rates alongside current figures, so that it was possible for discerning readers to note patterns and make predictions about risk. Cumulative data comprise a full column in an extant October 1603 bill, for example, and include annual totals from earlier plague years along with the six-month total from December 1602 to July 1603 and weekly figures from August and September 1603 (see Figure 4).[52] But even without this comparative data, the bills' weekly circulation invited readers, such as John Chamberlain, to track the fluctuations for themselves, to assess the past and present in order to predict and profit from the future.

## *A Perfect Close*

How then does this new urban temporality intersect with London comedies? And how might playgoers habituated to the periodicity of the weekly bills have experienced the stage's fascination with contemporary London, with plays that were themselves so "near and familiarly allied to the time" (3.1.521), as Mitis archly puts it in Jonson's first London comedy?[53] The insistent moralizing of Dekker's plague pamphlets suggests one possibility—that the relentless reporting of plague deaths may have prompted local audiences to see connections between the injustices associated with plague control and the commercial profiteering satirized by city comedy. Yet an equally likely possibility is that the regularized publication of mortality figures also sharpened the audience's apprehension of time, both as the subject of dramatic critique and as mode of theatrical experience elicited by the stage's performance of urban contemporaneity. In what follows, I turn to *The Roaring Girl* as a way of thinking about both categories of temporal experience. I begin by exploring the play's strikingly contradictory attitudes toward commercial time, reinforced by tensions between its explicit moral critiques and what Lawrence Manley aptly characterizes as the "ruthlessly positional logic" of satiric intrigue.[54] Then, in the section that follows, I consider the temporality of performance itself within the dislocating metatheatrics of the play's redoubling of the city scene, a metatheatrics that, I want to argue, points a way out of the limits of both comic convention and the regularized time of city commerce and mortality counts.

Like other city comedies, *The Roaring Girl* finds its subject in the hustle of contemporary London and, like others, its intrigue turns less on romantic desire than on the wheels of commerce. With the notable exception of its transvestite heroine, the plotting is standard citizen fare—generational conflict, thwarted love, grasping merchants, alluring city wives, predatory gallants—what T. S. Eliot dismissed as "cheap conventional intrigue."[55] The play begins with the time-worn formulas of New Comedy, as young Sebastian schemes to outwit his acquisitive father, Sir Alexander Wengrave, in order to secure both his inheritance and his bride of choice, the respectably modest Mary Fitzallard. The well-worn rhythms of generational conflict soon collide, however, with the market economy and a local cast of outspoken she-citizens and their uxorious husbands. As editors and critics often remark, there is no question of the place commerce holds in *The Roaring Girl*, for the playwrights take the novel step of making the stage over as an upscale market, in the style of London's fashionable exchanges. Stage directions are unusually explicit, calling for "*three shops open in a rank: the first a pothecary's shop, the next a feather shop, the third a sempster's shop*" (2.1.0 s.d.), an elaborate structure for the characteristically bare stage, and it is likely that the shop stalls remained in place throughout the performance, a powerful visual commentary on the urban nexus of social and commercial interests.[56]

Brimming with fashionable luxuries, the stage offers up a sumptuous bazaar of commodities—costly furniture, cushions, velvet ruffs, fine lawns and cambrics, imported tobacco, spangled feathers, gold chains, a diamond band, a viol—an alluring display that, as Jonathan Gil Harris suggests, interpellates consumer desire not only on stage but among the Fortune's own audiences.[57] *The Roaring Girl* goes a step further, however, to link this desire to the immediately recognizable, and often audible, measures of merchant's time. The play keeps its time mechanically, not by pastoral sundials or rustic church bells but by the rhythms of commerce—by the exchange bell (2.1.392) announcing the closing of business for the midday meal, by the clock at Savoy (3.1.29) sounding the time of Laxton's assignation with Moll in Gray's Inn Fields, and by Sir Alexander's much-prized German watch. It is this regularized urban clock-time that orders the activities of gallants and citizens alike, their buying and selling, their leisure, and their deceptions. Even Moll, who would seem to be above consumerist desires and the time pressures of commercial exchange, first enters the stage in a hurry, "to buy a shag ruff" (2.1.202) before the shops close at midday.

*The Roaring Girl* displays an unusual openness to the market's rhythms, depicting a collection of prosperous citizens and citizen-wives with a generosity often attributed to Dekker's hand in the play. Yet true to satiric comedy, the play also presents an assortment of urban predators who seek to profit from a time that can be manipulated and traded on for future gain.[58] It is no surprise, then, that *The Roaring Girl* adopts the genre's standard critique of urban commerce, setting competition against community and exploitation against social harmony. Nor should it be a surprise that the play also offers an equally predictable critique of urban timekeeping, setting the mechanized, sequential measures of the marketplace against the cyclical rhythms of a more pastoral temporality. Emblematic of the new urban time is the play's leading patriarch. Said to turn mercantile commercialism into "a habit of thought," the self-made Sir Alexander seeks to control and even possess time, as if to arrest its movement and his own mortality (his name is listed as "Went-graue" in the *dramatis personae*).[59] Materialized by his imported German watch, time becomes for Sir Alexander a precious object, an accoutrement of position and power. And when he plots against Moll, he uses the fashionable timepiece as a glittering lure to draw "her thief-whorish eye"(4.1.17) to the gallows. Moll is drawn to the watch—"A watch: what's o'clock here?" (128)—but what attracts her is its potential use-value, not its exchange-value. Seeing that the timepiece lacks accuracy, Moll rejects it at once, joking that a watch and a musician, which she is, "must both keep time well or there's no goodness in 'em" (131–32). The watch's failure to keep good time is playfully proleptic, an explanation of Sir Alexander's failure to keep up with his son's counter-plotting and a critique of merchant's time itself, especially its death-defying attempts to control future as well as current markets.

There is, as some have argued, a certain radicalism in *The Roaring Girl*'s critique of commercial capitalism, witnessed, for example, in Moll's modern-sounding colloquy on the plight of "distressed needlewomen and tradefallen wives," now a centerpiece of feminist criticism on the play.[60] But there's also a conservatism, particularly as the moralizing turns retrospective, invoking the pre-capitalist world of "traditional economic morality" that critics have long associated with satiric London comedies.[61] The play imagines a future, to be sure, but it is a future born largely of a longing for a world-that-was-lost. Rather than cordoning off the past to make room for the present and future, following the logic of mortality bills, this longing works to elide temporal modalities, invoking a recursive and supposedly natural time that both precedes and supersedes the commercial, urban present. Moll herself has been said to foster this nostalgia. As Katharine Maus writes in the *Norton* introduction to the play, the unusual heroine resuscitates "values that predate the rise of the metropolitan marketplace" and which the play affirms by representing "the energies of comic renovation as issuing from a place outside the city."[62]

Yet even as the play celebrates Moll's romantic adventurism and imagines its own version of the pastoral—in rogues "niggling" in fields and in the "brave sport" of duck hunting citizens heading out with guns and spaniels to Parlous Pond—it doesn't exactly resolve tensions between urban time and pastoral nostalgia. The opposing trajectories do sometimes converge in suggestive ways—in the collusion of Sebastian, Moll, and company to outwit Sir Alexander, for example, and perhaps in the protracted canting scene—but more often they exist in provocative tension. Indeed, what the play finally delivers is less the anticipated resolution of opposing temporalities—the triumph of a cyclical, pastoral time, say, over a calculated, future-directed merchant's time—than a pointed recognition of their complicity within the regulating sphere of the commercial city. The play thus begins to suggest a more unstable and dislocating critique than its moral judgments might seem to allow.

These temporal instabilities are provocatively on display in *The Roaring Girl*'s conclusion. Here, the sequential unfolding of intrigue and commerce appears to give way, with generic predictability, to a timeless universal of marriage and reconciliation, what Northrop Frye labels the "argument" of comedy and what the play's bland bride deems "a perfect close" (5.2.197).[63] Sir Alexander's possessive individualism magically dissolves into generosity and forgiveness as the old man suddenly finds solace in nature's cyclical returns, in the promise of "fertile lands," "a fair fruitful bride" (204), and an "eternity of boundless comforts" (176). Within this fantasy, the jostling marketplace reverts to rural community, unified not by the sequential trajectory of profits but by the perpetuity of future generations. Even the city wives, so central to the play's circulation of erotic and monetary desire, reappear here, regenerated as "kind gentlewomen, whose sparkling presence / Are glories set in marriage, beams of society"

(259–60). With Sir Alexander's closing request that this happiness be celebrated yearly in the community's collective memory, the notes of harmony extend to the audience as well:

> The happiness of this day shall be remembered
> At the return of every smiling spring;
> In my time now 'tis born, and may no sadness
> Sit on the brows of men upon that day,
> But as I am, so all go pleased away! (262–66)

Sir Alexander's imperative urges the audience to understand even the immediately present scene of reconciliation retrospectively, as an originary moment "born" in "my time now" and then projected into the future—as an event that "*shall be* remembered"—the basis for a reconstituted community unified by the nostalgic affirmation of newly discovered moral truths set against the fluctuating values of a future-directed market economy.

Yet even as Sir Alexander invokes a seemingly eternal world of pastoral returns, the play's intrigue plotting continues to resist, if not discredit, any endorsement of utopian harmony. No longer simply oppositional, pastoral romance and market-driven intrigue seem rather like two sides of the same coin, mutually supportive and complicit in the business of urban commerce. It is not magic or providential destiny, after all, or the supposedly natural course of true love that delivers this closing fantasy. Instead, the final promise of temporal escape hinges on the play's relentlessly sequential action of plots and counterplots, wagers, false reports, and manipulative deferrals. The intrigues even begin to push against the limits of English comic convention itself, deceiving the audience along with Sir Alexander by refusing to let them in on the ruse of Moll's comely bride-disguise.[64] The play's working out of comic transcendence thus delights in a version of the same deceptions and deferred resolutions perpetrated by Laxton's escalating blackmail earlier in the play. And just as the confession of the "lame gelding" (4.2.47) at the end of Act 4 seems unsatisfying, Sir Alexander's hearty embrace of rural utopia at the play's end seems equally unsatisfying, just one more trick in the unfolding of merchant's time, only here under the convenient cover of a time-honored pastoral retreat. Further undermining these closing harmonies is the play's mock staging of reconciliation only moments earlier, when Sir Alexander first tries on the language of harmony, pardoning all and welcoming "to my love and care for ever" (5.2.138) Sebastian and his masked bride (Moll disguised as Mary).

But once the substitute bride is unmasked, Sir Alexander immediately breaks his word by spitefully refusing to release Sir Guy Fitzallard from his costly pledge. "I'll work upon advantage as all mischiefs / Do upon me" (165–6), he vows, taking solace in the comforts of vengeful cruelty, which here take on a decidedly urban cast in the anti-communal pursuit of monetary advantage.

What I'm suggesting, then, is that rather than offering a retrospective position for satiric critique, this "perfect close" may itself be the object of critique, exposed as a regressive fantasy that sanctions and supports future-oriented economies of urban acquisition. There is, of course, a case to be made for the pastoral, not as a nostalgic ideal but as an actual place, flourishing in fields and pastures beyond London and its suburbs; by 1609, Middleton was himself residing in the rural village of Newington, famous for its gardens and peach orchards.[65] But geographic fact doesn't preclude Sir Alexander's opportunistic mythologizing. In the neofeudal mode of both popular romance and London civic pageantry, the patriarch's closing vision gestures toward resolving all conflict in a utopian fantasy of one-and-the-same, in effect denying or disavowing the actual contradictions, inequalities, and discontinuities that trouble urban society.[66] His strategy of suppressing social difference, moreover, involves a suppression of temporal difference in that it recovers an idealized and supposedly transcendent past for the present and future. Thus, rather than offering an alternative to the future-directed market, nostalgic retrospection is instead instrumental in its manipulation.

But does the play show a way out of the double bind of market-driven speculation and nostalgic retrospection, of calculating opportunism operating under the cover of a utopian pastoral? The answer, I suggest, may lie more with the dislocating effects of the play's contemporaneous performance than with its imperfect close, more with metatheatrical tricks and turns than with predictable moral judgments. Yet within the frame of the play itself, the cross-dressed, gender-bending, ever-protean Moll Cutpurse points a direction. Much has been said about Moll's liminality; indeed, her propensity for traversing and transgressing the boundaries of sex, gender, and class accounts for much of the play's popularity in recent years.[67] Similarly fluid and contradictory, I would argue, is her relation to urban time. Moll may invoke pre-capitalist values but, like the playwrights, she actively participates in city commerce. She bargains, makes wagers, takes profits, and shows herself proficient to drink with any Tearcat in his own language. Unlike the others, however, she seems to understand the limits of both merchant's time *and* its nostalgic underside. She sees the allure of Sir Alexander's watch and "brave booty" for what it is; likewise, she refuses the false promise of his closing invocation of cyclical generation, choosing instead to defer marriage for herself to a more progressive if not imaginary future of equity and justice—"This sounds like doomsday" (5.2.224), Lord Noland dryly comments. That Moll remains outside the "perfect close" celebrated at the play's end has been variously read as a sign of the limits as well as the freedoms offered by the play's arguably proto-feminist politics.[68] Still, the play's insistence on maintaining her position as outsider remains crucial, not only to its refusal to resolve questions of gender identity, as is commonly argued, but also to its refusal to resolve the temporal oppositions between future-directed commerce and retrospective fantasy.

Reiterating Moll's outsider status at the play's close, of course, is the sense that she will soon take up her other life as the real-life Mary Frith. That Moll seems to enjoy "a full existence outside the immediate dramatic context" has been one of the play's abiding fascinations.[69] This notion echoes in Eliot's praise for the character as "a real and unique human being," in R. C. Bald's claim that Middleton's city comedies were founded on "events from real life," and in the recent interest in the play's gender politics.[70] But insofar as Moll's double status as stage persona and historical personage has been notorious in provoking audiences and critics to look for the real in the fictive and the fictive in the real, it also invites awareness of a temporal slippage between the here-and-now of the present performance and the then-and-there of pasts and futures unfolding outside the bounded space of the Fortune's walls. Opening out from the play's "perfect close," and from the cyclical returns of Sir Alexander's valediction, Moll/Mary gestures to the dynamic temporalities of performing the urban contemporary.

## *Paying Expectation*

Even without the temporal dislocations of city comedy's contemporary traffic, theatrical time is polytemporal. Keir Elam, in *The Semiotics of Theatre and Drama*, identifies at least four temporal levels, including the double time of the dramatic narrative (the stage equivalent to *fabula* and *sjuzet*) and the multiple presents of a given performance. Here I want to focus on the interplay between two levels—the so-called "real time" of live performance, as actors literally make the play present to an audience, and the fictive time of the dramatic narrative, what Elam refers to as the "fictional *now* proposed by the dramatis personae—the temporal deixis which 'actualizes' the dramatic world" in a "perpetual present."[71] In its purchase on the contemporary urban scene, city comedy intensifies and exploits this interplay, often in disruptive metatheatrics that bring the "fictional *now*" into confrontation with the immediate present of the theater itself, so famously witnessed by Jonson's inductions and entre-acts, for example. *The Roaring Girl*'s novel doubling of Moll Cutpurse and the real-life Mary Frith pushes these tricks to the limits of theatrical representation, threatening to converge the "fictional *now*" with the real time of performance and thereby synchronizing the theater's multiple temporalities into a singular, living present. Yet, rather than simply fixing the moment, by stopping time and with it theatricality itself, this doubling may also work paradoxically to disrupt the audience's sense of simultaneity and thus to prompt them to become aware of themselves as temporal beings.

Time, Elizabeth Grosz astutely observes, is "neither fully 'present,' a thing in itself, nor is it a pure abstraction, a metaphysical assumption that can be ignored in everyday practice. . . . It is a kind of evanescence that appears only at those moments when our expectations are (positively or negatively) surprised. We can think it only when we are jarred out of our immersion in its continuity, when something untimely disrupts our expectations."[72] In its comic reversals and metatheatric hijinks, *The Roaring Girl* could be said to perform a version of the untimely, interrupting and dislocating temporal continuities and so provoking its audiences to "think time." Of course, as the mortality bills so powerfully document, Londoners did not need to go to the theater to experience the untimely so long as the threat of plague lingered on the outskirts of the city—"like stalking Tamburlaine," as Dekker described it.[73] Moreover, the government's strategic use of the bills may itself have been disruptive to the extent that it increased awareness of time's passage even as it attempted to institute regularity and order as a hedge against the unexpected. London city comedies could be said to model a similar cycle of control and disruption, and in some ways they do. But the stakes of playgoing and plague control are quite different and so too are the effects. For even as the play's timely narratives locate the city on stage, and thus momentarily control and fix its image, as *The Roaring Girl* so delightfully illustrates, the dislocating metatheatrics work against this fixity, making purchase on the unpredictable and the contingent with a freedom unavailable to the plague city. It is to these metatheatrics that I now turn.

*The Roaring Girl* opens by disrupting the theatrical scene, even before it has had a chance to begin, with a Prologue whose direct address to the audience marks out an immediate present seemingly poised between the world outside the theater and the performance to come. Hoping to shape audience expectation, the Prologue begins with a preemptive salvo: "A play expected long makes the audience look / For wonders—that each scene should be a book / Composed to all perfection" (1–3). What follows is at once a playful defense of the comedy's "mean" subject and a ramping up of speculation about her real-life identity, even as the Prologue insists on the difference between the play's so-called roaring girl and others within the city. Setting the stage against the world outside, and the here-and-now against the then-and-there, these gestures have the effect of protracting time within what might be called the anticipatory mode of the present. The Prologue reads this time on the bodies of the audience, describing their actions as suspended in the moment of expectation:

> I see attention sets wide ope her gates
> Of hearing, and with covetous listening waits
> To know what girl this roaring girl should be—
> For of that tribe are many. (13–16)

The effect is to turn the audience's attention from the stage to themselves, to make them aware of the immediate present as they watch themselves listening, awaiting the future. It is also to revel in the stage's power to draw out the anticipation, as the Prologue himself plays the expectation-game, withholding Moll's identity until the taunting flourish of the final couplet that ushers in the start of the performance—"But would you know who 'tis? Would you hear her name?— / She is called Mad Moll; her life our acts proclaim" (29–30). The Prologue's banter thus effects a series of dislocations even before the play has begun, forcing the spectators to think not only of the play's relation to the times but of their own dynamic relation to the performance's movements within time.

When replayed in an unusually arresting moment near the beginning of *The Roaring Girl*, the metatheatrics are even more disruptive in that rather than operating in prologues or entre-acts at the play's margins, they now interrupt unexpectedly from within the dramatic narrative itself. Sir Alexander's ostentatious after-dinner monologue in Act 1 provides the occasion, as the patriarch, pleased to show off his rooms and parlors to his guests, invites them to "look into [his] galleries" (1.2.14). Suddenly, in a theatrical *trompe l'oeil*, this fictive "prospect" opens out from the stage to take in the Fortune's own "sett square" galleries.[74] And as the gallants onstage peer out at the Fortune's audience, the trick wittily reverses the direction of their gaze, turning spectators into objects, now neatly arranged within Sir Alexander's gallery. Like many collectors, the old man proudly itemizes his holdings:

> Within one square a thousand heads are laid
> So close that all of heads the room seems made;
> As many faces there, filled with blithe looks,
> Show like the promising titles of new books
> Writ merrily, the readers being their own eyes,
> Which seem to move and to give plaudities;
> And here and there, whilst with obsequious ears
> Thronged heaps do listen, a cutpurse thrusts and leers
> With hawk's eyes for his prey—I need not show him. (1.2.19–27)

Re-presented as luxury commodities, the spectators' faces now stand on display alongside Sir Alexander's expensive furniture and household movables, the "Chairs, stools, and cushions" (1.2.46) portered in for the guests' comfort by serving men. And though Sir Alexander probably speaks from downstage, the effect is exactly the opposite of the fluid presentational space described by Robert Weimann, where the character-as-actor collaborates with the audience in asides, monologues, and clowning.[75] Imaginatively repositioning the audience *within* the illusionistic frame of the stage's *locus*, the monologue works here to striking effect, holding out to the Fortune's playgoers an identification so complete as to collapse them into the play and, for a moment at least, to stop time in an illusion of simultaneity.

For Sir Alexander, the possessive gesture hints at a refusal of mortality, a desire for control that reaches from his guests to his son's marriage to the audience itself. Yet by his own narrative, the old man admits the impossibility of stopping time's progress. The spectators' faces may show "like the promising titles of new books," but the books themselves are hardly static objects, artfully arranged in still-life paintings, say, or in private libraries. Instead, in what becomes a strangely playful figure, they are "Writ merrily, the readers being their own eyes, / Which seem to move and to give plaudities." The obsequious-eared playgoers may "seem" to applaud their representation on stage, but in reading themselves, they also resist Sir Alexander's objectification. Their eyes "move" to open a temporal and spatial distance between their place in the galleries (in the immediate present within the theater) and their place within the dramatic narrative (within the stage's "fictional *now*"). In the next line, with Sir Alexander's report of a cutpurse working his way through the transfixed crowd, the spell breaks altogether, jolting the spectators back to the immediate present within the theater, urging them to shift their gaze from the stage to themselves and each other, and to their purses. However momentary, this interruption in the audience's attention serves to dissolve Sir Alexander's illusion of simultaneity, his fantasy of controlling, if not stopping, time. The stage's Moll Cutpurse may be "perpetually real," to borrow from Eliot's praise for the character, but the Fortune's audience is not.[76]

Sir Alexander's narration thus ends up enacting the finitude it would transcend by interpellating the audience *into* temporal awareness, heightening their experience of time's passage. For though the patriarch intends otherwise, his lengthy monologue functions transversally, like the cutpurse (the play's Moll Cutpurse as well as the cutpurse supposedly spotted in the audience), as a metatheatrical interruption that cuts across both the onstage action and the time-space of the audience's relation to the stage. Forced to acknowledge their own movements within the theater—movements that no doubt differed from those Sir Alexander ascribes to them—some in the audience perhaps resist his fantasy of control, escaping as it were into the ordinariness of their own lives and their own mortality. In this sense, the playwrights' clever *trompe l'oeil* rehearses the complex transactions of the play as a whole. Like *The Roaring Girl*, the sequence verges on collapsing the theater into the dramatic narrative, and the immediate present into the "fictional *now*," by repositioning spectators as represented objects *within* the play. Yet the illusion of simultaneity is itself disruptive, paradoxically drawing attention to the distance and difference between the audience and their representation within the stage's fiction. In this play of identification and distance, the performance fractures the present moment into a here-and-now and a there-and-then, a dislocation that is itself both an effect and a condition of temporal movement. The effect is to mark out, and alienate, the audience's experience of the present within the present, in relation to the on-going performance.

In fracturing the present into "now" and "then," *The Roaring Girl*'s performances are in some sense homologous to the temporal work of the mortality bills. By provoking audiences both to identify with and separate themselves from stage representations, which are themselves already receding into the past of the present performance, the metatheatrics invite the kind of historical understanding that, in de Certeau's words, "exorcise[s] and confess[es] a presence of death amidst the living."[77] It is tempting, then, to imagine a reciprocity between the stage and the bills, a dynamic circulation in which the theatrical tricks of city comedies inflect as well as reflect the city's experience of the bills' temporal rhythms. But even as *The Roaring Girl*'s contemporaneous staging seems to provoke the same paradoxical temporalities as the mortality bills—opening up the non-coincidence of the present with itself *and* at the same time reiterating the audience's sense of themselves in that immediate and lived present—the effects of these engagements differ radically from those proposed by the weekly death counts. Like the bills, theatrical performance of the contemporary city has the potential to generate a commonality among the living, in part by marking off a present moment of duration that is separate from the past but extending into the future. But what is the shape of this future? In marked contrast to the mortality bills, *The Roaring Girl* could hardly be said to quantify the present and past so that futures might be calculated and predicted. Nor does the play join with Sir Alexander's closing invocation of a cyclical pastoral that might somehow transcend periodicity and finitude altogether. Instead, *The Roaring Girl*'s performance, as distinct from its plotting, suggests yet another order of futurity, one that opens out to a recursive logic of repetition, variation, and invention even within the sequential trajectories of death and commerce.

Delivered by the Epilogue, *The Roaring Girl*'s final address to the audience offers a glimpse of what this future might look like. The speech begins conventionally, with a cautionary tale about a foolish painter who, hoping to "mend" his life-like portrait of a woman so as "to please all," ends up creating a work "so vile, / So monstrous, and so ugly, all men did smile / At the poor painter's folly" (Epilogue, 11–15). While the analogy to the play seems obvious—especially as the playwrights and actors warn that they too "In striving to please all, please none at all" (30)—the underlying fear is that *The Roaring Girl*'s audience shares Sir Alexander's aesthetics, his habit of confusing persons and things and his desire to contract the world and time into a commodity that he might hold into the future. What is surprising about the Epilogue's appeal, then, is the stunning reversal of the closing lines, the offer to compensate the audience's disappointment by bringing back the "Roaring Girl herself" (35), presumably with Mary Frith, the real-life roaring girl, appearing on the Fortune's stage. At once humble and slyly arch, the Epilogue concludes the play with the promise that:

> . . . if what both [writers and actors] have done
> Cannot full pay your expectation,
> The Roaring Girl herself, some few days hence,
> Shall on this stage give larger recompense;
> Which mirth that you may share in, herself does woo you,
> And craves this sign: your hands to beckon her to you.
>
> (Epilogue, 33–38)

The solution seems to capitulate to an unsophisticated audience by promising them exactly what they want—Mary Frith *herself*, the "original" Moll-Cutpurse, unmediated either by author's pen or actor's voice and body—a desire *The Roaring Girl* has played to and on from the start.[78]

Paradoxically, however, the Epilogue's offer of "recompense" resists the implied promise to collapse distinctions of time and space within a living theater of the present. "Recompense" depends, after all, on a logic of substitution and equivalence rather than identification. Moreover, it adjudicates and calculates equivalence over time, offering "payment" in the present or future for something that occurred in the past (a loss, injury, or misdeed, perhaps). In the case of *The Roaring Girl*, the loss or injury lies in the recent present, now past, with "what both [the authors and actors] *have done*"—or not done—to "pay your expectation." The compensatory payment will come in the future, in the form of another, and different, performance "some few days hence." This is a clever marketing strategy, especially as the contractual language of compensation sets in motion a dramatic periodicity designed to fill the Fortune's amphitheater in days to come. Perhaps looking back to *2 Henry IV*'s Epilogue, with its promise to make amends by "continu[ing] the story," *The Roaring Girl* offers to make good on its own presumed failure to "pay expectation" with the promise of yet another production, thus setting in motion a line of credit that could conceivably extend in a succession of performances, each one compensating for the failed expectations of the last.[79] But if this proposition risks reiterating the stage's own commodification, with its assumption that theatrical pleasure might be quantified, calculated, and sold, it also points up the limitations of such accounting practices, the impossibility of ever balancing accounts within the fluid and unpredictable exchanges of theatrical performance.

*The Roaring Girl*'s future performances, the Epilogue suggests, will both repeat and supplement those of the past, thereby opening up possibilities for something other than either a calculated reprise or cyclical repetition of the same.[80] The repetition promised here is indeed far different from the seasonal returns endorsed by Sir Alexander in the play's close, when the patriarch imagines a future in the communal memory of the present moment—"this day shall be remembered" (5.2.262)—even as he commands the audience to "go pleased away" (5.2.266), a request that is at once a plea for approval and an insistence that they depart. The Epilogue pointedly reverses this farewell by inviting the audience to return to the theater "some few days hence." Looking to the future rather than the past, the Epilogue envisions a community constituted not so much by collective memory but by future performances that will bring audiences together with actors in "mirth that you may share in." Even comedy's requisite appeal for applause is here redirected toward the future, as the Epilogue urges the playgoers to use "your hands to beckon [Moll] to you," thus approving the performance to come rather than the one they have just heard. The invitation, of course, also leaves open the possibility of surprise, banking on a future in which the past might return playfully and unpredictably.

What may be the most startling revision of Sir Alexander's nostalgic retrospection, however, is the Epilogue's refusal to offer any guarantee of a return to origins. The naming of the "Roaring Girl herself" may seem to promise an exchange of Mary for Moll, the real for the fictive, the original for the copy. But following the logic of recompense, this alteration is not so much a restoration of what was lost as it is one in a sequence of substitutions—Mary for Moll for Mary—extending from past to future. In this, the play beckons to our own post-modern understandings of performance as a kind of substitution or "surrogation," what W. B. Worthen explains as an "ambivalent replaying of previous performers and performances" that "recalls and transforms the past in the form of the present." What performance involves, he writes, is "not the replaying of an authorizing text, a grounding origin, but the potential to construct that origin as a rhetorically powerful effect of performance."[81] While this notion of performance pointedly alters the priority of text to performance, it also serves to alter expectations about temporal sequence, allowing early modern spectators as well as contemporary critics to experience time in new and various ways. *The Roaring Girl*'s "recompense" could thus be said to offer more than simply an antidote to "merchant's time" or to death's finitude. For in structuring a dynamic movement that acknowledges and depends on the possibilities for differences and inequalities and change, theatrical "recompense" or substitution enacts a complex multi-temporality in which the past inflects the present even as the present recalls and reworks the past and so conditions possibilities for the future.

## *Telling Stories*

History has it that Mary Frith did indeed return to the stage in the weeks to come. Consistory Court records from January 27, 1612 claim that she "voluntarily confessed" to "being at a playe about 3 quarters of a yeare since at *the* ffortune in mans apparell & in her boot*es* & with a sword by her syde." A mirror of her theatrical counterpart, it seems, Frith "sat there vppon the stage in the publique viewe of all the people there pr*ese*nte in mans apparrell & playd vppon her lute & sange a songe."[82] Perhaps she performed an afterpiece, singing one of the "lewde Jigges songes" the Fortune was famous for (and in October 1612 was prohibited from performing) or maybe she actually impersonated herself in Middleton and Dekker's play, fingering her viol in Act IV and "spicing the written dialogue with extempore jests," as Paul Mulholland speculates.[83] Nor do her performances end here; rather, they foretell future appearances, including her scene of public penance at Paul's Cross following soon after her court appearance.

We know of the Paul's Cross spectacle from John Chamberlain, whose ongoing correspondence with Dudley Carleton regularly sprinkled tidbits of local gossip with court and city news, including updates on the mortality bills. Even for a prolific letter writer who claimed "never [to be] cloyed by particulars," Chamberlain's account is unusually detailed.[84] On February 12, 1612, he writes to Carleton:

> this last Sonday Mall Cut-purse a notorious bagage (that used to go in mans apparell and challenged the feild of divers gallants) was brought to the same place [Paul's Cross], where she wept bitterly and seemed very penitent, but yt is since doubted she was maudelin druncke, beeing discovered to have tipled of three quarts of sacke before she came to her penaunce: she had the daintiest preacher or ghostly father that ever I saw in pulpit, one Ratcliffe of Brazen Nose in Oxford, a likelier man to have led the revells in some ynne of court then to be where he was, but the best is he did extreem badly, and so wearied the audience that the best part went away, and the rest taried rather to heare Mall Cutpurse then him.[85]

This passage is often cited for what it documents about Frith's cross-dressing and her acting abilities, the latter so compelling in Chamberlain's estimation as to upstage the preacher. Frith's public behavior both at Paul's Cross and on the Fortune's stage is "deliberately theatrical," Anthony Dawson observes, blurring boundaries between social reality and *The Roaring Girl*'s fiction and thereby provoking "a kind of territorial dispute, in which the privilege of theatrical representation is contested."[86]

It is also the case, of course, that Frith's theatricality colludes with the stage, abetting the criss-crossing of performances, of substitutions and borrowings, that extend from the street to the stage and printed playbook and back again.[87] One effect of these repeat performances, certainly, is to reiterate and even exploit the linear calculations of "merchant's time." Indeed, as Gustav Ungerer concludes from the historical documents, Frith's performance at the Fortune is hardly extemporaneous but rather "a cooperative theatrical enterprise undertaken for the profit of all the parties involved."[88] Further profits were to be had from her penance at Paul's Cross. The Stationers' records suggest that the quarto was rushed into print by Nicholas Okes so as to coincide with the occasion, with the books to be sold by Garaband's bookstall within earshot of Paul's churchyard.[89] For a sixpence, a reader could purchase a souvenir quarto of the celebrated performance, illustrated with a likeness of the cross-dressed, pipe-smoking "Moll Cutpurse" herself on its title-page—to be enjoyed in "both gallery-room at the playhouse and chamber-room at your lodging," Middleton promises in his epistle to play-readers.[90]

But there's another temporality operating as well in these continuing and varied performances on stages and streets and in private chambers, one that in its reiterative openness suggests city comedy's capacity to exceed the limits of its own commercial ventures. Theatrical events are ongoing, Samuel Weber contends in *Theatricality as Medium*: "they can neither be contained within the place where they unfold nor entirely separated from it. They can be said, then, in a quite literal sense, to *come to pass*. They take place, which means in a particular place, and yet simultaneously also *pass away*—not simply to disappear but to happen somewhere *else*."[91] In its attention to theater's dislocations and times "out of joint" (to borrow from Derrida borrowing from *Hamlet*), Weber's formulation aptly describes *The Roaring Girl*'s circulations within metropolitan London. Simultaneously "taking place" and "passing away" to appear elsewhere, the play's proliferating performances give the slip to temporal and spatial boundaries, evading both the promise of theatrical self-presence and the threat of finitude and death within the city. Yet, at the same time, the dreadful rhythm marked out by the mortality bills continues to haunt the theater, perhaps lending a freedom to the temporal experience of performing the city on stage.

# *Epilogue*

## The Place of the Spectator

> In the following Act, the Office is opened and shown to the prodigal and his princess Pecunia, wherein the allegory and purpose of the author hath hitherto been wholly mistaken, and so sinister an interpretation been made, as if the souls of most of the spectators had lived in the eyes and ears of these ridiculous gossips that tattle between the Acts. But he prays you thus to mend it.
>
> —Ben Jonson, "To the Readers," *The Staple of News*

> [The spectator] observes, selects, compares, interprets. She links what she sees to a host of other things that she has seen on other stages, in other kinds of place. She composes her own poem with the elements of the poem before her.
>
> —Jacques Rancière, *The Emancipated Spectator*

Ben Jonson's note "To the Readers," inserted into the 1631 edition of *The Staple of News*, marks a decided intensification of his preoccupation with the reception of his work. Even without this note, the play is overloaded with critical apparatus, including an onstage audience that holds forth after every act in a series of intermeans. Returning to the device inaugurated in his first play with a London setting, Jonson envisions theatrical performance in terms of debate and disagreement. But here, in place of the urbane moderators of *Every Man Out of His Humor,* he presents a quartet of outspoken gossips, "*four gentlewomen lady-like attired*" (Induction, 0 s.d.), who prove themselves to be the very opposite of discretion and good judgment.[1] This obtrusive device is generally read as the playwright's struggle to regain control over the common stage, but if the note to readers is to be believed, it is a struggle Jonson risked losing. The note harshly criticizes the playgoing public together with the growing news industry, complaining that the author's "purpose" has "hitherto been wholly mistaken," and his meaning sinisterly misinterpreted ("To the Readers," 3). But it is the note's intrusive placement as much as its message that underscores the precariousness of the struggle over the play's reception. Coming not as prefatory matter but as an insertion, immediately prior to the controversial Staple scene of Act 3, the note pointedly disrupts the play text at a crucial moment. This is, as one critic remarks, "an extraordinary controlling mechanism even for Jonson," and so "bespeaks a fear of being unable to contain the effects of misreadings pronounced by characters of his own making."[2]

My interest in this intrusive bit of paratext is with the particular way Jonson's anxiety about his audience gets articulated in relation to the play's engagement with contemporary London. *The Staple of News* marks Jonson's return both to the city stage and to city subjects after nearly a decade of producing entertainments for the Jacobean court. Centered on the emerging news trade, there's a "dense topicality" to its satire.[3] But if topicality lends the play its currency, topicality is itself at issue in the play's critique of a news business that traffics in contemporary events and opinions. In Jonson's view, what drives the news office, or Staple, is the public's hunger for news and novelty—"the newest that thou hast" (3.2.19), the prodigal demands, in a refrain echoed by the stream of customers who come to the Staple to purchase news. This same appetite for newness also drives the play's onstage audience of gossips, who insist on the newest news from the stage as well. "Look your news be new and fresh . . . [not] stale or fly-blown" (Ind. 25–27), Gossip Tattle demands of the Prologue. The Prologue firmly resists, explaining that it is not the author's purpose to trade in news and gossip, "to know / How many coaches in Hyde Park did show / Last spring, what fare today at Medley's was, / If Dunstan or the Phoenix best wine has?" ("Prologue for the Stage," 13–16). Yet Jonson's handling of the Staple scene of Act 3 seems to belie this disclaimer by offering up a dizzying inventory of news to the Blackfriars' audience, from state politics to scientific discoveries and exotic tales of the new world, to news of pageants, coronations, and plague, including "news o'the stage" (3.2.198). And as Jonson takes potshots at Thomas Middleton's *A Game at Chess* and reports on the recent death of actor William Rowley only a few weeks before the play's opening, the headlines begin to seem less like parody and more like the real thing. Jonson is at pains to distance his play from the news it conveys—"consider the news here vented to be none of his news" ("To the Readers," 7–8), he protests—yet the immediacy of the reported events risks turning the satire into a vehicle for the play's own traffic in news and novelty.[4]

It is probably no coincidence that Jonson's concern with his audience intensifies at the moment the stage comes closest to replicating the city scene. The metatheatrics are in part a witty maneuver designed to play up the audience's experience of contemporaneity, but they also signal the playwright's struggle to control responses to this experience. In its pronounced self-consciousness, *The Staple of News* looks back to *Everyman Out of His Humor*, when Cordatus instructs the Globe's audience "to presuppose the stage the middle aisle in Paul's" (3.1.2–3).[5] Taken together, the metatheatrics of these two plays usefully frame this study's larger questions about theatrical mediation and the practice of new forms of urban collectivity. But they also raise a more specific question about the place of spectators within these mediating practices. Both plays, after all, grant spectators an unusual degree of visibility. Not only do they give local audiences new status as dramatic subjects; more pointedly, they directly address these audiences in inductions and intermeans, even going so far as to represent them on stage so as to make spectatorship itself a subject. In both plays, moreover, Jonson calls attention to a locus of instability in city plays by insisting on the spectators' visibility just when the stage verges on collapsing into the object it holds up for correction. Central to this instability is the question of audience response, for what Jonson's "ridiculous gossips" remind us is that city plays prompted audiences not just to identify with but to interpret the spectacle before them—to "tattle between the Acts" ("To the Readers," 5–6), as Jonson uncharitably puts it.

Implicit in Jonson's criticism of "mistaken" and "sinister" interpretations is an acknowledgment of the theater's constitutive dependence on its spectators. But what are the politics of this dependence? As this study has sought to show, in putting pressure on the relationship between the stage and its audience, city plays opened up a reflexive space more aligned with the multiplicity of Plato's *theatrocracy* than with the singular vantage point of a classical *theatron*, and my concern in individual chapters has been to explore this multiplicity in relation to new modes of urban experience and sociability. Here, at the close, I want to reflect more broadly on the mediating practices of the theater itself, and to do so by looking toward a contingent politics located in what Jacques Rancière calls "the question of the spectator," a question he puts in relation to intellectual and political emancipation.[6] Because theater figures centrally in Rancière's thinking about politics, aesthetics, and democratic practices, his work offers a resonant entry point into the political processes at stake for spectators of city plays. This is not simply because the spectator is central to Rancière's conception of politics, which it is, but also because his politics require a disruption of proper place that has affinities with the dislocations of "practicing" the city on stage and off.

Rancière begins with the seemingly commonplace assumption that politics hinges on a relationship between the stage and the audience. But what's not commonplace in his model is his framing of this relationship as a struggle or dispute, over who is recognized and heard, and who remains invisible and uncounted. Central to this struggle, and to Rancière's politics more generally, is the assertion of equality. In Rancière's account, however, "[e]quality is not a given that politics then presses into service," a fundamental or inalienable right, say, but is instead the very condition of politics, "inscribed in the setting up of a dispute, of a community existing solely through being divided."[7] Conceptualized in theatrical terms, this "disruptive equality" constitutes, and is constituted by, "conflict over the existence of a common stage and over the existence and status of those present on it."[8] Rancière uses the "common stage" to figure both the contested ground of politics and the improvised performances of unauthorized voices engaging in political *dissensus*. Theater and politics come together here in a two-fold alignment. Both display the potential for disruption on the part of those who have no part—the *dēmos*, or the *sans-part*, as Rancière defines them—and both give sensible form to this disruption by redistributing the audience's assigned places, making "a place for the out of place."[9] This is, of course, a very different notion of theater from the New Historicist or Foucauldian model of spectacle operating as an instrument of state power. But it is also different, Rancière reminds us, from nineteenth-century Romantic notions of theater as communitarian, idealized as a theater of "self-presence" that abolishes the separation between stage and audience.[10] What makes it different is the recognition it accords to spectators.

But did the early modern London theater grant a comparable recognition to its spectators? Or, to put it in Rancière's terms, did city audiences claim recognition and visibility for themselves? There's no shortage of examples to suggest that the stage was as much concerned with policing audiences as with emancipating them. The oft-cited Induction to *Bartholomew Fair* shows a playwright seemingly more inclined to agree with Plato's negative critique of a *theatrocracy*, in which playwrights cede power to audiences, than with Rancière's affirmations of democratic freedom.

Jonson's pre-performance contract indeed reads as an unapologetic attempt to prevent the disruptive "sovereignty of the audience" feared by Plato when he warns that theatrical license will lead to political license and throw the city into anarchy.[11] Jonson's contract not only binds "the said spectators and hearers" (Ind. 71) to the author's terms, it requires that they "remain in the places their money or friends have put them in" (74–75) for the duration of the play and, following this, that each spectator's judgment be commensurate with "the value of his place" (87).[12] Jonson's "Articles of Agreement" precisely invert Rancière's assertion of "disruptive equality" by insisting on predetermined hierarchies of distinction and difference. The contract would divide and fix spectators according to the price of their seats in a spatial policing that is the very opposite of Rancière's view of political action, which "makes visible what had no business being seen, and makes heard a discourse where once there was only place for noise."[13]

But would such a contract actually succeed in silencing the censure of "said spectators and hearers"? With a festive plot described as coming "about as close as Jonson ever gets to anything like an egalitarian conception," *Bartholomew Fair* suggests otherwise, threatening to disrupt the controlling authority of its opening premise and of the playwright himself.[14] Even within the Induction itself, the so-called contract is framed by the larger dispute between the bookholder and scrivener, who speak for "our author," and the vocal stagekeeper, who opens the play by speaking for and to the excluded demos, soliciting the judgments of the "understanding gentlemen o'the ground here" (Ind. 47–48). One might object that this dispute is only a fiction, a strategy of policing intended not to affirm the equality of the groundlings but rather to mock their ignorance, correct their misjudgments, and keep them in their place. But even if we assume that the play acknowledges the "part of those who have no part," who is to say that their visibility on stage is something other than mere spectacle, an illusory substitute for actual politics?[15] Richard Halpern takes up this line of argument in his critique of Rancière's reading of Greek tragedy, cautioning against an overly simple identification between aesthetic and political visibility. "The visibility granted by theater was rather compensatory," he argues of the women and slaves represented on the Greek stage, "a form of public exposure these groups received *in lieu* of democratic participation. . . . Perhaps theater does not, as Plato asserted, produce simulacra of persons but rather simulacra of their (political) visibility."[16]

Early-seventeenth-century playwrights seem far less circumspect about parsing differences between theatrical and political visibility. As New

Historicist work has documented across a range of plays, the political costs and consequences of theatrical visibility remained a pressing concern throughout the period. The stage's urban turn may have domesticated the stage by focusing on citizens rather than monarchs, but judging from the protestations of playwrights, questions persisted about the broader politics of theatrical visibility. For example, Thomas Dekker famously laments in *The Gull's Horn-Book* (1609) that the theater has become a place "so free in entertainment" that it "allows" a farmer's son the "selfsame liberty" as a courtier, and a "carman and tinker [to] claim as strong a voice in their suffrage, and sit to give judgment on the play's life and death as well as the proudest Momus among the Tribe of Critic."[17] Assuming a direct link between visibility, voice, and "suffrage," Dekker objects to the aesthetic judgments of laborers as a form of presumptuous political license. In *The Staple of News* Jonson extends this critique to include women among the offenders of decorum; even before the Prologue has finished his first line, the loud gossips commandeer the stage and prepare to "arraign" both the play and its "sweating" poet (Ind. 22, 65). Jonson's intention, surely, is "to ensure that no one in his real audience will share their feminized and devalued point of view."[18] But his note to readers in the 1631 edition suggests that the strategy failed with "most of the spectators" ("To the Readers," 4–5), who in fact aligned themselves with the gossips. And as Jonson solicits his readers to join with him against the tattling gossips and spectators, his note offers a rare glimpse of performance as a scene of politics in Rancière's sense of the term, as a conflict about who is seen and heard on the "common stage."[19]

My aim in this study has been to explore the stage's freedoms in relation to new and contested forms of urban practice, and to see city plays as marking out a space within which spectators could experience and experiment in the hypercomplexities of social change. Rancière's theatrical model adds yet another level to this accounting, however, by inviting us to look to "the politics of aesthetics," as he puts it, beginning with the question of dramatic form. Turning to *The Republic*, and to a polity founded on an orderly assignment of roles or occupations, Rancière points out the interconnection between Plato's exclusion of the demos from politics and his exclusion of theater.[20] What links these exclusions for Plato is the disorder that comes from "doing two things at once." In the case of politics, as Rancière points out, Plato objects that the artisans "cannot be *somewhere else* [participating in politics] because *work will not wait*."[21] Theater similarly requires its participants to "be somewhere else," quite literally in the case of artisans, but also imaginatively, in that participants must occupy multiple roles, "to play another identity than their 'own' identity."[22] For Plato, dramatic mimesis thus enacts a dangerously confusing duplicity, with deleterious effects on the ignorant and disorderly audiences, whom he describes as "the senseless element that cannot distinguish the greater from the less, but calls the same thing now one, now the other."[23] But for Rancière, mimesis is valuable precisely *because* it allows for the possibility of "doing two things at once," thereby confounding "the order of function and place."[24] Theater gives form to an aesthetic regime "based on the indetermination of identities, the delegitimation of positions of speech, the deregulation of partitions of space and time," a regime that for Rancière is identical to "the regime of democracy."[25]

In asking audiences "to presuppose" that the stage is the city, early modern plays about London give powerful form to theater's democratizing possibilities. They provoke local playgoers to confound "the order of function and place," and so to disturb "the clear partition of identities, activities, and spaces."[26] But in their insistent redoubling of the here-and-now of everyday London, city plays also deepen and complicate Rancière's model, most notably by requiring attention to what is missing from his account of dramatic mimesis—a consideration of theatrical forms of visibility *together with* dramatic content. Indeed, it is this nexus of theatrical form *and* explicitly urban subject matter, I suggest, that allows city spectators such unusual license and liberty. As prologues and epilogues would have us believe, the stage's heightened representations of city life encouraged a local population to claim their visibility, giving voice to opinions about the stage as well as the city. And the warrant for this claim, it seems, resides not with aristocratic privilege or classical learning but with everyday urban experience. *Bartholomew Fair*'s Induction is again instructive in that it opens with an untutored stagehand who immediately sets himself up as a critic, offering "to put in with my experience" (Ind. 28–29) with the author. The playwright's rebuttal, delivered by the Scrivener, then makes its own claim on experience, contending that the play traffics in "the present" (113) rather than in outworn "drolleries" that "make Nature afraid" (124–25). Put against the tired conventions of the popular stage, the Scrivener's appeal to experience slyly turns the tables in the comic face-off between a master-poet and his stagekeeper. But it also operates to solicit the local experiences and perceptions of audiences within the Hope theater, inviting a multiplicity of interpretations, opinions, and disputes about the city and theatrical practice.

With its onstage audience of opinionated gossips, *The Staple of News* offers an even more provocative example of a theatrical license. The play's extensive metatheatrical apparatus documents a range of spectators, including the "noblemen" and "grave wits" (Ind. 15–16), who will be offended "to see [the gossips] seated on the bench" (16–17), in places reserved for gentlemen. The "Prologue for the Court" acknowledges yet another audience in the figure of the king and court, whose judgment and "fair report" are far "above the vulgar sort" ("Prologue for Court," 6–7). But it is the "vulgar sort" who preside, and it is largely their commentary that mediates the play's performance. Like the stagekeeper in *Bartholomew Fair*, the gossips wish to put in with their experience with the play's absent poet, who it turns out is drunk backstage, having "torn the book in a poetical fury, and put himself to silence in dead sack" (Ind. 72–73). And like the stagekeeper, the gossips too pride themselves on their knowledge of popular traditions and are disappointed when the play fails to deliver up fools and devils or a Vice that "snap[s] at everybody he meets" with his wooden dagger (2 Int. 12–13). But as Gossip Mirth instructs, sounding a lot like Jonson, "That was the old way" (14), explaining that now the Vices "are attired like men and women o' the time" (16–17). The exchange clearly echoes the opening debate from *Bartholomew Fair*, but with a crucial difference in that it removes the master-poet, with his proxy contract, as an interlocutor. Instead Jonson allows the "vulgar sort" to sort it out among themselves between the acts, as the gossips debate the play's purpose and meaning.[27] The effect is to show a performance that simultaneously enacts and elicits disagreement. Whatever the author's purpose, the play succeeds in dividing and separating its spectators in a performance whose meaning "is owned by no one," to borrow again from Rancière, not the "sweating" poet or "the ridiculous gossips," and not even the king.

Written more than twenty-five years after the stage's urban turn, *The Staple of News* offers a retrospective on theater's ongoing experiment in urban contemporaneity. But Jonson's late play does more than simply reiterate the dislocating effects of mimetic redoubling operating in earlier plays. For in its vocal onstage audience, *The Staple of News* also invites us to reconsider the collective experience of playgoing itself. Rancière's work is again helpful in that its general conception of spectatorship reinforces the recent emphasis on the diversity and creativity of early modern audiences.[28] Rejecting the commonplace presupposition that theater is "an exemplary community form," based on the audience's shared experience of the performance, Rancière locates collectivity in the equality among spectators to observe and interpret the event.[29] "The collective power shared by spectators does not stem from the fact that they are members of a collective body or from some specific form of interactivity," he contends, but rather from "the power each of them has to translate what she perceives in her own way, to link it to the unique intellectual adventure that makes her similar to all the rest in as much as this adventure is not like any other."[30] And it is this shared power to interpret and translate that links spectators even as it keeps them separate. Granted, there's a contemporary ring to this talk of individuals sharing "unique intellectual adventures" that doesn't exactly fit with our sense of the London stage or its politics. Even so, in emphasizing the capacity for equality among "anonymous people, the capacity that makes everyone equal to everyone else," Rancière's model of the "emancipated spectator" usefully reflects on the politics of the stage within what was rapidly becoming a city of strangers, a diverse, differentiated, and mobile population no longer strictly bound by civic institutions or customs or by the parochial geography of neighborhoods.[31] What Rancière directs us to is the possibility that in its urban turn the early modern stage enabled spectators to engage in the freedoms of urban plurality, simultaneously identifying with and distancing themselves from each other as well as from the events on stage. And it is in this "unpredictable interplay of associations and disassociations," exercised through "irreducible distances," that Rancière locates what he calls the spectator's "emancipation."[32]

The gossips' final act is to censure the poet for his handling of the play's catastrophe. Each gossip offers her own variation on the how the scene should end, giving proof to the claim that the emancipated spectator "links what she sees to a host of other things that she has seen on other stages, in other kinds of place."[33] Together, the gossips then imagine the poet subjected to their punishment, placed in the stocks and forced to wear "large sheets of paper" or parchment skin "filled with news" (4 Int. 69, 72). The image is striking, particularly as it conjoins the spectators' triumph over the playwright with the triumph of the news business over theater, whose news is judged to be "Scurvy and stale" (3 Int. 14). Wearing news as his penance, the disgraced poet is a fitting emblem of the displacement of the dramatic poet by newsmongers, reinforcing D. F. McKenzie's conclusion that *The Staple of News* "marks the end of theater as the only secular mass medium, the end of the playhouse as the principal forum of public debate, the end of the actor's popular function as the abstract and brief chronicles of the time."[34] But what the play also marks, if only retrospectively, is the persistent power of the contemporary stage. In its "dense topicality," cleverly retailed by Jonson's extended parody of newsbooks, corantos, manuscript letters, and local tattle, *The Staple of News*, like other city plays, paradoxically insists that what the stage offers is not news. But in distancing itself from news, with its promise of immediacy and freshness, Jonson's play ends up reaffirming Samuel Weber's observation about theatrical mediation, that what "'happens' on the stage is not the communication of something new, in the sense of content, but a variation of something familiar through its repetition." At the same time, the play's boisterous gossips also reaffirm the corollary to this principle of repetition, dramatizing the ways theatricality's "reiterative openness" extends to spectators.[35] By Jonson's own account, his play offers neither "News" or "truths," but things "so like" truth that poetry might imitate "without scandal" ("Prologue for the Court," 14). In performing a version of the city "so like" truth, city plays mark out a space for the local population to engage in the politics of *dissensus* and "disruptive equality."

# *Notes*

## *Introduction: Presupposing the Stage*

1. Thomas Heywood, *An Apology for Actors* (London: 1612), sig. F3. By Darryll Grantley's tally, 21 of the surviving 140 Elizabethan plays are set in London, and include histories and tragedies as well as comedies, whereas close to half of the 182 Jacobean and Caroline comedies have London settings; in *London in Early Modern English Drama: Representing the Built Environment* (Basingstoke: Palgrave Macmillan, 2008), 7.

2. All citations from the play are from *Every Man Out of His Humour*, ed. Helen Ostovich, *The Revels Plays* (Manchester: Manchester University Press, 2001), an edition based on William Holme's 1600 edition (Q1). The first of Jonson's plays to be printed, *Every Man Out* appears to have sold well, published in three separate quarto editions in 1600 (Ostovich, 3–5).

3. Performed by the same company, *Every Man Out* and *Henry V* appeared in close proximity in late 1599, and so it is tempting to see Jonson engaging here in a bit of competitive dramaturgy that plays the local scene and its irreverent interlocutors against the epic machinery of Shakespeare's play.

4. A central location for finding employment within the city, the western or so-called *si-quis* door was, in Thomas Dekker's words, "pasted and plastered up with servingmen's supplications"; see *The Gull's Horn-Book*, in *Thomas Dekker*, ed. E. D. Pendry (Cambridge: Harvard University Press, 1968), 91.

5. According to Martin Butler, the Paul's Walk scene is "virtually the first quasi-realistic pastiche of everyday conversation in an identifiable city setting in any English play, and certainly the most elaborate"; see "Jonson's London and Its Theatres," in *The Cambridge Companion to Ben Jonson*, ed. Richard Harp and Stanley Stewart (Cambridge: Cambridge University Press, 2000), 23.

6. Steven Mullaney, "Affective Technologies: Toward an Emotional Logic of the Elizabethan Stage," in *Environment and Embodiment in Early Modern England*, ed. Mary Floyd-Wilson and Garrett A. Sullivan, Jr. (Basingstoke: Palgrave Macmillan, 2007), 71–89, esp. 74.

7. See, for example, the essays in *The Making of the Metropolis: London 1500–1700*, ed. A. L. Beier and Roger Finlay (London: Longman, 1986).

8. The anonymous author of "An Apologie of the Cittie of London," in *John Stow, A Survey of London*, ed. Charles Lethbridge Kingsford, 2 vols.

(Oxford: Clarendon Press, 1971), 2: 212, details the breadth of the migration into London even as he defends the city against those who charge it with "the losse and decay of many (or most) of the auncient Citties, Corporate Townes and markets within this Realme, by drawing from them to her selfe alone, say they, both all trade of traffique by sea, and the retayling of Wares, and exercise of Manuall Artes also" (211). For discussion of this new mobility, see Jeremy Boulton, *Neighbourhood and Society: A London Suburb in the Seventeenth Century* (Cambridge: Cambridge University Press, 1987); and Patricia Fumerton, *Unsettled: The Culture of Mobility and the Working Poor in Early Modern England* (Chicago: University of Chicago Press, 2006).

9. Richard Sennett, *The Fall of Public Man* (New York: W. W. Norton, 1974), 48. Sennett goes on to distinguish between two types of strangers within cities—first, those outsiders marked by ethnic, national, or linguistic differences and, second, the "unknown quantities" within, illustrated by the formation of new social classes within the city, the "mercantile bourgeoisie" in eighteenth-century London, for example.

10. Given that mortality rates exceeded birth rates in these years, immigration alone accounts for the rapid surge in population; Beier and Finlay, "Introduction: The significance of the metropolis," in *Making of the Metropolis*, 1–33, esp. 9. There is now a substantive body of work on the city's demography, including E. A. Wrigley and R. S. Schofield, *The Population History of England 1541–1871* (Cambridge: Cambridge University Press, 1981); Roger Finlay, *Population and Metropolis: The Demography of London 1580–1650* (Cambridge: Cambridge University Press, 1981); Roger Finlay and Beatrice Shearer, "Population Growth and Suburban Expansion," in *Making of the Metropolis*, 37–57; and Vanessa Harding, "The Population of London, 1550–1700: A review of the published evidence," *London Journal* 15 (1990): 111–28. See also Vanessa Harding's review of the literature on the city's demography and topography in "Early Modern London 1550–1700," *London Journal* 20 (1995): 34–45.

11. Margaret Pelling, "Skirting the city? Disease, social change and divided households in the seventeenth century," in *Londinopolis: Essays in the Cultural and Social History of Early Modern London*, ed. Paul Griffiths and Mark S. R. Jenner (Manchester: Manchester University Press, 2000), 154–75, esp. 154.

12. Discussions of the city's instability include Peter Clark and Paul Slack, *English Towns in Transition* (Oxford: Oxford University Press, 1976), and A. L. Beier, "Social Problems in Elizabethan London," in *The Tudor and Stuart Town: A Reader in English Urban History 1530–1688*, ed. Jonathan Barry (London: Longman, 1990), 121–38. For revisionist accounts emphasizing stability, see Frank Freeman Foster, *The Politics of Stability: A Portrait of the Rulers in Elizabethan London* (London: Royal Historical Society, 1977); Valerie Pearl, "Change and Stability in Seventeenth-Century London," *London Journal* 5 (1979), 3–34; and Steve Rappaport, *Worlds within Worlds: Structures of Life in Sixteenth-Century London* (Cambridge: Cambridge University Press, 1989). Subsequent work on London's civic structures—its government, livery companies, parishes, and wards—has

usefully complicated these debates by shifting emphasis away from fixed states of stability and disorder and concentrating instead on the processes or "pursuit of stability"; see Ian W. Archer, *The Pursuit of Stability: Social Relations in Elizabethan London* (Cambridge: Cambridge University Press, 1991), and M. J. Power, "A 'Crisis' Reconsidered: Social and Demographic Dislocation in London in the 1590s," *London Journal* 12 (1986): 134–45.

13. J. F. Merritt, "Introduction: Perceptions and portrayals of London 1598–1720," in *Imagining Early Modern London: Perceptions and Portrayals of the City from Stow to Strype, 1598–1720* (Cambridge: Cambridge University Press, 2001), 1–24, esp. 23. See also the introductions to other recent collections exploring the perceptions and experiences of local residents: *The Experience of Authority in Early Modern England*, ed. Paul Griffiths, Adam Fox, and Steve Hindle (New York: St. Martin's Press, 1996); *Londinopolis*, ed. Griffiths and Jenner; the excellent review of shifting approaches to community study in early modern England by Phil Withington and Alexandra Shepard, "Introduction: Communities in early modern England," in *Communities in Early Modern England: Networks, Place, Rhetoric*, ed. Shepard and Withington (Manchester: Manchester University Press, 2000), 1–15; J. F. Merritt, *The Social World of Early Modern Westminster* (Manchester: Manchester University Press, 2005); and the illuminating study of private spaces and lives by Lena Cowen Orlin, *Locating Privacy in Tudor London* (Oxford: Oxford University Press, 2007).

14. Keith Wrightson, "The Politics of the Parish in Early Modern England," in *Experience of Authority*, ed. Griffiths, Fox, and Hindle, 10–46, esp. 32.

15. Margaret Pelling, "Defensive tactics: networking by female medical practitioners in early modern London," in *Communities in Early Modern England*, ed. Shepard and Withington, 38–53, esp. 38–39, observes that many historians no longer think of "community" as referring to a group that is, by definition, harmonious, static, homogeneous, or geographically contained. See also Withington and Shepard's "Introduction" in *Communities in Early Modern*, 6.

16. "If London was a matter for all England, every English man and woman had a different 'London,'" Lena Cowen Orlin writes in her introduction to *Material London, ca. 1600*, ed. Lena Cowen Orlin (Philadelphia: University of Pennsylvania Press, 2000), 11, an observation that has become commonplace in recent work on early modern London.

17. Stow, *Survey*, 1: 165.

18. Rappaport, *Worlds*, 53. This number reflects a decline from the early 1550s, when seventy-five percent of the adult male population were citizens and "free" of a company, Rappaport estimates; the percentages would continue to decline, and by the 1640s, only half the male population were freemen. The companies, of course, controlled access to commerce within the city, enforcing production standards and employment practices along with the right to engage in retail trade. They also controlled access to citizenship within London, a status for which company membership was a prerequisite. While enfranchisement was sometimes granted on the basis of patrimony or purchased by "redemption,"

most gained the freedom by completing a formal seven-year apprenticeship, a route that ostensibly allowed them to become journeymen and eventually masters over apprentices in their own shops and perhaps one day to join the ranks of the livery.

19. Although occasionally widows enjoyed some benefits of company membership, many more women labored in family workshops without the benefit of wages; strangers, for their part, struggled to make a living, often by operating under the radar of company jurisdiction but also by lobbying the royal court and city government for increased economic privileges. For discussion of citizenship and its exclusions, see Rappaport, *Worlds*, 23–60; Archer, *Pursuit*, 58–148; and Fumerton, *Unsettled*, 12–32.

20. For discussions of London's social policies, including poor relief and plague control, see Archer, *Pursuit*; and Paul Slack, *The Impact of Plague in Tudor and Stuart England* (London: Routledge & Kegan Paul, 1985).

21. Michel de Certeau, *The Practice of Everyday Life*, trans. Steven Rendall (Berkeley: University of California Press, 1984), 94, posits the sixteenth century as the beginning of the "city" as concept: "'The city,' like a proper name, thus provides a way of conceiving and constructing space on the basis of a finite number of stable, isolatable, and interconnected properties."

22. Merritt, *Imagining*, 13, observes that rather than being fragmented into "a mosaic of little worlds," as Robert Park famously characterized twentieth-century cities, early modern London gave residents access to both neighborhood associations *and* the freedoms and perils of anonymity.

23. Boulton, *Neighbourhood and Society*, 206–27, 289–95, esp. 292.

24. See, for example, Boulton, *Neighbourhood and Society*; Ian Archer, *Pursuit*; Craig Muldrew, *The Economy of Obligation: The Culture of Credit and Social Relations in Early Modern England* (Basingstoke: Macmillan, 1998); Deborah E. Harkness, *The Jewel House: Elizabethan London and the Scientific Revolution* (New Haven: Yale University Press, 2007); and Paul Griffiths, *Lost London: Change, Crime, and Control in the Capital City, 1550–1660* (Cambridge: Cambridge University Press, 2008), as well as essay collections: *Communities in Early Modern England*, ed. Shepard and Withington; *Londinopolis*, ed. Griffiths and Jenner; *Imagining Early Modern London*, ed. Merritt; and the special edition of the *Huntington Library Quarterly* 71 (2008), ed. Deborah Harkness and Jean E. Howard.

25. Joseph P. Ward, *Metropolitan Communities: Trade Guilds, Identity, and Change in Early Modern London* (Stanford: Stanford University Press, 1997), 27–44, makes the case for viewing London companies within a "metropolitan" community. He also notes that members of the Grocers' Company "lived and worked throughout the metropolis," as did members of numerous other companies, including the Vintners' and Brewers' companies.

26. See, for example, Daniel Woolf, *The Social Circulation of the Past: English Historical Culture 1500–1730* (Oxford University Press, 2003), who describes England's "historical culture" as "the perceptual and cognitive web of relations between past, present, and future" (9).

27. See, for example, Andrew McRae, *Literature and Domestic Travel in Early Modern England* (Cambridge: Cambridge University Press, 2009), which explores English domestic travel, and mobility more generally, in relation to the formation of English nationhood. For comparable work on the city of Bristol, see David Harris Sacks, *The Widening Gate: Bristol and the Atlantic Economy, 1450–1700* (Berkeley: University of California Press, 1991).

28. Henri Lefebvre, *The Production of Space*, trans. Donald Nicholson-Smith (Oxford: Blackwell, 1991), 86.

29. Lefebvre, 86–87. See also John Agnew's persuasive critique of arguments that see the nation-state as simply displacing traditional or local spatial configurations, in "Representing Space: Space, scale, and culture in social science," in *Place/Culture/Representation*, ed. James Duncan and David Ley (London: Routledge, 1993): 251–71.

30. Agnew, "Representing Space," 253.

31. Agnew, "Representing Space," 263–64.

32. Steven Mullaney's now classic study, *The Place of the Stage: License, Play, and Power in Renaissance England* (Chicago: University of Chicago Press, 1988), has been central to this debate.

33. See the foundational study of L. C. Knights, *Drama & Society in the Age of Jonson* (London: Chatto & Windus, 1937), which explores England's "development of capitalist enterprise" in conjunction with drama of the period. For alternative approaches to drama and society that productively complicate the moral economies of earlier work on Jonson and city comedy, see Don Wayne, "Drama and Society in the Age of Jonson: Shifting Grounds of Authority and Judgment in Three Major Comedies," in *Renaissance Drama* n.s. 13 (1982): 103–29; and Jonathan Haynes, *The Social Relations of Jonson's Theater* (Cambridge: Cambridge University Press, 1992).

34. Brian Gibbons, *Jacobean City Comedy: A Study of Satiric Plays by Jonson, Marston and Middleton*, 2nd ed. (London: Methuen, 1980), 4.

35. Lawrence Manley, *Literature and Culture in Early Modern London* (Cambridge: Cambridge University Press, 1995), 15–16. For leading discussions of the commercial theater and city commerce, see Jean-Christophe Agnew, *Worlds Apart: The Market and the Theater in Anglo-American Thought, 1550–1750* (Cambridge: Cambridge University Press, 1986); Douglas Bruster, *Drama and the Market in the Age of Shakespeare* (Cambridge: Cambridge University Press, 1992); Theodore B. Leinwand, *Theatre, Finance, and Society in Early Modern England* (Cambridge: Cambridge University Press, 1999); Janette Dillon, *Theatre, Court and City, 1595–1610: Drama and Social Space in London* (Cambridge: Cambridge University Press, 2000); and Jean E. Howard, *Theater of a City: The Places of London Comedy, 1598–1642* (Philadelphia: University of Pennsylvania Press, 2007).

36. Bruster, *Drama and the Market*, 10.

37. Knights, *Drama and Society*, 7.

38. Howard, *Theater of a City*, 39.

39. Manley, *Literature and Culture*, 14.

40. Merritt, introduction to *Imagining*, 23.

41. See, for example, John Michael Archer, *Citizen Shakespeare: Freemen and Aliens in the Language of the Plays* (Basingstoke: Palgrave Macmillan, 2005), who astutely explores citizenship in Shakespeare and early modern London as constituted by struggle and conflict, a "category of multilayered belonging" (16).

42. Karen Newman, *Cultural Capitals: Early Modern London and Paris* (Princeton: Princeton University Press, 2007), 44.

43. See Mary Bly, "Playing the Tourist in Early Modern London: Selling the Liberties Onstage," *PMLA* 122 (2007): 61–71, and "Carnal Geographies: Mocking and Mapping the Religious Body," in *Masculinity and the Metropolis of Vice, 1550–1650*, ed. Amanda Bailey and Roze Hentschell (Basingstoke: Palgrave Macmillan, 2010), 89–113; Adam Zucker, *The Places of Wit in Early Modern English Comedy* (Cambridge: Cambridge University Press, 2011). For other recent work on spatial relations, see John Twyning, *London Dispossessed: Literature and Social Space in the Early Modern City* (Basingstoke: Macmillan, 1998); Ian Munro, *The Figure of the Crowd in Early Modern London: The City and Its Double* (Basingstoke: Palgrave Macmillan, 2005); Howard, *Theater of a City*; Grantley, *London in Early Modern English Drama*; Bailey and Hentschell, ed., *Masculinity and the Metropolis of Vice*; Julie Sanders, *The Cultural Geography of Early Modern Drama, 1620–1650* (Cambridge: Cambridge University Press, 2011); and Natasha Korda, *Labors Lost: Women's Work and the Early Modern English Stage* (Philadelphia: University of Pennsylvania Press, 2011).

44. Hannah Arendt, *The Human Condition*, 2nd edition (Chicago: University of Chicago Press, 1998), 7. "Plurality is the condition of human action," Arendt writes, "because we are all the same, that is, human in such a way that nobody is ever the same as anyone else who ever lived, lives, or will live" (8).

45. Ben Jonson, *Every Man in His Humour*, ed. Robert S. Miola, *The Revels Plays* (Manchester: Manchester University Press, 2000).

46. T. S. Eliot, *Essays on Elizabethan Drama* (New York: Harcourt, Brace, and Company, 1932), 93–94.

47. Manley, *Literature and Culture*, 2.

48. Manley, *Literature and Culture*; see also Lorna Hutson's nuanced analysis of intrigue plotting and market processes, "The Displacement of the Market in Jacobean City Comedy," *London Journal* 14 (1989): 3–16.

49. Mary Thomas Crane, "What Was Performance?" *Criticism* 43 (2002): 169–87, esp. 172–73; defenders of the early modern stage, Crane explains, tended to understand theater as involving material practice, using terms like performance, practice, exercise, or use, whereas critics of the stage deployed terms like showing or playing, which suggested frivolity and deceit.

50. Crane, 175.

51. E. K. Chambers, *The Elizabethan Stage*, 4 vols. (Oxford: Clarendon Press, 1923), 4: 325.

52. The OED defines "practice" as repeated performances of an activity or skill with the aim of proficiency (2.a.b.c) and as the pursuit or performance of one's occupation, profession, or trade (1.a.b.c.).

53. Alfred Harbage, *Shakespeare and the Rival Traditions* (New York: Macmillan, 1952).

54. Howard, *Theater of a City*, 3.

55. Cordatus's move from presupposing performances to an authorized volume of knowledge neatly encapsulates a version, in reverse, of the paradigm William N. West lays out in his capacious study, *Theatres and Encyclopedias in Early Modern Europe* (Cambridge: Cambridge University Press, 2002). West's study charts developments between encyclopedia and theater that, by the seventeenth century, produced a new standard of knowing, involving "the performance of knowledge" (2). West categorizes *Every Man Out of His Humor* as a hybrid form, "a theatricalization of the encyclopedic combinatory method" (147).

56. As West points out, the opening cry of "Make room!" serves in morality plays and interludes as "a physical, actual displacement of ordinary activity," and an intervention "literally from *within* the crowd, not from one side of it"; these plays thus "present themselves not as descriptions drawn from a distance, but as events, as interventions into the larger world around them" (*Theatres and Encyclopedias*, 113).

57. See Robert Weimann's classic essay, "Bifold Authority in Shakespeare's Theatre," *Shakespeare Quarterly* 39 (1988): 401–17, and *Author's Pen and Actor's Voice: Playing and Writing in Shakespeare's Theatre*, ed. Helen Higbee and William West (Cambridge: Cambridge University Press, 2000), and West's *Theatres and Encyclopedias*.

58. West, *Theatres and Encyclopedias*, 141.

59. Samuel Weber, *Theatricality as Medium* (New York: Fordham University Press, 2004), 116. In a related argument, Weber elegantly deconstructs Debord's assertion in *The Society of the Spectacle*—" 'The world the spectacle holds up to view is at once *here* and *elsewhere*' "—to point out that the usage of " 'at once' constitutes the challenge of theatricality to every system of thought based on the priority of identity and self-presence" (*Theatricality as Medium*, 13). See also John Guillory, "Enlightening Mediation," in *This Is Enlightenment*, ed. Clifford Siskin and William Warner (Chicago: University of Chicago Press, 2010), 37–63, esp. 56, which traces the Western preference for representation over that of medium back to a passage in Aristotle's *Poetics*, which, in emphasizing mimesis, sets aside "the question of 'in what' form a representation is transmitted."

60. Weber, *Theatricality as Medium*, 7.

61. Weber, *Theatricality as Medium*, 15.

62. Weber, *Theatricality as Medium*, 24.

63. West, *Theatres and Encyclopedias*, 47–48. In Chapter 2, "The idea of a theatre," West traces conflicting notions of the word "theater" in this period, as a primarily visual medium or common "looking place," or, following Aristotle, as imitative and active.

64. Plato, *The Laws*, trans. A. E. Taylor, 700–701a, in Plato, *The Collected Dialogues*, ed. Edith Hamilton and Huntington Cairns (Princeton: Princeton University Press, 1973), 1924; quoted in Weber, *Theatricality as Medium*, 33.

65. Plato, *The Laws*, 701a–c, quoted in Weber, *Theatricality as Medium*, 33. For Plato, the theatrocracy was worse than democracy, which was at least, in his view, "confined to art, and composed of free men."

66. Jacques Rancière, *The Emancipated Spectator*, trans. Gregory Elliott (London: Verso, 2009), 2.

67. See, for example, Jeremy Lopez, *Theatrical Convention and Audience Response in Early Modern Drama* (Cambridge: Cambridge University Press, 2003), which relies on the evidence of play texts, and Erika T. Lin, *Shakespeare and the Materiality of Performance* (New York: Palgrave Macmillan, 2012), which examines the early modern stage's presentational or non-mimetic practices and conventions. For an exemplary exception to this emphasis on play texts and theatrical materiality, see Charles Whitney, *Early Responses to Renaissance Drama* (Cambridge: Cambridge University Press, 2006), which examines the fragmentary responses of individual playgoers from various social ranks.

68. Henry S. Turner, "Toward a New Theatricality?" *Renaissance Drama*, n.s. 40 (2012): 29–35, esp. 35.

69. The few studies of London plays that do include histories tend to focus on what Howard calls "chronicle comedies," the celebratory civic plays such as Dekker's *Shoemaker's Holiday* or Heywood's *If You Know Not Me You Know Nobody, Part 2* whose London engagements are more obvious and more sustained; see Jean E. Howard, "Competing Ideologies of Commerce in Thomas Heywood's *If You Know Not Me You Know Nobody, Part II*," in *The Culture of Capital: Property, Cities, and Knowledge in Early Modern England*, ed. Henry S. Turner (London: Routledge, 2002), 163–82.

## *1. Extending Credit and the* Henry IV *Plays*



1. Quotations from *1 Henry IV* follow the Arden Shakespeare, *King Henry IV, Part 1*, ed. David Scott Kastan (London: Thomson Learning, 2002); quotations from *The Famous Victories of Henry V* follow *The Oldcastle Controversy: Sir John Oldcastle, Part 1 and The Famous Victories of Henry V*, ed. Peter Corbin and Douglas Sedge (Manchester: Manchester University Press, 1991).

2. E. K. Chambers, *Shakespeare: A Survey* (London: Sidgwick & Jackson, 1925), 118, cited in *A New Variorum Edition of Shakespeare: Henry the Fourth, Part 1*, ed. Samuel Burdett Hemingway (Philadelphia: J. B. Lippincott, 1936), 402.

3. In *1 Henry IV*, where nearly a third of the lines appear in comic scenes, David Kastan points out that twentieth-century critics have tended to follow Fredson Bower's lead in subordinating "subplot to main plot, commoners to aristocrats, comedy to history"; Kastan adds, however, that "the actual achievement of the play seems to me less neat and stable than this suggests—not therefore less good or less interesting but less willing to organize its disparate voices

into hierarchies . . . ." (15). For a recent exception to this emphasis on parody plotting, see Alan Stewart, "Shakespeare and the Carriers," *Shakespeare Quarterly* 58 (2007): 431–64, who closely examines the role of carrier in the play and in the late 1590s.

4. Quotations from *2 Henry IV* follow the Arden Shakespeare, *King Henry IV, Part 2*, ed. A. R. Humphreys (London: Methuen, 1966). In identifying material credit with commoners rather than kings, Shakespeare departs from *Holinshed's Chronicles*, which abound with references to Henry IV's money problems, detailing the parliamentary debates about subsidies and taxes needed to maintain the king's wars. See *Holinshed's Chronicles of England, Scotland, and Ireland* (1587), ed. Henry Ellis, 6 vols. (London: J. Johnston, 1808), 3: 27–31.

5. Although more concerned with politics than economics, most New Historicist discussions of the *Henry IV* plays tend to regard economic interests as inherently oppressive. See, for example, Stephen Greenblatt's influential essay "Invisible Bullets," which, in its revised version in *Shakespearean Negotiations: The Circulation of Social Energy in Renaissance England* (Berkeley: University of California Press, 1988), 21–65, applies late-sixteenth-century "evangelical colonialism" to Lancastrian domestic policy. By contrast, Jean E. Howard and Phyllis Rackin, in *Engendering a Nation: A feminist account of Shakespeare's English histories* (New York: Routledge, 1997), 160–85, assume a more complicated model of economic politics, one that sees the commercial activity of the tavern as having the potential to challenge fixed hierarchical structures.

6. H. R. Coursen, *The Leasing Out of England: Shakespeare's Second Henriad* (Washington: University Press of America, 1982), 3.

7. Sandra K. Fischer, "'He means to pay': Value and Metaphor in the Lancastrian Tetralogy," *Shakespeare Quarterly* 40 (1989): 149–64, esp. 152–53.

8. Even Lars Engle, in *Shakespearean Pragmatism: Market of His Time* (Chicago: University of Chicago Press, 1993), 127, although he locates Shakespeare's pragmatism in the transactions of the early modern market, attends primarily to matters of kingship, arguing that the plays show how "royal power is pragmatically produced in, and to some extent by, an economy of credit and negotiation." Jesse Lander, "'Crack'd Crowns' and Counterfeit Sovereigns: The Crisis of Value in *1 Henry IV*," *Shakespeare Studies* 30 (2002): 137–61, also concentrates on sovereign authority, but his essay persuasively links the crisis of value in *1 Henry IV* with Tudor difficulties with inflation and the fluctuating value of coins.

9. For early modern interpretations of credit, I am indebted to Craig Muldrew, *The Economy of Obligation: The Culture of Credit and Social Relations in Early Modern England* (New York: St. Martin's Press, 1998). See also Theodore B. Leinwand, *Theater, finance and society in early modern England* (Cambridge: Cambridge University Press, 1999); Victoria Kahn, *Wayward Contracts: The Crisis of Political Obligation in England, 1640–1674* (Princeton: Princeton University Press, 2004); Ceri Sullivan, *The Rhetoric of Credit: Merchants in Early Modern Writing* (Madison: Fairleigh Dickinson University Press, 2002); and Amanda Bailey, *Of*

*Bondage: Debt, Property, and Personhood in Early Modern England* (Philadelphia: University of Pennsylvania Press, 2013).

10. Muldrew emphasizes that mobility might be downward as well as upward, as debt loads grew (3). For a discussion of credit networks operating on the city's periphery, see Marjorie K. McIntosh, "Money Lending on the Periphery of London, 1300–1600," *Albion* 20 (1988): 557–71.

11. For this brave act, the story goes, Walworth was knighted by the king, an honor extended to all subsequent mayors, and his dagger placed in the city's shield. See T. Nelson, *The Device of the Pageant* (1590), and Robert Withington, "The Lord Mayor's Show for 1590s," *Modern Language Notes* 33 (1918): 8–13.

12. Arthur B. Ferguson, *The Chivalric Tradition in Renaissance England* (Washington: Folger Books, 1986), 78. The city elite, Ferguson writes, "were able to see themselves in the light of the current chivalric romanticism because they accepted hierarchy as ordained and the values of the aristocracy, its conventions, and its ways of weighing dignity and honor, as given. Indeed, their own tradesmen-heroes usually turn out to be themselves of aristocratic origin." See also Laura Stevenson, *Praise and Paradox: Merchants and Craftsmen in Elizabethan Popular Literature* (Cambridge: Cambridge University Press, 1984), 6, who writes that "Elizabethan praise of bourgeois men was expressed in the rhetoric—and by extension, in the terms of social paradigms—of the aristocracy."

13. Lawrence Manley, *Literature and Culture in Early Modern London* (Cambridge: Cambridge University Press, 1995), 130. "It was within and through the context of this complex neofeudal situation that the new fictions of urban settlement were elaborated," Manley contends.

14. Manley, *Literature and Culture*, 128. See also Stevenson, *Praise and Paradox*, 107–8.

15. Many plays in the period connected the city and court through the marketplace, though not necessarily in the context of English history; see Janette Dillon, *Theatre, Court and City, 1595–1610: Drama and Social Space in London* (Cambridge: Cambridge University Press, 2000), 15, whose wide-ranging study explores the "mobility of relations between court and city" in relation to the market and the theater.

16. See E. K. Chambers, *The Elizabethan Stage*, 4 vols. (Oxford: Clarendon Press, 1923), 2: 443–45, for a history the Boar's Head in the sixteenth and seventeenth centuries. The plays, of course, do not directly identify the tavern with the Boar's Head, but editors and playgoers have long taken the prince's query about Falstaff's whereabouts in *2 Henry IV*—"Doth the old boar feed in the old frank?"—together with Bardolph's answer, "At the old place, my lord, in Eastcheap" (2.2.138–40), as proof enough.

17. John Stow, *A Survey of London*, ed. Charles Lethbridge Kingsford, 2 vols. (Oxford: Clarendon Press, 1971), 1: 216–17. Stow tries to set the record straight by recounting an incident in the eleventh year of Henry's reign, when the king's sons visited Eastcheap for a late night breakfast and got into a ruckus requiring the mayor, sheriffs, and citizens to restore order.

18. John Wheeler, *A Treatise of Commerce* (Middelburge, 1601), sigs. B1r–B2v.

19. Thomas Tusser, *Five hundreth pointes of good husbandrie* (London, 1586), 21.

20. In the words of the preacher in Sir Thomas Wilson's *A Discourse Upon Usury* , ed. R. H. Tawney (New York: Harcourt Brace, 1925), 202, self-interest was replacing neighborliness, as men lent money more to "seeke their owne gain, than anything the benefit of theire Christian neyghbour."

21. Wilson, 232. See also Richard Johnson, who reminds his readers in *Look on Me, London* (1613) that during the reign of Henry III, the "good cittizens of London, in one night, slew five hundred Jewes, for that a Jew tooke of a Christian a penny in the shilling usury, and ever after got them banished the citty," quoted from *Illustrations of Early English Popular Literature*, ed. J. Payne Collier, 2 vols. (New York: Benjamin Blom, 1966), 2: 22–23.

22. Muldrew, *Economy of Obligation*, 315.

23. Kahn, *Wayward Contracts*, 7.

24. Muldrew, *Economy of Obligation*, emphasizes the increasing importance of personal wealth in establishing credit during this period; according to one late-sixteenth-century writer: "'commonly no man is accompted worthy of much honor, or of great trust and credit, unlesse he be rich'" (153). See also Susan Dwyer Amussen, *An Ordered Society: Gender and Class in Early Modern England* (Oxford: Basil Blackwell, 1988), 152–53.

25. Thomas Lodge, *An Alarum against Vsurers* (1584) in *The Complete Works of Thomas Lodge*, 4 vols. (Glasgow: Robert Anderson, 1883), 1: 13. See also Wilson, who warns of the dangers to the commonwealth when a landed gentleman is "eaten up by an usurer" (356).

26. Roger Hacket, *A Sermon Needfull for Theese Times* (Oxford, 1591), sig. B3r.

27. See Richard L. Greaves, *Society and Religion in Elizabethan England* (Minneapolis: University of Minnesota Press, 1981), 609.

28. Stow, 1: 225.

29. Charles Gibbon, quoted from Norman Jones, *God and the Moneylenders: Usury and Law in Early Modern England* (Oxford: Basil Blackwell, 1989), 148.

30. Miles Mosse, *The Arraignment and Conviction of Usurie* (London,1595), 28–30.

31. For a valuable overview of the usury debate and the compromise of the 1571 statute, see Tawney's introduction in Wilson, *Discourse Upon Usury*, 157.

32. Edward Misselden, *The Circle of Commerce* (London,1623), 17 (quoted from the 1969 Da Capo Press facsimile edition).

33. As William Scott later declared , the citizen was "made compleat" by his "just, pleasing, profitable wayes" (*An Essay of Drapery or the Compleate Citizen* [London, 1635], sig. B2v). See also Joyce Oldham Appleby, *Economic Thought and Ideology in Seventeenth-Century England* (Princeton: Princeton University Press, 1978).

34. See Kahn, *Wayward Contracts*, who in discussing these debates points to the link between commerce, contract, and debt in the period. Contract law, she writes, "developed in response to the increasing commercialism of English society and the astonishing explosion of legal actions for debt" (41).

35. Johannes Nider, *On the Contracts of Merchants* (1468), trans. Charles H. Reeves, ed. Ronald B. Shuman (Norman: University of Oklahoma Press, 1966), 7–8.

36. Christopher St. Germain, *Doctor and Student* (1531), ed. T. F. T. Plucknett and J. L. Barton (London: The Selden Society, 1974), 228.

37. Thomas Elyot, *The boke named the Governour*, quoted from Muldrew, *Economy of Obligation*, 135.

38. *A Godlie Treatice Concerning The lawfull use of ritches* (London, 1578), sig. L2$^{r}$.

39. William West, *Symbolaeographia* (London, 1590), sig. ¶¶.1 (quoted here from the 1975 Theatrum Orbis Terrarum facsimile of the Bodleian copy).

40. Wilson, 287.

41. See, for example, Lodge, *An Alarum*, and Richard Johnson, *Look On Me, London*.

42. This remark is attributed to Philip Henslowe by the Lady Elizabeth's Men in a formal petition charging him with oppressive financial practices; quoted from E. K. Chambers, *Elizabethan Stage*, 1: 367.

43. C. W. Brooks, *Pettyfoggers and Vipers of the Commonwealth: The 'Lower Branch' of the Legal Profession in Early Modern England* (Cambridge: Cambridge University Press, 1986), 57–71. A tally of cases before the Court of Common Pleas in Michaelmas Term 1606, for example, shows that "men below the rank of gentlemen were involved as plaintiffs in 71 percent of all litigation, and that they were a good deal more likely to sue their social superiors than to be sued by them" (Brooks, 61).

44. Muldrew is careful to emphasize the limits of this equality, however, noting that the "powerful justificatory force of contract did nothing to address the increasing inequality of accumulation, but it did give the poor equality of *access* to right" (*Economy of Obligation*, 318).

45. Muldrew, *Economy of Obligation*, 133. See Mervyn James, *Society, Politics and Culture: Studies in Early Modern England* (Cambridge: Cambridge University Press, 1986), 274–75.

46. Michael D. Bristol, *Carnival and Theater: Plebian Culture and the Structure of Authority in Renaissance England* (London: Methuen, 1985), 3.

47. For discussions of alehouses and taverns, see Andrew McRae, *Literature and Domestic Travel in Early Modern England* (Cambridge: Cambridge University Press, 2009); Peter Clark, *The English Alehouse: A Social History 1200–1830* (London and New York: Longman, 1983); Theodore B. Leinwand, "Spongy plebs, mighty lords, and the dynamics of the alehouse," *Journal of Medieval and Renaissance Studies* 19 (1989): 159–84; Patricia Fumerton, "Not Home: Alehouses, Ballads, and the Vagrant Husband in Early Modern England," *Journal of Medieval and Early Modern Studies* 32 (2002): 493–518.

48. Thomas Dekker, "The Gull's Horn-Book," *Thomas Dekker*, ed. E. D. Pendry (Cambridge: Harvard University Press, 1968), 103.

49. *Acts of the Privy Council, AD 1596–1597*, ed. John Roche Dasent (London: Majesty's Stationary Office, 1902), 26: 95.

50. For an especially insightful discussion of the Coventry scene that reads Falstaff as "both exploiter and spokesman for the exploited," see Charles Whitney, "Festivity and Topicality in the Coventry Scene of *1 Henry IV*," *English Literary Renaissance* 24 (1994): 410–48, esp. 425. See also Harry Berger Jr., "The Prince's Dog: Falstaff and the Perils of Speech-Prefixity," *Shakespeare Quarterly* 49 (1998): 40–73.

51. For Falstaff, and perhaps for Shakespeare, bad faith becomes a marker of high social status. "Falstaff is the first major joke by the English against their class system; he is a picture of how badly you can behave, and still get away with it, if you are a gentleman—a mere common rogue would not have been nearly so funny," William Empson remarks in his essay, "Falstaff," in *Essays on Shakespeare*, ed. David B. Pirie (Cambridge: Cambridge University Press, 1986), 29–78, esp. 46.

52. Fischer, 152.

53. Greenblatt, 52–53.

54. Coursen, 109.

55. Greenblatt, 44.

56. As Elliot Krieger, *A Marxist Study of Shakespeare's Comedies* (New York: Barnes and Noble, 1979), remarks on Francis's dilemma: "Service according to an objective, regulative time schedule, as a force opposed to the subjective, whimsical demands for immediate gratification imposed by a master, works, in *1 Henry IV*, as a liberating force" (156).

57. Engle, 111.

58. Long associated with the dangers of unregulated commerce, engrossers garnered even more opprobrium in the late 1590s when the government blamed the dearth of corn on the monopolistic practices of these "bad-disposed persons" who, like those who caused the death of Robin Ostler, preferred "their own private gain above the public good" (*Tudor Royal Proclamations, The Later Tudors [1588–1603]*, ed. Paul L. Hughes and James F. Larkin, 3 vols. [New Haven: Yale University Press, 1969], 3: 194).

59. See David Scott Kastan's discussion of Henry IV's "utopian solution to the problems of difference," in "'The King Hath Many Marching in His Coats,' or, What Did You Do During the War, Daddy?" in *Shakespeare Left and Right*, ed. Ivo Kamps (London: Routledge, 1991), 242.

60. Samuel Johnson, quoted from *The Second Part of Henry the Fourth: A New Variorum Edition*, ed. Matthias A. Shaaber (Philadelphia: J.B. Lippincott, 1940), 319.

61. See Muldrew, *Economy of Obligation*, 95–119. For a study that focuses explicitly on debt bonds, on stage and off, see Bailey, *Of Bondage*.

62. For general discussions of the law of contract, see J. H. Baker, *An Introduction to English Legal History* (London: Butterworths, 1971), 174–204; A. W. B. Simpson, *A History of the Common Law of Contract: The Rise of the Action of Assumpsit* (Oxford: Clarendon Press, 1975); and *Anson's Law of Contract*, ed. A. G. G. Guest (Oxford: Clarendon Press, 1969).

63. This is not to suggest that *assumpsit* ignored the materiality of the exchange. The concept of "consideration" served to link the promise to an actual exchange—that is, the circumstances motivating the promise—and in this sense fulfilled a function similar to, though not identical with, *quid pro quo*. For further discussion of the complicated relationship between *quid pro quo* and consideration in the sixteenth century, see Simpson, *Common Law of Contract*, 316–488; and J. H. Baker, "Origins of the 'Doctrine' of Consideration, 1535–1585," in *The Legal Profession and the Common Law: Historical Essays* (London: Hambledon Press, 1986), 369–91.

64. For discussions of Slade's Case, see Edward Coke, *The Reports of Sir Edward Coke*, ed. George Wilson, 7 vols. (London: J. Rivington, 1777), 2: 91–95; A. W. B. Simpson, "The Place of Slade's Case in the History of Contract," *The Law Quarterly Review* 74 (1958): 381–96; H. K. Lücke, "Slade's Case and the Origin of the Common Counts, Parts 1–3," *The Law Quarterly Review* 81 (1965): 422–45, 539–61, and *Law Quarterly Review* 82 (1966): 81–96; J. H. Baker, "New Light on *Slade's Case*, Part I," *Cambridge Law Journal* 29 (1971): 51–67; Baker, "New Light on *Slade's Case*, Part II," *Cambridge Law Journal* 29 (1971): 213–36; Baker and S.F.C. Milsom, *Sources of English Legal History in Private Law to 1750* (London: Butterworth, 1986), 420–41; David Ibbetson, "Assumpsit and Debt in the Early Sixteenth Century: The Origins of the Indebitatus Count," *Cambridge Law Journal* 41 (1982): 142–61, and Ibbetson, "Sixteenth Century Contract Law: *Slade's Case* in Context," *Oxford Journal of Legal Studies* 4 (1984): 295–317.

65. In the words of legal scholar J. H. Baker, the question was, simply put: "Did a contract contain in itself an undertaking to perform the duty which it generated, even though the contracting parties did not use the express words 'I promise' or 'I undertake'?" (Baker, "New Light, Part II," 226).

66. Coke, *Reports*, 94b.

67. As Francis Bacon and others argued on behalf of the defendant, *assumpsit* required deceit, and failure to pay did not necessarily constitute the intention to deceive. Coke's response put the matter bluntly: "It is clear that when a man contracts with another to pay money or to do anything, and does not perform it, this is a deceit." Quoted from Baker, "New Light, Part I," 62.

68. Baker, "New Light, Part I," 55.

69. Baker, "New Light, Part II," 220.

70. In allowing the action of *assumpsit* in matters of debt, Coke's ruling allowed plaintiffs to avoid the corrupt practice of wager of law associated with actions of debt. By the 1590s, compurgation, or wager of law, was being openly abused by the practice of hiring professional oath-helpers, or "knights of the post," as they were dubbed, in place of the friends and neighbors who had traditionally testified to a defendant's reputation or trustworthiness (Baker, "New Light, Part II," 228). As Coke writes on Slade's Case: "for now experience proves that mens consciences grow so large that the respect of their private advantage rather induces men (and chiefly those who have declining estates) to perjury" (Coke, *Reports*, 95b).

71. As Victoria Kahn persuasively concludes: "If in the older view of obligation, promises were to be kept because of a transcendent moral law ("pacta sunt servanda"), in Slade promises were to be kept because they had been articulated in the shared medium of language and ratified by the exchange of other material signs" (*Wayward Contracts*, 47). See also the trenchant discussion of Slade's case by David Harris Sacks, "The Promise and the Contract in Early Modern England: Slade's Case in Perspective," in *Rhetoric and Law in Early Modern Europe*, ed. Victoria Kahn and Lorna Hutson (New Haven: Yale University Press, 2001), 28–53.

72. While disputes involving marriage contracts usually came under the jurisdiction of the church courts, when deceit or bad faith was involved in promises of land, movables, or money made in connection with a marriage, then the case was actionable under *assumpsit*. See Baker, ed. *The Reports of Sir John Spelman*, 2 vols. (London: Selden Society, 1978), 2: 269, 277, and Lücke, "Slade's Case, Part 1," 435–37.

73. If Falstaff's deployment of erotic credit here and elsewhere in the *Henriad* recalls feudal relations of service, it also points to the ways in which eroticism is not necessarily antithetical to commercial exchange and contract. See, for example, Walter Benn Michaels, "The Phenomenology of Contract," in his *The Gold Standard: The Logic of Naturalism* (Berkeley: University of California Press, 1987), 115–36.

74. As Jonathan Crewe observes in his essay, "Reforming Prince Hal: The Sovereign Inheritor in *2 Henry IV*," *Renaissance Drama*, n.s. 21 (1990): 225–42, the peaceful succession in this play rests on the likeness, or equivalence, between father and son: "what this situation allows is that wildness . . . can *consensually* be transferred from the scapegrace son to the father as original usurper, on one hand allowing it to be buried with the corpse and on the other permitting the instantly reformed son to become the legitimate heir" (236).

75. See Lorna Hutson, "Not the King's Two Bodies: Reading the 'Body Politic' in Shakespeare's *Henry IV*, Parts 1 and 2," in *Rhetoric and Law*, ed. Kahn and Hutson, who similarly reads the Prince's intentions and promises within the context of assumpsit.

76. West, *Symbolaeographia* (London, 1590), sig. ¶¶.1.

77. See Laurie E. Osborne, "*Crisis of Degree* in Shakespeare's *Henriad*," *Studies in English Literature 1500–1900* 25 (1985): 337–59.

78. Robert Weimann, "Thresholds to Memory and Commodity in Shakespeare's Endings," *Representations* 53 (1996): 1–20, esp. 2.

79. Luke Wilson, "Promissory Performances," *Renaissance Drama*, n.s. 25 (1994): 59–87.

80. For a discussion of the shift from patronage to commerce, see Kathleen E. McLuskie, "The Poets' Royal Exchange: Patronage and Commerce in Early Modern Drama," *The Yearbook of English Studies* 21 (1991): 53–62.

81. Weimann, "Thresholds," 17.

82. Weimann, "Thresholds," 4.

83. Weimann, "Thresholds," 1.

2. *Differentiating Collaboration: Protest and Playwriting and* Sir Thomas More



1. Quotations from the play follow *Sir Thomas More: The Arden Shakespeare, Third Series*, ed. John Jowett (London: Methuen, 2011).

2. Jowett, introduction to *Sir Thomas More*, 39. For other recent discussions of the play's London setting, see Tracey Hill, "'The Cittie is in an uproare': Staging London in *The Booke of Sir Thomas More*," *Early Modern Literary Studies* 11.1 (2005): 2.1–19. Two cudgel-carrying apprentices, for example, speak of meeting at the Artillery Yard at Bunhill and of going to breakfast in St. Anne's Lane, with the "head drawer at the Mitre by the Great Conduit" (*Sir Thomas More*, OT1b.4–5).

3. Much has been written about the topicality of anti-alien sentiments in the 1590s, a point I take up later in this chapter. For another point of intersection, see Richard Rowland, *Thomas Heywood's Theatre, 1599–1639: Locations, Translations, and Conflict* (Farnham: Ashgate, 2010), who writes that in recreating early-sixteenth-century Cheapside on stage, the playwrights "simultaneously evoke the Cheapside in which a crowd of almost two thousand wrecked the pillories in the disturbances of the mid–1590s," thereby inviting potential audiences "to reconstruct" past acts of resistance "imaginatively in the streets in which they still lived and worked" (30–31).

4. See Jowett, *Sir Thomas More*, 139.

5. Jowett observes that Tilney "expressed his strongest hostility" in the play to these lines, marking out Lincoln's speech horizontally, line by line, and again with a vertical line and a large X in the left margin (*Sir Thomas More*, 357).

6. Paul Slack, introduction to *Rebellion, Popular Protest and the Social Order in Early Modern England* (Cambridge: Cambridge University Press, 1984), 1. Following the work of E. P. Thompson and Natalie Zemon Davis, recent work avoids seeing protest simply as disorderly or chaotic or as a spontaneous combustion of festive revelry. See also Richard Wilson's discussion of the Southwark riots of 1592, where "clothing workers . . . turned, for want of an ideology, to a time-honoured cultural script"—the Midsummer festival—immediately taken by the authorities as a sign not of revelry but of rebellion ("A Mingled Yarn: Shakespeare and the Cloth Workers," in *Will Power: Essays on Shakespearean Authority* [Detroit: Wayne State University Press, 1993], 22–44, esp. 35).

7. See Jeffrey Masten, *Textual Intercourse: Collaboration, Authorship, and Sexualities in Renaissance Drama* (Cambridge: Cambridge University Press, 1997); Gordon McMullan, *The Politics of Unease in the Plays of John Fletcher* (Amherst: University of Massachusetts Press, 1994); Brian Vickers, *Shakespeare, Co-Author: A Historical Study of Five Collaborative Plays* (Oxford: Oxford University Press, 2002); and Heather Anne Hirschfeld, *Joint Enterprises: Collaborative Drama and the Institutionalization of the English Renaissance Theater* (Amherst: University of Mas-

sachusetts Press, 2004). See also earlier foundational work: Gerald Eades Bentley, "Collaboration," in *The Profession of Dramatist in Shakespeare's Time 1590–1642* (Princeton: Princeton University Press, 1971), 197–234; and Stephen Orgel, "What Is a Text?" in *Research Opportunities in Renaissance Drama* 24 (1981): 3–6.

8. Bentley, 199. According to Neil Carson, *A Companion to Henslowe's Diary* (Cambridge: Cambridge University Press, 1987), 82 percent of the plays performed at the Rose in spring/summer 1598 and 60 percent of those performed in fall/winter 1598 were collaboratively written (57).

9. Eric Rasmussen, "The Revision of Scripts," in *A New History of Early English Drama*, ed. John D. Cox and David Scott Kastan (New York: Columbia University Press, 1997), 442.

10. Paul Werstine, "Close Contrivers: Nameless Collaborators in Early Modern London Plays," *Elizabethan Theatre* 15 (2002): 3–20, esp. 7.

11. W. W. Greg, ed., *The Book of Sir Thomas More* (Oxford: Malone Society, 1911).

12. The recent rejection of attribution in favor of collaborative writing and theatrical practice in *Sir Thomas More* was brilliantly launched by Scott McMillin, *The Elizabethan Theatre and "The Book of Sir Thomas More"* (Ithaca: Cornell University Press, 1987); see also Elizabeth Pittenger, "Aliens in the Corpus: Shakespeare's Books in the Age of the Cyborg," in *Prosthetic Territories: Politics and Hypertechnologies*, ed. Gabriel Brahm, Jr. and Mark Driscoll (Boulder: Westview Press, 1995), 204–18; Jeffrey Masten, "*More* or Less: Editing the Collaborative," *Shakespeare Studies* 29 (2001): 109–31; and Werstine, "Close Contrivers."

13. Speculation about Shakespeare and *More* began with Richard Simpson, "Are There Any Extant MSS. in Shakespeare's Handwriting?" in *Notes and Queries* 4th ser., 8 (July 1, 1871): 1–3. For an admirably concise and balanced account of the debate over Hand D, see Jowett, who concludes that "currently, the case for Shakespeare looks more secure than ever. But the collaborative nature of playmaking, and of revising this play in particular, should be kept in view. Shakespeare was revising another dramatist's work. Revision takes many forms" (*Sir Thomas More*, 437–53, esp. 452). For recent arguments against the attribution of Hand D to Shakespeare, see: Arthur F. Kinney, "Text, Context, and Authorship of *The Booke of Sir Thomas Moore*" in *Pilgrimage for Love: Essays in Early Modern Literature in Honor of Josephine A. Roberts*, ed. Sigrid King (Tempe: Arizona Center for Medieval and Renaissance Studies, 1999), 133–60; and Paul Werstine, "Shakespeare, *More* or Less: A. W. Pollard and Twentieth-Century Shakespeare Editing," *Florilegium* 16 (1999): 125–45.

14. See Margreta de Grazia and Peter Stallybrass, "The Materiality of the Shakespearean Text," *SQ* 44 (1993): 255–83, esp. 277–79; and Werstine, who refers to the *More* manuscript as "the site upon which the metaphysics of authorship has been centred for most of this century" ("Close Contrivers," 7). For reconsiderations of Shakespeare as "co-author," see Vickers, as well as the critique of the "new orthodoxy" of collaborative studies by Jeffrey Knapp, "What Is a Co-Author?" in *Representations* 89 (2005): 1–29.

15. John Jowett, ed., introduction to *The Life of Timon of Athens by William Shakespeare and Thomas Middleton* (Oxford: Oxford University Press, 2004), 144.

16. Harold Jenkins, "Supplement to the Introduction," in *The Book of Sir Thomas More*, ed. W. W. Greg (1911; rpt. Oxford: Malone Society, 1961), xl; Carol A. Chillington, "Playwrights at Work: Henslowe's, Not Shakespeare's, *Book of Sir Thomas More*," *ELR* 10 (1980): 439–79, esp. 439–40; see also Greg's observation that "no attempt is made to sew the loose ends into decent continuity" (*Book of Sir Thomas More* [1911], xv).

17. Vittorio Gabrieli and Giorgio Melchiori, eds., *"Sir Thomas More": A Play by Anthony Munday and Others* (Manchester: Manchester University Press, 1990), 30. Percy Simpson, for example, dismissed this and similar plays as "dramatised biography . . . a narrowing down of the chronicle play proper, which in Shakespeare's hands acquired a national significance" ("The Play of 'Sir Thomas More' and Shakespeare's Hand In it," *The Library*, 3rd ser., 8 [1917]: 79–96, esp. 80).

18. The *Riverside Shakespeare*, like many complete works, reprints only the lines by Hand D, and its editor, G. Blakemore Evans, judges the play to be "negligible," a chronicle history of "bourgeois sympathies" that "never rises above more or less competent mediocrity," in "*Sir Thomas More*: The Additions Ascribed to Shakespeare," in G. Blakemore Evans, gen. ed., *The Riverside Shakespeare*, 2d ed. (Boston: Houghton Mifflin, 1997), 1775–79, esp. 1777.

19. Refusing to study the manuscript as "a collection of paleographical clues" (17), McMillin radically expanded the scholarly conversation about *More*, reframing questions about collaboration in relation to theatrical practices rather than attribution. The Revels text of *Sir Thomas More*, edited by Gabrieli and Melchiori, soon followed, offering an accessible version of the play. Jowett's *Arden 3* edition offers the benefits of an extensive critical and editorial apparatus, and a text that clearly tracks the various hands and revisions for readers, presenting a play that is at once complex *and* navigable.

20. Jeffrey Masten, "Playwrighting: Authorship and Collaboration," in *A New History of Early English Drama*, 357–82; esp. 366. Masten's work has been central to my thinking about collaboration; my differences from him are intended as additions to the conversation he has so ably reframed.

21. Charles R. Forker and Joseph Candido, "Wit, Wisdom, and Theatricality in *The Book of Sir Thomas More*," *Shakespeare Studies* 13 (1980): 85–104, esp. 86.

22. David Bevington, *Tudor Drama and Politics: A Critical Approach to Topical Meaning* (Cambridge: Harvard University Press, 1968), 256; see also William B. Long, "The Occasion of *The Book of Sir Thomas More*," in *Shakespeare and "Sir Thomas More": Essays on the play and its Shakespearean interest*, ed. T. H. Howard-Hill (Cambridge: Cambridge University Press, 1989), 45–56.

23. Étienne Balibar, "Citizen Subject," in *Who Comes after the Subject?*, ed. Eduardo Cadava, Peter Connor, and Jean-Luc Nancy (New York: Routledge, 1991), 33–57, esp. 40. Following recent theoretical work on citizenship, this essay adopts a broad definition of "citizen" that extends from "citizenship-as-legal-status" to include a more modern notion of "citizenship-as-activity"; see, for

example, Will Kymlicka and Wayne Norman, "Return of the Citizen: A Survey of Recent Work on Citizenship Theory," in *Theorizing Citizenship*, ed. Ronald Beiner (Albany: SUNY Press, 1995): 283–322. This is not to deny the hierarchies and exclusions that restricted London citizenship to those adult males admitted to "the freedom" of a livery company (and thereby excluded most women and servants, wage laborers, and some professionals alongside the city's "alien" populations) but rather to render more visible the complex processes constituting the collective actions of London's differentiated urban population. See John Michael Archer, *Citizen Shakespeare: Freemen and Aliens in the Language of the Plays* (New York: Palgrave Macmillan, 2005), 1–22.

24. Although the play, as I argue, constructs the category of citizen broadly—as a condition of both status and activity—the text itself tends to reserve the term for the city elite, as in More's request for a watch of "substantial citizens" (6.214) to keep order at the city gates, while referring to the protesters as "the commons" (1.130; 3.8) or "the people" (3.87). Scholarship on the play, however, tends to refer to the protestors, as well as the commons, as "citizens"; for example, Gabrieli and Melchiori not only refer to the crowd as citizens in the introduction to the Revels edition (6, 30) but also emend several of the rebels' speech prefixes to read "*Another citizen*" (2.3.5) and "*Some citizens*" (1.41); likewise, Jowett's Arden3 edition adds "citizens" to speech prefixes the manuscript (Addition II) designates "all."

25. Londoners used the term "stranger" interchangeably with "alien" to refer to those born abroad while "foreigner" typically designated the English non-free; see Ian W. Archer, *The Pursuit of Stability: Social Relations in Elizabethan London* (Cambridge: Cambridge University Press, 1991), 131.

26. Ian W. Archer, "Responses to Alien Immigrants in London, c. 1400–1650," in *Le Migrazioni in Europa secc. XIII–XVIII*, ed. Simonetta Cavaciocchi, Istituto Internazionale di Storia Economica "F. Datini" (Prato, Italy: Le Monnier, 1994), 755–74, esp. 755. For discussions of London's history of anti-alien sentiment, see also Lien Bich Luu, *Immigrants and the Industries of London, 1500–1700* (Aldershot: Ashgate, 2005); Laura Hunt Yungblut, *Strangers Settled Here Amongst Us: Policies, Perceptions and the Presence of Aliens in Elizabethan England* (London: Routledge, 1996); and Andrew Pettegree, *Foreign Protestant Communities in Sixteenth-Century London* (Oxford: Clarendon Press, 1986).

27. While debate continues about the extent of London's xenophobia, most agree that the alien issue figures importantly in ongoing struggles between the city and the Crown. As Yungblut characterizes it, weak monarchs in the fifteenth century often held out regulation of aliens as a bargaining chip, or bribe, to secure London's political and monetary support (66–70). The Elizabethan government, by contrast, was generally supportive of alien immigration for economic and religious reasons; moneylenders providing the largest sums to the Crown were aliens, and Cecil hoped to use alien artisans in a project of home production designed to reduce England's dependence on foreign goods (90).

28. Repertory 3, fol. 164ᵛ, in Repertories of the Court of Aldermen, Corporation of London Record Office, quoted in Susan Brigden, *London and the Reformation* (Oxford: Clarendon Press, 1989), 129–33, esp. 132. See also the accounts of the unrest in Steven Rappaport, *Worlds within Worlds: Structures of Life in Sixteenth-Century London* (Cambridge: Cambridge University Press, 1989), 15–17; and Martin Holmes, "Evil May-Day, 1517: The Story of a Riot," *History Today* 15 (1965): 642–50.

29. For discussions of the political uses of anti-alien sentiment and Ill May Day, see Archer, "Responses"; and George Unwin, *The Gilds and Companies of London*, 4th ed. (London: Frank Cass and Co., 1963), 243–66.

30. John Strype, *Annals of the Reformation*, 4 vols. (Oxford: Clarendon Press, 1824), 4:234–35.

31. These lines are from a manuscript discovered in 1971, reproduced by Arthur Freeman, in "Marlowe, Kyd, and the Dutch Church Libel," *ELR* 3 (1973): 44–52, esp. 51 (ll. 46, 49, 39–41).

32. Debate continues about the dates of the original text along with the revisions and additions. Many argue that the original text was written between 1592 and 1595, although Jowett argues for a later date sometime around 1600; some, including Gabrieli and Melchiori, assign an early date to the revisions, in the mid 1590s, but there is now increasing consensus that the manuscript was revised in 1603–4. For useful reviews of the question, see Gabrieli and Melchiori, *Sir Thomas More*, 11–12; Gary Taylor, "The date and auspices of the additions to *Sir Thomas More*," in *Shakespeare and "Sir Thomas More,"* 131–50; and Jowett, *Sir Thomas More*, 424–33.

33. Alfred W. Pollard, introduction to *Shakespeare's Hand in the Play of "Sir Thomas More,"* ed. Pollard et al. (Cambridge: Cambridge University Press, 1923), 1–40, esp. 4.

34. Jowett, *Sir Thomas More*, 139.

35. See, for example, Buchanan Sharp, "Popular Protest in Seventeenth-Century England," in *Popular Culture in Seventeenth-Century England*, ed. Barry Reay (New York: St. Martin's, 1985), 271–308, esp. 285–86, which distinguishes between "a theatre of riot" and "a theatre of rebellion," in which protestors cross "a fine line" between "normal" riots that "sustained the existing social and political order" and rebellion, which threatened to turn that order upside down.

36. My approach counters Richard Wilson's argument about the Cade scenes of *2 Henry VI*. Taking "[a]uthority and authorship" to be "synonymous in Shakespearean politics," Wilson claims that the playwright legitimated the "bourgeois 'order'" of his commercial playhouse by misrepresenting rebellious London artisans as an illiterate, carnivalesque mob (*Will Power*, 27–28, 30).

37. Alastair Bellany, "Libels in Action: Ritual, Subversion and the English Literary Underground, 1603–42," in *The Politics of the Excluded, c. 1500–1850*, ed. Tim Harris (Basingstoke, Hampshire: Palgrave, 2001), 99–124; and "'Raylinge Rymes and Vaunting Verse': Libellous Politics in Early Stuart England, 1603–1628," in *Cul-*

*ture and Politics in Early Stuart England*, ed. Kevin Sharpe and Peter Lake (Stanford: Stanford University Press, 1993), 285–310.

38. *Acts of the Privy Council of England, New Series*, ed. John Roche Dasent, 32 vols. (1901; repr., Nendeln: Kraus Reprint, 1974), 24:201.

39. *Acts of the Privy Council*, 24:222.

40. C. F. Tucker Brooke, ed., *The Life of Marlowe and "The Tragedy of Dido Queen of Carthage,"* in R. H. Case, gen. ed., *The Works and Life of Christopher Marlowe*, 6 vols. (London: Methuen, 1930–33), 1:105. Kyd's text (British Library Harleian MS 6849) appears as Appendix 5, "Kyd's Letter to Sir John Puckering," 1:103–6.

41. British Library Harleian MS 6848, quoted in Brooke, 1:56.

42. "Kyd's Letter," in Brooke, 1:104.

43. Quotations from Shakespeare's plays (exclusive of *Sir Thomas More*) follow *The Riverside Shakespeare.*

44. Masten, "Playwriting," 361.

45. "Kyd's Letter," in Brooke, 1:105.

46. "Kyd's Letter," in Brooke, 1:106.

47. Michel Foucault, "What Is an Author?" *Language, Counter-Memory, Practice: Selected Essays and Interviews*, ed. Donald F. Bouchard, trans. Donald F. Bouchard and Sherry Simon (Ithaca: Cornell University Press, 1977), 113–38.

48. My assumptions here differ from those of both Masten and Wayne Koestenbaum, who understand collaborative writing in opposition to the "modern author." Building on Foucault, Masten's interest is in play texts located "at a historical moment prior to the emergence of the author in its modern form" (*Textual Intercourse*, 13), whereas Koestenbaum explores the "double writing" of the late-nineteenth and early-twentieth centuries, reading collaboration as "a symptom of the monolithic author's decline" (*Double Talk: The Erotics of Male Literary Collaboration* [New York: Routledge, 1989], 8).

49. Within the London context, the pseudonym may refer not only to Marlowe's popular stage hero but also to his theatrical afterlife in what David Riggs has described as "an urban legend of plebian self-assertion," collaboratively authored in London's alehouses, streets, and marketplaces (*The World of Christopher Marlowe* [London: Faber and Faber, 2004], 220).

50. Masten, *Textual Intercourse*, 19.

51. Masten, *Textual Intercourse*, 21.

52. Marcy L. North, *The Anonymous Renaissance: Cultures of Discretion in Tudor-Stuart England* (Chicago: University of Chicago Press, 2003), 14.

53. North, 18.

54. Raphael Holinshed, *The Third Volume of Chronicles . . .* (London, 1587), fol. 840.

55. Edward Hall, *The Unyon of the Two Noble and Illustre Famelies of Lancastre and Yorke* (London: Richard Grafton, 1550), fol. 60[r] (sig. KKk.6[r]). Abbreviations in quotations from Hall's chronicle are silently expanded.

56. Hall, fol. 60ᵛ (sig. KKk.6ᵛ) (emphasis added).

57. Hall, fol. 61ʳ (sig. LLl.1ʳ). Hall's description, in detailing the events leading up to the outbreak, suggests collective action more deliberative and extensive than "a spontaneous riot," as Rappaport characterizes it (15–17, esp. 16).

58. Hall, fol. 61ʳ, 62ʳ (sigs. LLl.1ʳ, LLl.2ʳ).

59. Ethan H. Shagan, "Rumours and Popular Politics in the Reign of Henry VIII," in *Politics of the Excluded*, 30–66, esp. 35, 32

60. Hall, fol. 62ʳ (sig. LLl.2ʳ).

61. Hall, fol. 63ʳ (sig. LLl.3ʳ).

62. For a discussion of the play's multiple inversions of class, gender, and ethnic hierarchies, see Peter Stallybrass, "The World Turned Upside Down: Inversion, Gender and the State," in *The Matter of Difference: Materialist Feminist Criticism of Shakespeare*, ed. Valerie Wayne (Ithaca: Cornell University Press, 1991), 201–20.

63. Balibar, 51–52.

64. The apposition of "mechanic" and "organic" is borrowed from Samuel Taylor Coleridge's comparison of Beaumont and Fletcher to Shakespeare; see *Coleridge's Literary Criticism*, ed. J. W. Mackail (Oxford: Oxford University Press, 1908), 250; quoted in McMullan, 137.

65. Fredson Bowers, *The Dramatic Works in the Beaumont and Fletcher Canon*, 7 vols. (Cambridge: Cambridge University Press, 1966–96), 1:vii; quoted in McMullan, 149.

66. Jeffrey Masten, "My Two Dads: Collaboration and the Reproduction of Beaumont and Fletcher," in *Queering the Renaissance*, ed. Jonathan Goldberg (Durham: Duke University Press, 1994), 280–308, esp. 289, 303, 298.

67. *"Brief Lives," Chiefly of Contemporaries, Set Down by John Aubrey, between the Years 1669 and 1696*, ed. Andrew Clark, 2 vols. (Oxford: Clarendon Press, 1898), 1:95–96; quoted in Masten, "My Two Dads," 303.

68. Aristotle's definition comes from Montaigne's "Of Friendship," in *The Essayes or Morall, Politike and Millitairie Discourses of Lo: Michaell de Montaigne . . . now done into English*, trans. John Florio (London, 1603), fol. 94 (sig. I5ᵛ); quoted in Masten, *Textual Intercourse*, 32. Masten reads Montaigne's essay alongside Richard Brathwait's *The English Gentleman* (London, 1630).

69. Masten, *Textual Intercourse*, 35.

70. Masten, it should be noted, does build difference into his discussion of *More* (while cautioning that the play should not be taken as representative of collaborative playwriting). Borrowing from Stuart Hall's model of identification, which operates *across* difference, Masten calls for editing practices that, rather than searching for "'alien hands,'" would read "across hands" ("*More* or Less," 124, 116).

71. Jacques Derrida, *Politics of Friendship*, trans. George Collins (London: Verso, 1997), viii; see especially the critique of Montaigne's "double singularity" in the chapter "He Who Accompanies Me," 171–93. For a nuanced reading of Renaissance friendship that incorporates difference into a "rhetoric of likeness,"

see Laurie Shannon, *Sovereign Amity: Figures of Friendship in Shakespearean Contexts* (Chicago: University of Chicago Press, 2002).

72. Jacques Derrida, "The Politics of Friendship," *Journal of Philosophy* 85 (1988): 632–44, esp. 640–41.

73. *Nichomachean Ethics*, 1155a23–24, quoted in Jill Frank, *A Democracy of Distinction: Aristotle and the Work of Politics* (Chicago: University of Chicago Press, 2005), 147; my discussion of Aristotelian friendship is indebted to Frank's illuminating chapter on "The Polity of Friendship" (138–80) and to Danielle S. Allen's "Brotherhood, Love, and Political Friendship," in *Talking to Strangers: Anxieties of Citizenship since "Brown v. Board of Education"* (Chicago: University of Chicago Press, 2004), 119–39.

74. Sir Thomas Smith, *De Republica Anglorum*, ed. Mary Dewar (Cambridge: Cambridge University Press, 1982), 57.

75. Smith, 57.

76. McMillin, 20, 18, 49.

77. Giorgio Melchiori, "*The Booke of Sir Thomas Moore:* A Chronology of Revision," *SQ* 37 (1986): 291–308, esp. 296.

78. Evidence for Shakespeare's hand in Addition II, Richard Simpson concluded in 1871, "depends on the Shakespearian flavour, which only a critical taste can thoroughly discriminate" (3); it should be noted, however, that Simpson did not distinguish between Hands D and C in these passages.

79. R. W. Chambers, "The Expression of Ideas—Particularly Political Ideas—in the Three Pages, and in Shakespeare," in *Shakespeare's Hand*, 142–87, esp. 142; see also R. W. Chambers, "Some Sequences of Thought in Shakespeare and in the 147 Lines of 'Sir Thomas More,'" *MLR* 26 (1931): 251–80, and the recent extension of Chambers by John W. Velz, "*Sir Thomas More* and the Shakespeare Canon: Two Approaches," in *Shakespeare and "Sir Thomas More,"* 171–95.

80. Jenkins, "Supplement," xxxvii–xxxviii.

81. Chambers, "Expression of Ideas," 142.

82. Greg, *Book of Sir Thomas More*, xiii.

83. Werstine, "Close Contrivers," 11–15.

84. Greg, *Book of Sir Thomas More*, ix.

85. McMillin, 154–59.

86. McMillin, 159.

87. Chambers, "Expression of Ideas," 181.

88. Forker and Candido, 100–1.

89. Thomas Hobbes, *The Elements of Law: Natural & Politic*, ed. Ferdinand Tönnies (Cambridge: Cambridge University Press, 1928), 98 (2.2.11).

90. P. Maas, "Henry Finch and Shakespeare," *Review of English Studies*, n.s. 4 (1953), 142. Finch's position here echoes his similarly vocal opposition to an anti-recusant bill the month before, in February 1593 (J. E. Neale, *Elizabeth I and Her Parliaments 1584–1601* [London: Jonathan Cape, 1957], 280–85), suggesting the mutual interests of strangers and recusants, including Protestant nonconformists.

See also Donna Hamilton, "'Aliens and Strangers,' the Common Lawyers and *The Book of Sir Thomas More*," an unpublished paper presented at the Shakespeare Association of America annual meeting, 1994; Hamilton points out the broad use of "aliens and strangers" in the period to refer to "anyone whom the conformists regarded as posing a threat to church unity."

91. McMillin, 103; for other discussions of *More*'s verbal and structural parallels, see Alistair Fox, "The Paradoxical Design of *The Book of Sir Thomas More*," *Renaissance and Reformation* 17 (1981): 162–73; Gabrieli and Melchiori, 29–32; and Forker and Candido, passim.

92. Gabrieli and Melchiori, who generally exclude C's emendations of D's speech headings, justify the assignment of these lines to Lincoln based on the length of the speech ("too long for choral delivery"), although they suggest that "Doll or George Betts would have been better choices" (2.3.153n). Jowett retains D's "All" alongside C's "Lincoln," and notes: "Hand C consolidates the role, makes Lincoln a more acquiescent figure as the scene progresses and adds irony to his later execution" (*Sir Thomas More*, 196, n. 159).

93. Richard Wilson, "Making Men of Monsters: Shakespeare in the Company of Strangers," *Shakespeare* 1 (June 2005): 8–28, esp. 22.

94. The attack on imported vegetables suggests a double displacement of the standard carnival inversion of "displaced abjection," in which "one 'low' group defends itself either by asserting its claims to uphold hierarchical values or by demonising another low group" (Stallybrass, 211).

95. Wilson, "Making Men," 22.

96. The Clown's part dominates the first sixty-four lines of Addition II (Fol. 7[a]), attributed to Hand B; Greg, *Book of Sir Thomas More*, Addition II, 1–64n.

97. Greg, *Book of Sir Thomas More*, xiii.

98. In "Hand D in 'Sir Thomas More': An Essay in Misinterpretation," *Shakespeare Survey* 38 (1985): 101–14, esp. 106, Giorgio Melchiori makes the case that C, "a company bookkeeper," misunderstood D's intentions (C not having access to Munday's original from which D presumably worked). Building on this argument, Gary Taylor and Stanley Wells attempt to recover D's intentions for the *Oxford Shakespeare* by purging C's emendations: "If readers are interested primarily in Hand D's work, they should be able to read that work in the final form which Hand D gave to it, before it had been massaged by Hand C" (*William Shakespeare: A Textual Companion*, ed. Stanley Wells, Gary Taylor, John Jowett, and William Montgomery [Oxford: Clarendon Press, 1987], 461–62). Melchiori and the *Revels* edition do include C's assignment of lines to the Clown, as well as lines 265–66 to Lincoln, as noted earlier; and Jowett's *Arden 3* edition retains *both* C and D's speech prefixes, allowing readers to see when C overwrites D.

99. The *Norton Shakespeare*, gen. ed. Stephen Greenblatt (New York: W. W. Norton, 1997), 2013.

100. In this performance, the author too may double as actor (see More's remark, "We'll see how Master Poet plays his part" [9.69]), recalling Orgel's

observation that "Shakespeare can be distinguished from most other playwrights only because he was in on more parts of the collaboration" (6); see also Knapp, who distinguishes Shakespeare's single authorship from his collaborative fellowship as an actor-playwright (12–19), as well as the excellent discussion of the "discontinuities" between "author's pen" and "actor's voice" by Robert Weimann, "Playing with a Difference: Revisiting 'Pen' and 'Voice' in Shakespeare's Theater," *SQ* 50 (1999): 415–32.

101. "All but one of the speaking roles in the revised More can be played by thirteen men and five boys" (79), McMillin conjectures, working out an "index of possibilities" (77) for casting that has citizens and strangers from the first part of the play doubling back across ranks in the latter.

## *3. Trading in Tongues: Language Lessons and* Englishmen for My Money

1. Alexander Leggatt, *Citizen Comedy in the Age of Shakespeare* (Toronto: University of Toronto Press, 1973), 7.

2. This entry is followed by another, in May 1998, recording an additional 20 shillings to "horton in pte of payemente of his boocke called a womon will haue her wille," cited by Albert Croll Baugh, introduction to "William Haughton's *Englishmen for My Money or A Woman Will Have Her Will*" (PhD dissertation, University of Pennsylvania, 1917), 25. According to Baugh, Haughton regularly collaborated with Dekker and Chettle; *Englishmen* is his only "unaided" play.

3. See Angela Stock, "Stow's *Survey* and the London Playwrights," in *John Stow (1525–1605) and the Making of the English Past: Studies in Early Modern Culture and the History of the Book*, ed. Ian Gadd and Alexandra Gillespie (London: British Library, 2004), 89–98. Crutched Friars, or "Crossed Friers," lies within Aldgate Ward, which Stow describes as housing three churches, the halls of the Bricklayers, the Fletchers, and the Ironmongers, as well as fourteen almshouses. "At the east end of this lane," he writes, "in the way from Aldgate toward the Crossed Friers, of old time were certaine tenements called the poore Iurie, of Iewes dwelling there" (*A Survey of London*, ed. Charles Lethbridge Kingsford, 2 vols. [Oxford: Clarendon Press, 1971], 1: 149). For discussions of Pisaro as a Jew, see Edmund Valentine Campos, "Jews, Spaniards, and Portingales: Ambiguous Identities of Portuguese *Marranos* in Elizabethan England," *ELH* 69 (2002): 599–616; Alan Stewart, "'Euery Soyle to Mee Is Naturall': Figuring Denization in William Haughton's *English-men for My Money*," *Renaissance Drama* 35 (2006): 55–81; and Lloyd Edward Kermode, *Aliens and Englishness in Elizabethan Drama* (Cambridge: Cambridge University Press, 2009), 121–33.

4. See Kermode's discussion of *Wealth and Health, Like Will to Like*, and *The Tide Tarrieth No Man* in his chapter, "Discovering the alien in Elizabethan moral drama," in *Aliens and Englishness*, 23–58.

5. Quotations from the play follow the Revels edition of *Englishmen for My Money*, in *Three Renaissance Usury Plays*, ed. Lloyd Edward Kermode (Manchester: Manchester University Press, 2009).

6. Sir Philip Sidney, *The Defense of Poesy*, in *The Norton Anthology of English Literature*, 9th ed. vol. B (New York: W. W. Norton, 2012), 1079.

7. Jean E. Howard, *Theater of a City: The Places of London Comedy, 1598–1642* (Philadelphia: University of Pennsylvania Press, 2007), 38. See also Crystal Bartolovich, "London's the Thing: Alienation, the Market, and *Englishmen for My Money*," *Huntington Library Quarterly* 71 (2008): 137–55.

8. R. Porder, *A Sermon of Gods Fearefull Threatnings for Idolatrye. . . Preached in Paules Churche the XVI Daye of Maye 1570*, cited in Ian Archer, "Responses to Alien Immigrants in London, c. 1400–1650," *Instituto Internazionale* 25 (1994): 755–74, esp. 756.

9. *The Merchant of Venice: The Arden Shakespeare*, ed. John Drakakis (London: Methuen, 2010), which Haughton's play seems at times to echo within a contemporary London setting (3.3.26).

10. Richard Carew, "The Excellencie of the English tongue," in William Camden, *Remaines Concerning Britaine* (London, 1614), 36–44, esp. 39.

11. See, for example, Howard, *Theater of a City*, 38–48, and Stewart, "'Euery Soyle,'" 55–81, esp. 74–75.

12. Thomas Dekker, *The Dead Terme*, in *The Non-Dramatic Works of Thomas* Dekker, ed. Alexander B. Grosart, 5 vols. (New York: Russell & Russell, 1963), 4: 51; like others in the period, Dekker likens Paul's Walk's "confusion of languages" to the Tower of Babel. See A. J. Hoenselaars, "Reconstructing Babel in English Renaissance Drama: William Haughton's *Englishmen for My Money* and John Marston's *Antonio and Mellida*," *Neophilologus* 76 (1992): 464–79.

13. Steven Mullaney, *The Place of the Stage: License, Play, and Power in Renaissance England* (Chicago: University of Chicago Press, 1988), 82.

14. Étienne Balibar, "Citizenship without Community?" in *We, the People of Europe? Reflections on Transnational Citizenship*, trans. James Swenson (Princeton: Princeton University Press, 2004), 51–77, esp. 76.

15. Balibar positions his argument in relation to Carl Schmitt's nationalist position and Jürgen Habermas's cosmopolitanism, invoking an opposition that he then shows to be not without paradoxes; for inasmuch as progressive communities aim to institute "belonging" and "identification" by appealing to a "common good" or "universalist content," their construction of community is not without exclusions—both in the form of the community itself (as unified and normative, say) and in the processes by which this community is formed (Balibar, 52–61).

16. Balibar, 77.

17. Emma Smith, "'So much English by the Mother': Gender, Foreigners, and the Mother Tongue in William Haughton's *Englishmen for My Money*," *Medieval and Renaissance Drama in England* 13 (2001): 165–81, esp. 172. For other discussions of language as a marker of identity in the play, see Elizabeth Schafer, "William Haughton's *Englishmen for My Money*: A Critical Note," *RES* 41 (1990): 536–38; A. J. Hoenselaars, *Images of Englishmen and Foreigners in the Drama of Shakespeare and His Contemporaries: A Study of Stage Characters and National Identity in English Renaissance Drama, 1558–1642* (Rutherford: Fairleigh Dickinson

University Press, 1992), 54–58; Diane Cady, "Linguistic Dis-ease: Foreign Language as Sexual Disease in Early Modern England," in *Sins of the Flesh: Responding to Sexual Disease in Early Modern Europe*, ed. Kevin Sienna (Toronto: Centre for Reformation and Renaissance Studies, 2005): 159–86; and Stewart, "'Euery Soyle,'" which explores language in relation to denization issues.

18. Paula Blank, *Broken English: Dialects and the Politics of Language in Renaissance Writings* (London: Routledge, 1996), 44–45. See also Bryan A. Garner, "Shakespeare's Latinate Neologisms," *Shakespeare Studies* 15 (1982): 149–70.

19. Thomas Wilson, *The Arte of Rhetorique*, quoted in Richard Foster Jones, *The Triumph of the English Language* (Stanford: Stanford University Press, 1953), 101.

20. Jones, *Triumph*, and Blank, *Broken English*.

21. Richard Helgerson, *Forms of Nationhood: The Elizabethan Writing of England* (Chicago: University of Chicago Press, 1992), 22. See also Helgerson, "Language Lessons: Linguistic Colonialism, Linguistic Postcolonialism, and the Early Modern English Nation," *The Yale Journal of Criticism* 11 (1998): 289–99.

22. Samuel Daniel, "A Defence of Rime," in *The Renaissance in England* (Massachusetts: D. C. Heath, 1954), 662, quoted in Carla Mazzio, "Staging the Vernacular: Language and Nation in Thomas Kyd's *The Spanish Tragedy*," *SEL* 38 (1998): 207–32, esp. 208.

23. Richard Mulcaster, *Mulcaster's Elementarie*, ed. E. T. Campagnac (Oxford: Clarendon Press, 1925), 173–74.

24. Mulcaster, *Elementarie*, 287. Or, as William Camden put it, looking back over a century of vernacular expansion, English "hath beene beautified and enriched out of other good tongues, partly by enfranchising and endenizing strange words, partly by refining and mollifying olde words, partly by implanting new wordes with artificial composition" (*Remains Concerning Britain*, ed. R. D. Dunn [Toronto: University of Toronto Press, 1984], 29, cited in Neil Rhodes, *Shakespeare and the Origins of English* [Oxford: Oxford University Press, 2004], 127).

25. Carew, "Excellencie," 41.

26. Richard Verstegan, quoted in Blank, *Broken English*, 45; "the sense that the new trade in words did not represent enrichment but a kind of cultural bankruptcy," Blank writes, "circulated alongside celebrations of the 'commonwealth' of the new English" (46).

27. Roger Ascham, *Toxophilus* (1545), in *The English Works of Roger Ascham*, ed. William Aldis Wright (Cambridge: Cambridge University Press, 1904), xiv.

28. Pierre Bourdieu, *Language and Symbolic Power*, ed. John B. Thompson, trans. Gino Raymond and Matthew Adamson (Cambridge: Harvard University Press, 1991), 57.

29. Blank, *Broken English*, 38. See also James R. Siemon, *Word Against Word: Shakespearean Utterance* (Amherst: University of Massachusetts Press, 2002); and Robert N. Watson, "Coining Words on the Elizabethan and Jacobean Stage," *Philological Quarterly* 88 (2009): 49–75.

30. Robert Robinson, *The Art of Pronuntiation*, 1617, in *The Phonetic Writings of Robert Robinson*, ed. E. J. Dobson (London: Oxford University Press, 1957), 6.

31. John Florio, *His Firste Fruites* (1578; Amsterdam: Da Capo Press, 1969), 50; and John Eliot, *Ortho-epia Gallica. Eliots Fruits for the French* (1593; Menston: Scolar Press, 1968), sig. B.

32. M. St. Clare Byrne, introduction to *The French Littelton*, by Claudius Holyband (Cambridge: Cambridge University Press, 1953), xv. Hollyband's school was costly compared to the Merchant Taylor's, Byrne notes, but "it gave value for money in the shape of an eight-hour school-day."

33. Claude Desainliens [Claudius Hollyband], *The French School-master* (1573; Menston: Scolar Press, 1972), title page.

34. John Palsgrave, *Lesclarcissement de la langue francoyse*, 1530 (Menston: Scolar Press, 1969); and Giles Duwes, *An Introductorie for to lerne to rede, to pronounce, and to speke French trewly* (1533; Menston: Scolar Press, 1972), title page. See also Kathleen Lambley, *The Teaching and Cultivation of the French Language in England During Tudor and Stuart Times* (Manchester: Manchester University Press, 1920).

35. Hollyband, *French Schoolmaster* (1573), title page; subsequent references to *The French Schoolmaster* follow this edition and are cited parenthetically within the text.

36. Claude Desainliens [Claudius Hollyband], *The French Littelton* (1576; Menston: Scolar Press, 1970), sig. ii$^{v}$; subsequent references to *The French Littelton* are cited parenthetically within the text.

37. *A plaine pathway to the French tongue* (1575; Menston: Scolar Press, 1968), title page and sig. Biii.

38. *Plaine pathway*, sig. A2.

39. Although Hollyband, substituting French for Latin, closely follows Roger Ascham's title page for *The Scholemaster* (1570), he distinguishes his audience from Ascham's by specifying that *The French Schoolmaster* is intended for those who "studie priuatly in their owne study or houses." By contrast, Ascham intends his text "*for the priuate bryngingup of youth in Ientlemen and Noble mens houses.*" Ascham believes his book can be used "without a Scholemaster," but in contrast to Hollyband, he reserves this use for those who have already received formal training but now need a refresher in the language (*English Works of Roger Ascham*, 171).

40. Robert Cawdrey, *A Table Alphabeticall* (1604; Amsterdam: Da Capo Press, 1970), sig. A3.

41. Richard Mulcaster, *Positions Concerning the Training Up of Children*, ed. William Barker (Toronto: University of Toronto Press, 1994), 148.

42. Mulcaster, *Positions*, 148.

43. Eliot, *Ortho-epia Gallica*, 3.

44. Eliot continues on in this dialogue to rant against the many Italian and French men "who teach their languages for wages in the Citie of London," criticizing their "proud" and "capricious" manner and linking them to Machiavelli and Peter Aretine (*Ortho-epia*, 3–4).

45. Eliot, *Ortho-epia*, sig. A3[v]. Lambley, *Teaching and Cultivation*, 171–78, reads Eliot's satiric tone as a protest against the monopoly by the French and Italians on language instruction in London in these years. Frances A. Yates, *John Florio: The Life of an Italian in Shakespeare's England* (New York: Octagon Books, 1968), 139–73, argues that Eliot particularly targets Florio's *Second Fruits.* See also F. Yates, "The Importance of John Eliot's *Ortho-epia Gallica*," *Review of English Studies* 7 (1931): 419–30.

46. Eliot, *Ortho-epia*, 3–4.

47. R. C. Simonini, Jr., "The Italian Pedagogy of Claudius Hollyband," *Studies in Philology* 49 (1952): 144–54, esp. 146. Simonini writes that Hollyband was "the first teacher to provide England with suitable and practical textbooks for learning French, and his books were so successful that they were in general use for nearly a hundred years."

48. *Returns of Aliens in the City and Suburbs of London 1523–1571*, Publications of the Huguenot Society of London, 10/1 (London: Huguenot Society, 1900), 471. See also Mark Eccles, "Claudius Hollyband and the Earliest French-English Dictionaries," *Studies in Philology* 83 (1986): 51–61, esp. 51.

49. Laura Hunt Yungblut, *Strangers Settled Here Amongst Us: Policies, Perceptions and the Presence of Aliens in Elizabethan England* (London: Routledge, 1996), 23.

50. "A Complaynt of the Cytizens of London against the great number of strangers in and about this cytty," S.P.D., *Elizabeth*, vol. 81, no. 29, in *Tudor Economic Documents*, ed. R. H. Tawney and Eileen Power, 3 vols. (London: Longmans, Green, and Co., 1935) 1: 308.

51. *Tudor Economic Documents*, 1: 308–9.

52. Quoted in Yungblut, *Strangers*, 87.

53. Quoted in Yungblut, *Strangers*, 89.

54. Eccles, "Claudius Hollyband," 51. Steve Rappaport, *Worlds Within Worlds: Structures of Life in Sixteenth-Century London* (Cambridge: Cambridge University Press, 1989), 42, notes that few strangers sought out denizen status, with only forty-two letters of denization, on average, granted each year between 1509 and 1602. For sample denization letters, see *The Publications of the Huguenot Society of London*, 8 (London: Huguenot Society, 1893), i–vi.

55. See Andrew Pettegree, *Foreign Protestant Communities in Sixteenth-Century London* (Oxford: Clarendon Press, 1986), 289–91; Stewart, "'Euery Soyle,'" 63–65; Jacob Selwood, "'English-Born Reputed Strangers': Birth and Descent in Seventeenth-Century London," *Journal of British Studies* 44 (2005): 728–53.

56. The 1571 citizens' complaint, for example, objected to strangers, including denizens, being admitted to companies, claiming that they are "a common wealth within themselves," and "though they be demized or borne heere amongst us, yett they keepe themselves severed from us" (*Tudor Economic Documents*, 1: 309). In *The Pursuit of Stability: Social Relations in Elizabethan London* (Cambridge: Cambridge University Press, 1991), 134, Ian Archer writes that city custom regarding aliens was "amplified by a series of Henrician statues" in the aftermath of Ill May Day 1517: "Non-denizens were forbidden to set up workshops at all, and denizens

limited as to the number of journeymen they could employ, and banned from employing stranger apprentices." Many aliens simply continued to operate outside city jurisdiction, avoiding the trouble and expense of denization.

57. Eccles, "Claudius Hollyband," 58–59.

58. Alan Stewart observes that "[i]n practice as well as etymologically, the status of a denizen was always precarious, despite the legal definition. Although the act of being denizated should have made a stranger English, in reality, a denizen continued to be perceived as a form of stranger" ("'Euery Soyle,'" 62).

59. Stewart cites references to denizen plants in Michael Drayton and Barnaby Googe, among others ("'Euery Soyle,'" 60–61).

60. Florio, *His Firste Fruites*, C.i.v. Corroborating Florio's dialogue is that of Giordano Bruno, in which the Italian interlocutor pretends ignorance of English "in order to avoid rude encounters"; quoted in Frances A. Yates, "Italian Teachers in Elizabethan England," *Journal of the Warburg Institute* 1 (1937): 103–16, esp. 103.

61. Thomas Middleton and Thomas Dekker, *The Roaring Girl*, ed. Paul A. Mulholland (Manchester: Manchester University Press, 1987).

62. *Thomas Dekker*, ed. E. D. Pendry (Cambridge: Harvard University Press, 1968), 94. See also Janette Dillon, *Theatre, Court and City, 1595–1610: Drama and Social Space in London* (Cambridge: Cambridge University Press, 2000), 73–78.

63. For a discussion of urban hospitality, see Felicity Heal, *Hospitality in Early Modern England* (Oxford: Oxford University Press, 1990), 300–51; citing Hollyband's feast sequence, Heal contends that hospitality was an important part of urban as well as rural culture.

64. See, for example, *The Colloquies of Erasmus*, trans. Craig R. Thompson (Chicago: University of Chicago Press, 1965), and the dialogues of Vives, in *Tudor School-Boy Life: The Dialogues of Juan Luis Vives*, trans. Foster Watson (London: Frank Cass, 1970).

65. Hollyband's readers probably didn't need reminding that abundance, when linked to luxury, carried strong negative associations. Indeed, copious lists more often served to censure than to promote consumption, as in this oft-quoted passage by Thomas Smith typical of the period's critique: "their shops glisteres and shine of glasses, as well looking as drinking, yea, all manner [of] vessels of the same stuff: painted cruses, gay daggers, knives, swords, and girdles, that is able to make any temperate man to gaze on them, and to buy somewhat, though it serve no purpose necessary" (*A Discourse of the Common Weal of this Realm of England*, ed. E. Lamond [1581; Cambridge: Cambridge University Press, 1954], 64).

66. John Brinsley, *Lvdvs Literarivs: or The Grammar Schoole* (London, 1622), 212.

67. One might wonder, of course, about the cultural politics of a study session in which *The French Schoolmaster*'s dedicatee, Master Robert Sackville, must frame his tongue to fit the part of one of the prosperous merchants in Hollyband's dialogues.

68. *Collected Works of Erasmus: Literary and Educational Writings*, vol. 26, ed. J. K. Sowards (Toronto: University of Toronto Press, 1978) 4: 370. Others extolled

the health benefits of speaking aloud. Mulcaster, for example, called for "exercise of the voice," or "lowd speaking," that "practiseth and stirreth the inward partes, and vocall instrumentes" (*Positions*, 65). See also Gina Bloom, *Voice in Motion: Staging Gender, Shaping Sound in Early Modern England* (Philadelphia: University of Pennsylvania Press, 2007).

69. Robinson, *Phonetic Writings*, 6 and title page.

70. *Collected Works of Erasmus*, 26: 421.

71. Bourdieu, *Language*, 86.

72. Ascham, *English Works*, 229. Many at the time believed that the English were unusually susceptible to foreign cultures, for better and for worse. As Fynes Morrison wrote: "the English are naturally inclined to apply themselves to the manners and customs of any foreign nations with whom they live and converse"; quoted in Mary Floyd-Wilson, *English Ethnicity and Race in Early Modern Drama* (Cambridge: Cambridge University Press, 2003), 58.

73. Central to Hollyband's pedagogy, this alienation suggests a version of the performative force described by Judith Butler, *Excitable Speech: A Politics of the Performative* (London: Routledge, 1997), 146–47. Pushing beyond what she takes to be the limits of Bourdieu's notion of performative language, Butler argues that bodily speech acts have the capacity to resist as well as adopt the cultural norms: "But is there a sure way of distinguishing between the imposter and the real authority? Are there moments in which the utterance forces a blurring between the two, where the utterance calls into question the established grounds of legitimacy, where the utterance, in fact, performatively produces a shift in the terms of legitimacy as *an effect* of the utterance itself?" See also Lynn Enterline, *Shakespeare's Schoolroom: Rhetoric, Discipline, Emotion* (Philadelphia: University of Pennsylvania Press, 2012); focused on affective registers of pedagogy's role in inculcating notions of masculinity in the period, Enterline examines the techniques of *prosopopoeia*, or impersonation, in translation exercises to argue that grammar schools instilled "habits of alterity" in their pupils and "a highly mediated relation to emotion, a tendency to experience what passes for deep personal feeling precisely by taking a detour through the passions of others (particularly those classical figures offered as examples for imitation)" (25).

74. Andrew Fleck, "'Ick verstaw you niet': Performing Foreign Tongues on the Early Modern English Stage," *Medieval and Renaissance Drama in England* 20 (2007): 204–21, argues that this patois allowed uneducated audiences to understand "foreign languages" onstage; Hoenselaars also minimizes the negative stereotypes of broken English, arguing that it serves simply "to increase the comic effect of the foreigners' courtship" (*Images*, 56). Far more the norm among critical work on the play, however, is Janette Dillon's observation that "[l]anguage, and racially stereotyped modes of speaking are repeatedly the excuse for comic abuse," in *Language and Stage in Medieval and Renaissance England* (Cambridge: Cambridge University Press, 1998), 174.

75. G. K. Hunter, "Elizabethans and Foreigners," *Shakespeare Survey* 17 (1964): 37–52, esp. 43.

76. Hunter describes the play as a "run-of-the-mill comedy" in which "[f]oreignness is no part of the moral structure, but is only an intriguing local colour" ("Elizabethans," 43–44).

77. The play's staging of foreign languages has dominated recent critical work on the play (see note 17). Reversing this emphasis, my approach concentrates on the play's native English speakers and *their* attempts to negotiate foreign tongues.

78. *Henry V, The Shoemaker's Holiday*, and *The Merry Wives of Windsor* (and possibly *Sir Thomas More*) quickly follow *Englishmen for My Money*. See Wilson O. Clough, "The Broken English of Foreign Characters of the Elizabethan Stage," *Philological Quarterly* 12 (1933): 255–68; R. C. Simonini, "Language Lesson Dialogues in Shakespeare," *Shakespeare Quarterly* 2 (1951): 319–29; Fleck, "'Ick verstaw'"; and John Michael Archer's discussion of "urban language" in Shakespeare's civil comedies in *Citizen Shakespeare: Freemen and Aliens in the Language of the Plays* (Basingstoke: Palgrave Macmillan, 2005).

79. Hoenselaars, "Reconstructing Babel," 473.

80. In one of the few discussions of these linguistic impersonations, Hoenselaars contends that even though "to a modern reader" Frisco and Anthony provide "an ironic counterpoint" to the foreign merchants, the play itself "does not comment on this irony." In Hoenselaars's reading, the absence of irony registers "a double standard, providing the play with the flaw by which patriotism thrives—namely, a blindness to one's own national weaknesses" (*Images*, 58). Kermode disagrees, asserting that the play links patriotism with the English language so that the "Englishmen's inability to speak foreign languages is the play's proof of such skills' lack of worth" (*Aliens*, 126). By contrast, I argue that because of its linguistic self-consciousness, the play invites contemporary London audiences to critique both positions, exposing the city's chauvinistic ignorance of other tongues.

81. Among the meanings of "natural" listed by the *Oxford English Dictionary* that might apply to Frisco's use of the term is that of a "natural fool," or "a person having a low learning ability or intellectual capacity" (II.7.), as well as "a person or thing of or from a designated region; a native" (III.19.a).

82. Many of Anthony's "strange" words—exasperate, nominate, provoke, and audience, for example—are to be found in *A Table Alphabeticall* (1604), Robert Cawdrey's soon to be published dictionary of "hard" English words, "borrowed from the Hebrew, Greeke, Latine, or French," as the title page advertises.

83. Schafer, "William Haughton's *Englishmen*," 536–37.

84. In the *Revels* edition of *Englishmen for My Money*, Kermode suggests that "[p]art of the essential comedy here is the awareness that English actors are playing at being foreigners; this constant awareness adds another layer of irony to the scenes in which Englishmen and foreigners pretend to be each other, in a linguistic version of cross-dressing" (*Three Renaissance Usury Plays*, 66).

85. As Adam Zucker reminds us, balconies were not yet a feature of London architecture in this period; see *The Places of Wit in Early Modern Comedy* (Cambridge: Cambridge University Press, 2011), 118–23.

86. Kermode, *Aliens*, 5.
87. Kermode, *Aliens*, 85.
88. Kermode, *Aliens*, 128–29.
89. Carew, "Excellencie," 39.

## 4. *The Place of the Present: Making Time and* The Roaring Girl

1. Thomas Middleton and Thomas Dekker, *The Roaring Girl*, ed. Paul A. Mulholland (Manchester: Manchester University Press, 1987), 68. All quotations from *The Roaring Girl* follow this edition.

2. See, for example, Douglas Bruster, *Drama and the Market in the Age of Shakespeare* (Cambridge: Cambridge University Press, 1992); Janette Dillon, *Theatre, Court and City, 1595–1610: Drama and Social Space in London* (Cambridge: Cambridge University Press, 2000); Jean E. Howard, *Theater of a City: The Places of London Comedy, 1598–1642* (Philadelphia: University of Pennsylvania Press, 2007); and Amanda Bailey, *Of Bondage: Debt, Property, and Personhood in Early Modern England* (Philadelphia: University of Pennsylvania Press, 2013).

3. Jacques LeGoff, "Merchant's Time and Church's Time in the Middle Ages," in *Time, Work, and Culture in the Middle Ages*, trans. Arthur Goldhammer (Chicago: University of Chicago Press, 1980): 29–42, esp. 35. See also David Harvey's discussion on time and space in *The Condition of Postmodernity: An Enquiry into the Origins of Cultural Change* (Oxford: Blackwell, 1990), 201–39.

4. L. C. Knights, *Drama and Society in the Age of Jonson* (London: Chatto and Windus, 1937).

5. For an astute discussion of the defining tensions of city comedy in relation to romance, see Lawrence Manley's chapter, "The Uses of Enchantment: Jacobean City Comedy and Romance," in *Literature and Culture in Early Modern London* (Cambridge: Cambridge University Press, 1995), 431–77. For other discussions of city comedy's tensions, see Susan Wells, "Jacobean City Comedy and the Ideology of the City," *ELH* 48 (1981): 37–60; and Anne Barton, "London Comedy and the Ethos of the City," *London Journal* 4 (1978), 158–80. See also Barton's discussion of comic *emplotment* in this essay: Comedy "has always been given to resurrecting the dead," Barton observes. "But such unlikely returns acquire a special quality when . . . characters literally climb out of their coffins in Cheapside, in a house at Crutched Friars, or just behind Charing Cross. This both is and is not London, a world simultaneously familiar and strange" (160–61).

6. Walter Cohen, *Drama of a Nation: Public Theater in Renaissance England and Spain* (Ithaca: Cornell University Press, 1985), 284.

7. These figures derive from the annual mortality bills. Paul Slack records 25,045 plague burials in 1603 within the city and liberties, *The Impact of Plague in Tudor and Stuart England* (London: Routledge and Kegan Paul, 1985), 151; the mortality tables of John Graunt, in *The Economic Writings of Sir William Petty, Together with the "Observations Upon the Bills of Mortality,"* ed. Charles Henry

Hull, 2 vols. (Cambridge: Cambridge University Press, 1899), 2:407, calculate 14,748 plague deaths between 1604 and 1611.

8. In the first published study of the bills, John Graunt observed in 1662 that extant evidence of the continuous publication of London's weekly bills begins on December 29, 1603 (*Economic Writings*, 2: 335), and several sources, including John Bell's *London's Remembrancer* (1665), corroborate Graunt's claims. Contesting this widely accepted date, Stephen Greenberg, "Plague, the Printing Press, and Public Health in Seventeenth-Century London," *Huntington Library Quarterly* 67 (2004): 508–27, esp. 517, has located surviving bills from July 14–21, 1603; printed by the printer for the City of London, this series of bills continued uninterrupted for twenty-three weeks (both the Houghton Library and the British Library have the complete twenty-three week run). For useful overviews of the mortality bills, see Hull, introduction to *Economic Writings*, 1: lxxx–xci; F. P. Wilson, *The Plague in Shakespeare's London* (Oxford: Clarendon Press, 1927), 189–208; and Leeds Barroll, *Politics, Plague, and Shakespeare's Theater: The Stuart Years* (Ithaca: Cornell University Press, 1991), 217–26.

9. E. K. Chambers, "Documents of Control," in *The Elizabethan Stage*, 4 vols. (Oxford: Clarendon Press, 1923), 4: 313. While the Privy Council often reacted directly to London's high mortality figures, it was not above using plague as a pretext for social control; see Barbara Freedman, "Elizabethan Protest, Plague, and Plays: Rereading the 'Documents of Control,'" *English Literary Renaissance* 26 (1996): 17–45.

10. Barroll, *Politics*, 70–116, 211–32; although Barroll concentrates on Shakespeare's late career, his richly suggestive study is one of the few to explore relations between the London theater and the ongoing plague.

11. Quoted in Barroll, *Politics*, 100.

12. This is not to suggest a causal link between mortality bills and theatrical fashion—city comedies were, of course, already popular on the London stage prior to the bills' regular appearance in 1603—but it is to recognize these two widely divergent representations of London as simultaneous, conjoined by the times and their audience members and readers, many of whom followed the playing seasons together with the plague bills.

13. I offer the term "temporal stories" as a supplement to the "spatial stories" so powerfully elaborated by Michel de Certeau, *The Practice of Everyday Life*, trans. Steven Rendall (Berkeley: University of California Press, 1984), 115–30.

14. For a detailed discussion of the play's date, see P. A. Mulholland, "The Date of *The Roaring Girl*," *R.E.S.*, n.s. 28 (1977): 18–31.

15. Katharine Maus, ed., *The Roaring Girl*, in *English Renaissance Drama: A Norton Anthology*, ed. David Bevington et al. (New York: W. W. Norton, 2002), 1371; as Maus also observes, given censorship laws against representing political figures on stage, it is not surprising that "the first positively identifiable living person to be translated into a quasi-fictional dramatic realm was someone the authorities had no interest in protecting."

16. Paul Ricoeur, *Time and Narrative*, trans. Kathleen McLaughlin and David Pellauer, 3 vols. (Chicago: University of Chicago Press, 1985), 2: 101.

17. *Your Five Gallants*, in *Thomas Middleton: The Collected Works*, ed. Gary Taylor and John Lavagnino (Oxford: Clarendon Press, 2007). Trade in second-hand clothing was rightly suspected of spreading infection (Slack, *The Impact of Plague*, 238); see also Dekker's reference in *A Rod for Run-awayes* (1625) to a broker whose trade "was enough to cut off the kindred, his Clothes smelt of infection" (*The Plague Pamphlets of Thomas Dekker*, ed. F. P. Wilson [Oxford: Clarendon Press, 1925], 155).

18. By the early seventeenth century, the highest mortality rates had begun to shift from the inner city to London's impoverished and densely populated suburban parishes; see Slack, *Impact of Plague*, 151–64.

19. John Graunt, *Natural and Political Observations*, in *Economic Writings*, ed. Hull, 2: 333.

20. Thomas Dekker, *London Looke Back, at That Yeare of Yeares 1625* (1630), in *Plague Pamphlets*, ed. Wilson, 181.

21. Ricoeur draws here on Heidegger's notion of "within-time-ness" to distinguish between time as an abstract measure and the "preoccupation that determines the meaning of this time" (*Time and Narrative*, 1: 62–63).

22. *Time and Narrative*, 1: 65.

23. The early seventeenth century saw a marked increase in debate about the plague—its causes, treatments, methods of control—and, as Slack observes, the mortality bills "did most to stimulate discussion and analysis of plague" (*Impact of Plague*, 239).

24. According to Paul Slack, "Metropolitan Government in Crisis: The Response to Plague," in *London 1500–1700: The Making of the Metropolis*, ed. A. L. Beier and Roger Finlay (London: Longman, 1986): 60–81, the impetus for social control came from the Privy Council; by contrast, city rulers tended to resist the council's aggressive plague orders, partly because of the high costs of mobilizing the quarantines, pesthouses, and medical teams envisioned by the council but also because "they were aware that new kinds of social regulation were as likely to aggravate as to prevent disorder" (75). For more on the plague orders and the city's response, see Wilson, *Plague in Shakespeare's London*, 14–84; also Richelle Munkoff, "Searchers of the Dead: Authority, Marginality, and the Interpretation of Plague in England, 1574–1665," *Gender and History* 11 (1999): 1–29; and "Reckoning Death: Women Searchers and the Bills of Mortality in Early Modern London," in *Rhetorics of Bodily Disease and Health in Medieval and Early Modern England*, ed. Jennifer C. Vaught (Farnham: Ashgate, 2010), 119–34.

25. Foucault, *Security, Territory, Population*, ed. Michel Senellart, trans. Graham Burchell (London: Palgrave, 2007), 66–67. For Foucault, this shift is part of a larger shift from sovereignty to government, from sovereign discipline (associated with plague and quarantine) to government security (associated with eighteenth-century smallpox epidemics, for example). Slack's plague research suggests that mortality bills allowed for security as well as surveillance, laying a

foundation for the government to collect data, estimate probabilities, and calculate risks.

26. de Certeau, *Practice*, 93. Insofar as the bills' weekly publication promotes a temporal or sequential mapping of plague deaths, the particular form of the bill itself, which presents an *alphabetical* list of plague deaths by parish—rather than a geographical "survey" along the lines of Stow's perambulation, say—resists rather than enables an easy spatial mapping of the plague's movement within the city.

27. Wilson, *Plague in Shakespeare's London*, 189. A London draper and haberdasher by trade, Graunt is considered a founder of modern statistics, and in the book's conclusion he points to possible governmental applications (what we might call social engineering): Just as it is "good to know the *Geometrical* Content, Figure, and Situation of all the Lands of a *Kingdom*" together with its resources, he writes, it is "no less necessary to know how many People there be of each Sex, State, Age, Religion, Trade, Rank, or Degree, *&c.* by the knowledge whereof, Trade and Government may be made more certain and Regular" (*Economic Writings*, ed. Hull, 2: 396).

28. The "enclosed, segmented space" of quarantine constitutes "a compact model of the disciplinary mechanism," figured architecturally by Bentham's Panopticon, Foucault famously argues in *Discipline and Punish: The Birth of the Prison*, trans. Alan Sheridan (New York: Vintage Books, 1979), 197.

29. Greenberg, "Plague, the Printing Press, and Public Health," 518. In this remarkable essay of bibliographic sleuthing based on the 1603 mortality bill series, Greenberg concludes that John Windet, printer to the City of London, was able to turn out such a remarkably large print run each week by using two different presses.

30. Graunt, in *Economic Writings*, 2: 347. In the book's dedication, Graunt humbly leaves it up to the Privy Council to make policy based on his observations, "as they are of little or none [use] to me, which is no more than the fairest *Diamonds* are to the *Journeyman Jeweller* that works them, or the poor *Labourer* that first digg'd them from the Earth" (2: 320).

31. William Petty, *A Treatise of Taxes* (London, 1662), in *Economic Writings*, ed. Hull, 1: 80. See also Peter Buck, "Seventeenth-Century Political Arithmetic: Civil Strife and Vital Statistics," *Isis* 68 (1977): 67–84, esp. 76. For both Petty and Graunt, political arithmetic was instrumental not only in enabling government regulation but also in garnering consent from the population itself; as Buck argues, both men understood that "repression was most effective when men also accepted and enforced its dictates on themselves because they were in agreement with their rulers about the prerequisites for order." See also Julian Hoppit, "Political Arithmetic in Eighteenth-Century England," *Economic History Review*, 49 (1996): 516–40.

32. In 1609, for example, the Parish Clerks' Company took measures to ensure that no one leaked the numbers to the public before they had been seen by government officials; on Thursday mornings, bills were to be first delivered

to the mayor at 8 a.m. before being released for general circulation two hours later (J. C. Robertson, "Reckoning with London: Interpreting the *Bills of Mortality* before John Graunt," *Urban History* 23 [1996]: 325–50, esp. 336).

33. Margaret Healy, *Fictions of Disease in Early Modern England: Bodies, Plagues and Politics* (Basingstoke: Palgrave, 2001), 94.

34. "Elegy 14: A Tale of a Citizen and his Wife," *John Donne: The Complete Poems*, ed. A. J. Smith (Middlesex: Penguin Books, 1973), 114–16. Critics also objected that the bills had themselves become a commodity in the plague business; see, for example, Thomas Nash's remark that Gabriel Harvey was employed by city printer John Wolf to write "that eloquent *post-script* for the Plague Bills, where he talkes of the series, the classes, & the premisses, & presenting them with an exacter methode hereafter, if it please God the Plague continue" (*The Works of Thomas Nashe*, ed. Ronald B. McKerrow, 5 vols [Oxford: Basil Blackwell, 1958] 3: 89, qtd. in Matthias A. Shaaber, *Some Forerunners of the Newspaper in England, 1476–1622* [Philadelphia: University of Pennsylvania Press, 1929], 161).

35. Quoted in Slack, *Impact of Plague*, 149. In April 1603, for example, the mayor, writing to the Privy Council, pointed to the latest figures to show that the king had received " 'unjust information' " about rising infection rates; in early December that same year, directors of the new East India Company cited weekly numbers to show that trade was beginning to resume in the city (cited in Robertson, "Reckoning," 325–27).

36. Le Goff cites an instructive fourteenth-century Franciscan ruling against merchants taking profits: "*in doing so he would be selling time* and would be committing usury *by selling what does not belong to him*" (*Time, Work, and Culture*, 29–30).

37. Thomas Dekker, *A Rod for Run-awayes* (1625), in *Plague Pamphlets*, ed. Wilson, 143, 151–52. For the controversy surrounding Henoch Clapham's ill-fated insistence on attributing plague to divine providence alone, see Slack, *Impact of Plague*, 234–35.

38. See, for example, Hull, "Introduction," *Economic Writings*, 1: lxxv–xci; Ian Hacking, *The Emergence of Probability: A Philosophical Study of Early Ideas about Probability, Induction, and Statistical Inference* (Cambridge: Cambridge University Press, 1975); and I. Sutherland, "John Graunt: A Tercentary Tribute," *Journal of the Royal Statistical Society*, ser. A, 126 (1963): 537–56.

39. Robertson, "Reckoning," 349. Erin Sullivan contends that implicit in this mapping was an image of the body politic, so that as the bills anatomized the sick "body" of London, they opened up "new discursive possibilities for the exploration of spiritual affliction" ("Physical and Spiritual Illness: Narrative Appropriations of the Bills of Mortality," in *Representing the Plague in Early Modern England*, ed. Rebecca Totaro and Ernest B. Gilman [London: Routledge, 2011]: 76–94, esp. 84).

40. Benedict Anderson, *Imagined Communities: Reflections on the Origin and Spread of Nationalism* (London: Verso, 1991), 34–36, borrowing here from Walter Benjamin's characterization of modern simultancity as "marked not by

prefiguring and fulfilment, but by temporal coincidence, and measured by clock and calendar" (24).

41. Daniel Woolf, "News, History and the Construction of the Present in Early Modern England," in *The Politics of Information in Early Modern Europe*, ed. Brendan Dooley and Sabrina Baron (London: Routledge, 2001): 80–118, esp. 108.

42. For an excellent analysis of early London news, see Joad Raymond, *Pamphlets and Pamphleteering in Early Modern Britain* (Cambridge: Cambridge University Press, 2003); Raymond emphasizes that while there was "no outright ban on domestic or foreign news publications," various royal proclamations called for licensing and censorship: "Hence printed publications of domestic news tended to be restricted to sensation, disasters, crimes, and official publications, including proclamations and the monarch's speeches. . . . Foreign political news could usually be reported in detail. Domestic political commentary was avoided, and parliamentary proceedings, crucially, were not reported" (130).

43. According to Raymond, it was the mortality bills, not newsbooks, that first developed "exact periodicity" in London; news publications did not achieve this degree of precise periodicity until late 1641 (*Pamphlets*, 107–8). See also C. John Sommerville, *The News Revolution in England: Cultural Dynamics of Daily Information* (Oxford: Oxford University Press, 1996). Sommerville similarly regards London mortality bills as a precursor of periodical news (65–67).

44. *The Letters of John Chamberlain*, ed. Norman Egbert McLure, 2 vols. (Philadelphia: American Philosophical Society, 1939), 1: 264, 267, 271. Ralph Josselin of Essex similarly tracked London's death rates during the devastating epidemic of 1665, recording the numbers in weekly diary entries and with increasing alarm: "June. 11. God good in our health and peace, the plague increaseth to 43. this weeke. . . . June. 18. plague increasd to 112. . . . June. 25. plage increasd to 168. . . . July: 2. plague increased to 267. bill 684: my son have leave to continue in the country, god in mercy preserve us, and heale the city. . . . July. 9. God good in our preservacon, the plague feares the London they flie before it and the country feares all trade with London. died. 1006. of the plague. 470 the Lord stay his heavy hand" (*The Diary of Ralph Josselin 1616–1683*, ed. Alan Macfarlane [London: Oxford University Press for The British Academy, 1976], 518–32, esp. 518–19).

45. As Woolf observes, one of the consequences of "the creation of a meaningful present" is a "permanent separation of news from history" ("News," 98). Although Woolf identifies this separation with the onset of periodical news later in the seventeenth century, the mortality bills certainly suggest that distinctions between past and present, if not between history and news, were already possible at the century's start.

46. Ben Jonson, *The Staple of News*, ed. Anthony Parr (Manchester, UK: Manchester University Press, 1988).

47. Michel de Certeau, *The Writing of History*, trans. Tom Conley (New York: Columbia University Press, 1988), 101, 87.

48. Vanessa Harding, *The Dead and the Living in Paris and London, 1500–1670* (Cambridge: Cambridge University Press, 2002), 6; for plague-time burial prac-

tices, see Harding, "Burial of the Plague Dead in Early Modern London," *Epidemic Disease in London*, ed. J. A. I. Champion (Centre for Metropolitan History Working Papers Series, No. 1, 1993): 53–64.

49. Dekker, *Plague Pamphlets*, ed. Wilson, 72, from the dedicatory epistle to Sir Nicholas Nemo, "*alias* Nobody." Dekker's pamphlets repeatedly return to the horrors of mass graves; see, for example, the description from *The Wonderfull Yeare* (1603) of a "Mucke-pit" where "[t]hreescore that not many houres before had euery one seuerall lodgings very delicately furnisht, are now thrust altogether into one close roome: a litle litle noisom roome: not fully ten foote square" (*Plague Pamphlets*, 29).

50. Woolf, "News," 96.

51. Ben Jonson, *The Alchemist (The New Mermaids)*, ed. Elizabeth Cook (New York: Norton, 1991). The ensuing quibble over whether the number applies to the liberties, as Subtle assumes, or "within the walls," as Face insists, perhaps mocks the precision with which some may have attempted to interpret the bills even as it underscores the widening differences in mortality rates between city and suburbs.

52. In the 1630s, newsletter writer John Flower repeatedly used comparisons as a basis of prediction and speculation; for example, in the summer of 1630, he reported that the death tolls "'increased greatlie the last week, in w[hi]ch there died of it threescore and seventeen, w[hi]ch is allmost as manie more as died of it the week before and there are ten parishes more infected than were then,'" so that "'men fear that it rather increaseth than decreaseth'" (quoted in Robertson, "Reckoning," 342).

53. Ben Jonson, *Every Man Out of His Humour*, ed. Helen Ostovich (Manchester: Manchester University Press, 2001).

54. Manley, *Literature and Culture*, 436; see also Lorna Hutson, "The Displacement of the Market in Jacobean City Comedy," *London Journal* 14 (1989): 3–16, esp. 10. Hutson brilliantly explores ways in which classical intrigue comedy offers "a perfect temporal analogy of the boundless market." My own thinking about temporality in city comedy is indebted to the foundational work of both Hutson and Manley on comic emplotment. For discussions of Dekker's plague pamphlets, see Healy, who observes that Dekker uses a "mercantile and marketplace language" to establish a "moral dichotomy" between "greed and luxury" and "God's wrath and plague" (*Fictions of Disease*, 110), and John Twyning, *London Dispossessed: Literature and Social Space in the Early Modern City* (Basingstoke: MacMillan, 1998), 158–70.

55. T. S. Eliot, *Essays on Elizabethan Drama* (New York: Harcourt, Brace, 1932), 85. By contrast, Eliot famously opines, the play's heroine suggests "a real and unique human being."

56. As a standing property, the shops would have given a "symbolic visual focus to the stage," Scott McMillin notes of the play in "Middleton's Theatres," in *Thomas Middleton: The Collected Works*, 1:84.

57. Jonathan Gil Harris, *Sick Economies: Drama, Mercantilism, and Disease in Shakespeare's England* (Philadelphia: University of Pennsylvania Press, 2004), 180.

See also Harris, "Properties of Skill: Product Placement in Early English Artisanal Drama," in *Staged Properties in Early Modern English Drama*, ed. Jonathan Gil Harris and Natasha Korda (Cambridge: Cambridge University Press, 2002), 35–66.

58. See Gail Kern Paster's now-classic discussion of the "City as Predator" in *Idea of the City in the Age of Shakespeare* (Athens: University of Georgia Press, 1985), 150–77. *The Roaring Girl*'s ambivalent take on city commerce is often explained as the collaborative joining of Middleton's trademark brand of satiric comedy with Dekker's more sentimental vision of community and social transformation; see, for example, Harris, *Sick Economies*, 176–77, and Maus, ed., *English Renaissance Drama*, 1373.

59. Mulholland, ed., introduction to *Roaring Girl*, 25, 72, n. 1.

60. See, for example, Simon Shepherd, *Amazons and Warrior Women: Varieties of Feminism in Seventeenth-Century Drama* (Brighton: Harvester Press, 1981), 67–92, esp. 73, who suggests that the play draws on the radical strain of the Long Meg stories, in which "Meg stands as a form of lower-class resistance against the dominant order of society"; Linda Woodbridge, *Women and the English Renaissance: Literature and the Nature of Womankind, 1540–1620* (Urbana: University of Illinois Press, 1986), 254–55; Mary Beth Rose, "Women in Men's Clothing: Apparel and Social Stability in *The Roaring Girl*," *English Literary Renaissance* 14 (1984): 367–91; and Jean E. Howard, "Sex and Social Conflict: The Erotics of *The Roaring Girl*," in *Erotic Politics: Desire on the Renaissance Stage*, ed. Susan Zimmerman (New York: Routledge, 1992): 170–90. For alternative readings, see also recent discussions on women's work by Mario DiGangi, "Sexual Slander and Working Women in *The Roaring Girl*," *Renaissance Drama*, n.s. 32 (2003): 147–76; and Natasha Korda, "The Case of Moll Frith: Women's Work and the 'All-Male' Stage," *Early Modern Culture* (2004): 1–16.

61. Knights, *Drama and Society*, 7.

62. Maus, *English Renaissance Drama*, 1375.

63. Northrop Frye, "The Argument of Comedy," *English Literary Essays 1949*, ed. D. A. Robertson (New York: Columbia University Press, 1959): 58–73.

64. As Hutson persuasively argues, English intrigue comedy prior to Jonson eschewed classical comedy's celebration of "error as opportunity" and with it the practice of deliberately "withholding or concealing a part of a story or argument" from the audience as well as the mark or victim on stage ("Displacement," 10).

65. Gary Taylor, "Thomas Middleton: Lives and Afterlives," in *Thomas Middleton*, ed. Taylor and Lavagnino, 1: 39. In Dekker's plague pamphlets, the rural countryside is imagined as a refuge by those fleeing the city, although it is hardly the utopian paradise of pastoral fantasy: Witness the macabre tale in *The Wonderfull Yeare* (1603) of a London citizen who drops dead of plague at a country inn and no one can be found to bury him (*Plague Pamphlets*, ed. Wilson, 55–59).

66. This reading coincides with Lawrence Manley's astute characterization of the genre's abiding tension between intrigue and romance. "Much of the history of city comedy," he writes, "is a history of dissent against romance dynam-

ics of the kind represented in Dekker's plays, an exposure of the positional logic—the bourgeois bias—which supports their apparently non-positional, utopian recovery of social and ethical harmony from the threat of purely adversarial struggle" (*Literature and Culture*, 444).

67. For an analytical review of the importance of *The Roaring Girl* in recent work on social identity and subject formation, see Bryan Reynolds and Janna Segal, "The Reckoning of Moll Cutpurse: Transversal Reimaginings of *The Roaring Girl*," in *Transversal Enterprises in the Drama of Shakespeare and His Contemporaries: Fugitive Explorations* (Basingstoke: Palgrave, 2006): 27–63.

68. Both Rose, "Women in Men's Clothing," and Howard, "Sex and Social Conflict," discuss the cultural ambivalence registered by Moll's exclusion from the new society at the play's end. For a critique of the recent tendency to romanticize marginality, see Deborah Jacobs, "Critical Imperialism and Renaissance Drama: The Case of *The Roaring Girl*," in *Feminism, Bakhtin, and the Dialogic*, ed. Dale M. Bauer and Susan Jaret McKinstry (Albany: SUNY Press, 1991): 73–84.

69. Anthony B. Dawson, "Mistris Hic & Haec: Representations of Moll Frith," *SEL* 33 (1993): 385–404, esp. 399.

70. Eliot, *Essays*, 85; R. C. Bald, "The Sources of Middleton's City Comedies," *JEPG* 33 (1934): 373–87, esp. 373. See also Valerie Forman's provocative analysis of the play's "enhanced forms of realism and the fiction of the 'individual'" as compensatory for the "increasingly abstract and 'dematerialized' social relations of the play's credit and commodity-driven economy," *Renaissance Quarterly* 54 (2001): 1531–60, esp. 1532.

71. Keir Elam, *The Semiotics of Theatre and Drama* (London: Methuen, 1980), 117–18. The "fictional *now*" or *discourse time* is both "perpetual" and "unrepeatable," Elam writes, citing Peter Szondi's observations on the dynamic present of dramatic action: "the present passes and is transformed into the past, but as such ceases to be the present. . . . The passage of time in the drama is an absolute succession of 'presents.'"

72. Elizabeth Grosz, *The Nick of Time: Politics, Evolution, and the Untimely* (Durham, N.C.: Duke University Press, 2004), 5.

73. Thomas Dekker, "The Wonderful Year," in *Thomas Dekker, Stratford-Upon-Avon Library* 4, ed. E. D. Pendry (Cambridge: Harvard University Press, 1968): 46.

74. Diverging from London's traditionally round playhouses, the Fortune's contract called for the new playhouse to be "sett square," suggesting the rational proportions of a u-shaped gallery space illustrated by Sebastiano Serlio's architectural renderings; see John Orrell, "The Architecture of the Fortune Playhouse," *Shakespeare Survey: An Annual Survey of Shakespeare Studies and Production*, 47, ed. Stanley Wells (Cambridge: Cambridge University Press, 1994): 15–28, esp. 15.

75. In Robert Weimann's now-classic formulation, in "Bifold Authority in Shakespeare's Theater," *Shakespeare Quarterly* 37 (1988): 459–75, the Elizabethan platform stage marked out two separate but interacting locations: the upstage or

*locus*-centered "world of the play," set off by its distance or "aloofness from the audience," and the downstage *platea*, the "world of its production and performance," enacted in a self-reflexive dramaturgy that brought audiences into the performance, making them collaborators of a sort with the downstage actors.

76. Eliot, *Essays*, 93.

77. de Certeau, *Writing of History*, 87. One might argue that the homology works to reiterate the stage's own equivocal relationship to the dead, as a theater of memory, say, or a "haunted stage." See, for example, Marvin Carlson, *The Haunted Stage: The Theater as Memory Machine* (Ann Arbor: University of Michigan Press, 2003).

78. If the epilogue is delivered by the actor playing Moll, as some editors assume (notably Mulholland and Cook), the offer seems doubly ironic.

79. *The Roaring Girl*'s performances could thus be said to mirror its plot, aptly described by Valerie Forman as "creating a series of interchangeable equivalences out of not only objects, but desires and social relations themselves" ("Marked Angels," 1533).

80. The "recompense" of future performances suggests what Derrida calls a "gift" of justice—giving "*beyond* the due, the debt, the crime, or the fault. . . . without restitution, without calculation, without accountability." And it is the disjointure of the present—"the non-contemporaneity of present time with itself" (Hamlet's "time is out of joint")—that paradoxically both requires and allows for the gift of justice and a possible future (Jacques Derrida, *Specters of Marx: The State of Debt, the Work of Mourning and the New International*, trans. Peggy Kamuf [London: Routledge, 1994], 29–30). See also Derrida, *Given Time: I. Counterfeit Money*, trans. Peggy Kamuf (Chicago: University of Chicago Press, 1992); and Elizabeth Grosz, *Time Travels: Feminism, Nature, Power* (Durham, N.C.: Duke University Press, 2005), 67–70.

81. W. B. Worthen, "Drama, Performativity, and Performance," *PMLA* 113 (1998): 1093–107, esp. 1101, elaborating on the term "surrogation," coined by Joseph Roach in *Cities of the Dead: Circum-Atlantic Performance* (New York: Columbia University Press, 1996), 1–31.

82. "Officium Domini Contra Mariam Frith," from the *Consistory of London Correction Book*, reprinted in *The Roaring Girl*, ed. Mulholland, 262.

83. Mulholland, "Date of *The Roaring Girl*," 22.

84. *Letters of John Chamberlain*, 1: 112.

85. *Letters of John Chamberlain*, 1: 334. In the sentence immediately following Frith's penance, Chamberlain notes Thomas Bodley's agreement with the Stationers "to have one copie of every booke that shalbe printed for his librarie" and his plans to begin building at Oxford—a juxtaposition of cultures typifying the capaciousness of Chamberlain's ear for local news.

86. Dawson, 389–90; see also Stephen Orgel's discussion of theatrical performance in relation to gender, "The Subtexts of *The Roaring Girl*," in *Erotic Politics*, ed. Zimmerman, 12–26.

87. The dramatic persona Moll Cutpurse also returned to the stage, with a cameo later that summer at Blackfriars in Nathan Fields's *Amends for Ladies* and mention in numerous other plays and verse, including Dekker's *If This Be Not Good, the Devil Is In It* (1611). In 1662 Mary/Moll achieved national status in the biography *The Life and Death of Mrs. Mary Frith. Commonly called Mal Cutpurse*; rehabilitated for the times as a royalist, she is said to have wounded General Fairfax during a robbery on Hounslow Heath; see Melissa Mowry, "Thieves, Bawds, and Counterrevolutionary Fantasies: *The Life and Death of Mrs. Mary Frith*," *Journal for Early Modern Cultural Studies* 5 (2005): 26–48.

88. Gustav Ungerer, "Mary Frith, Alias Moll Cutpurse, in Life and Literature," *Shakespeare Studies*, 28 (2000): 42–84, esp. 59.

89. Mulholland, ed., *The Roaring Girl*, 1.

90. Breaking with the standard practice of relying on generic woodcuts to decorate title-pages, *The Roaring Girl*'s quarto is the second printed play to use an illustration directly related to its content (the first, *The History of the Two Maids of Moreclack* [1609], was also published by Thomas Archer with Nicholas Okes); see John H. Astington, "Visual Texts: Thomas Middleton and Prints," in *Thomas Middleton and Early Modern Textual Culture: A Companion to the Collected Works*, ed. Taylor and Lavagnino (Oxford: Clarendon Press, 2007), 231–32.

91. Samuel Weber, *Theatricality as Medium* (New York: Fordham University Press, 2004), 7.

*Epilogue: The Place of the Spectator*

1. All citations from the play are from *The Staple of News*, ed. Anthony Parr (Manchester: Manchester University Press, 1988).

2. Don E. Wayne, "The 'exchange of letters': Early modern contradictions and postmodern conundrums," in *The Consumption of Culture 1600–1800: Image, Object, Text*, ed. Ann Bermingham and John Brewer (London: Routledge, 1997): 143–65, esp. 158.

3. Anthony Parr sees this topicality as the "main obstacle to modern performance" of the play (introduction to *Staple of News*, 50).

4. While the play is often read in relation to the rise of printed news in the period, there has been much debate about the complicated ambivalence of Jonson's insistence on distinguishing his dramatic art from what he sees as the crass commercializing of information, the very antithesis of a public sphere of discerning newsreaders. See, for example, D. F. McKenzie, "*The Staple of News* and the Late Plays," in *A Celebration of Ben Jonson*, eds. William Blissett, Julian Patrick, R. W. Van Fossen (Toronto: University of Toronto Press, 1973): 83–128; Parr, Introduction, 22–31; Mark Z. Muggli, "Ben Jonson and the Business of News," *Studies in English Literature, 1500–1900* 32 (1992): 323–40; Karen Newman, "Engendering the News," *The Elizabethan Theatre* XIV, ed. A. L. Magnusson and C. E. McGee (Toronto: University of Toronto Press, 1991): 49–69; Julie Sanders, *Ben Jonson's Theatrical Republics* (New York: St. Martin's Press, 1998);

Don E. Wayne, "'Pox on Your Distinction!' Humanist Reformation and Deformations of the Everyday in *The Staple of News*," in *Renaissance Culture and the Everyday*, ed. Patricia Fumerton and Simon Hunt (Philadelphia: University of Pennsylvania Press, 1999): 67–91; Stuart Sherman, "Eyes and Ears, News and Plays: The Argument of Ben Jonson's *Staple*," in *The Politics of Information in Early Modern Europe*, ed. Brendan Dooley and Sabrina A. Baron (London: Routledge, 2001): 23–40; Paul Yachnin, "The house of fame," in *The Culture of Playgoing in Shakespeare's England: A Collaborative Debate*, Anthony B. Dawson and Paul Yachnin (Cambridge: Cambridge University Press, 2001); and Jane Rickard, "A Divided Jonson? Art and Truth in *The Staple of News*," *English Literary Renaissance* 42 (2012): 294–316.

5. Ben Jonson, *Every Man Out of His Humor*, ed. Helen Ostovich, The Revels Plays (Manchester: Manchester University Press, 2001).

6. Jacques Rancière, *The Emancipated Spectator*, trans. Gregory Elliot (London: Verso, 2009), 2.

7. Rancière, *Dis-agreement: Politics and Philosophy*, trans. Julie Rose (Minneapolis: University of Minnesota Press, 1999), 32–33.

8. Rancière, *Dis-agreement*, 26–27. The term "disruptive equality" comes from Peter Hallward's astute review of Rancière's theatrical politics, "Staging Equality: Rancière's Theatrocracy and the Limits of Anarchic Equality," in *Jacques Rancière: History, Politics, Aesthetics*, ed. Gabriel Rockhill and Philip Watts (Durham: Duke University Press, 2009): 140–57, esp. 142.

9. Hallward, "Staging Equality," 148.

10. Rancière, *Emancipated Spectator*, 5–6.

11. Plato, *The Laws*, 700–1 a, quoted in Samuel Weber, *Theatricality as Medium* (New York: Fordham University Press, 2004), 33.

12. Ben Jonson, *Bartholomew Fair*, The New Mermaids, ed. G. R. Hibbard (London: A & C Black, New York: Norton, 1977).

13. Rancière, *Dis-agreement*, 30.

14. Don Wayne, "Drama and Society in the Age of Jonson: An Alternative View," *Renaissance Drama*, n.s. 13 (1982): 103–29, esp. 120. See also Jonas A. Barish, *Ben Jonson and the Language of Prose Comedy* (Cambridge: Harvard University Press, 1967), 235.

15. Rancière, "Ten Theses on Politics," in *Dissensus: On Politics and Aesthetics*, ed. and trans. Steven Corcoran (London: Continuum, 2010), 33.

16. Richard Halpern, "Theater and Democratic Thought: Arendt to Rancière," *Critical Inquiry* 37 (2011): 545–72, esp. 569.

17. Thomas Dekker, "The Gull's Horn-Book," in *Thomas Dekker*, ed. E. D. Pendry (Cambridge: Harvard University Press, 1968), 98.

18. Newman, "Engendering the News," 68.

19. As Don Wayne observes: "Jonson's note warning the reader to discount his characters' pronouncements in a previous scene suggests that, by 1631, at least some members of the audience were laughing *with* the characters at the author's expense!" ("Pox on Your Distinction," 81).

20. Rancière, "The Thinking of Dissensus," quoted in Hallward, "Staging Equality," 143.

21. Rancière, *The Politics of Aesthetics: The Distribution of the Sensible*, trans. Gabriel Rockhill (London: Continuum, 2004), 12. See also "On Art and Work," included in this collection: "The democratic distribution of the sensible makes the worker into a double being. It removes the artisan from 'his' place, the domestic space of work, and gives him 'time' to occupy the space of public discussions and take on the identity of a deliberative citizen. The mimetic act of splitting in two, which is at work in theatrical space, consecrates this duality and makes it visible. The exclusion of the mimetician, from the Platonic point of view, goes hand in hand with the formation of a community where work is in 'its' place" (43).

22. Rancière, "The Thinking of Dissensus," quoted in Hallward, 143.

23. Plato, *The Republic* 605b–c, quoted in Hallward, "Staging Equality," 143.

24. Hallward, "Staging Equality," 144.

25. Rancière, *The Politics of Aesthetics*, 13–14.

26. Rancière, *The Politics of Aesthetics*, 13.

27. Several discussions of the play emphasize the diversity of the onstage audience. See, for example, D. F. McKenzie, "*Staple*," and Nova Myhill, "Taking the Stage: Spectators as Spectacle in the Caroline Private Theaters," in *Imagining the Audience in Early Modern Drama, 1558–1642*, ed. Nova Myhill and Jennifer A. Low (Basingstoke: Palgrave Macmillan, 2011): 37–54.

28. In *Early Responses to Renaissance Drama* (Cambridge: Cambridge University Press, 2006), Charles Whitney counters studies that focus on the collective responses of audiences, gleaned from the evidence of play texts, by redirecting attention to individual responses, both in and outside the theater. The responses he examines "tell us something about both individual particularity and larger patterns . . . . demonstrating the actual diversity and creativity of early reception" (2). For a review of debates about early modern audiences, see Myhill and Low, "Audience and Audiences," in *Imagining the Audience.*

29. Rancière, *Emancipated Spectator*, 5.

30. Rancière, *Emancipated Spectator*, 16–17; see also Hallward, who observes that Rancière "is not interested, as a rule, in the domain of theater or anywhere else, in the group dynamics of collective mobilization, determination, or empowerment: the model in each case is provided by the isolated process of intellectual *self*-emancipation" (154).

31. Rancière, *Emancipated Spectator*, 17.

32. Rancière, *Emancipated Spectator*, 17.

33. Rancière, *Emancipated Spectator*, 13.

34. McKenzie, "*Staple*," 126.

35. Samuel Weber, *Theatricality as Medium*, 24.

# Index